ENQUIRIES INTO RELIGION
AND CULTURE

THE WORKS OF CHRISTOPHER DAWSON

General Editor: Don J. Briel

Christopher Dawson

ENQUIRIES INTO RELIGION
AND CULTURE

with an introduction by Robert Royal

The Catholic University of America Press
Washington, D. C.

First published in 1933 by Sheed and Ward, London
This edition is published by arrangement with Mr. Julian Scott, literary
executor of the author
Copyright © 1933 by Julian Scott
Introduction copyright © 2009 by The Catholic University of America Press
All rights reserved

The paper used in this publication meets the minimum requirements of
American National Standards for Information Science—Permanence of Paper
for Printed Library Materials, ANSI z39.48-1984.

∞

LIBRARY OF CONGRESS CATALOGING-IN-PUBLICATION DATA
Dawson, Christopher, 1889–1970.
Enquiries into religion and culture / Christopher Dawson ; with an
introduction by Robert Royal.
p. cm. — (The works of Christopher Dawson)
Includes bibliographical references and index.
ISBN 978-0-8132-1543-3 (pbk. : alk. paper)
1. Religion. 2. Civilization. I. Title. II. Series.
BL55.D27 2009
201'.7–dc22
2008039756

Contents

Introduction

ROBERT ROYAL

Human intelligence usually comes in one of several kinds. The person who is a genius in mathematics or physics is often not as notable in the very different disciplines of history or literature. This is understandable because the stark and necessary abstractions of the former two categories are quite different from the fluid, multidimensional, and imaginative truths of the latter. This basic divide typically exists too among people who think about religion. Philosophers and theologians tend toward the more analytical end of the spectrum while scripture scholars, spiritual writers, and Church historians tend toward the synthetic. Both kinds of intelligence are necessary to human life, but it is rare to find them united in a single person. And when that person also shows a high degree of genuine intuition and great gifts as a writer in conveying those truths to all sorts of readers who are far from being geniuses, it is a rare event indeed. All of this is what continues to keep us interested, even years after his death, in the historical work of Christopher Dawson.

This volume may be an even better example of his genius than his best-known books such as *Progress and Religion*, *The Making of Europe*, and *Religion and the Rise of Western Culture*. Those volumes are beautifully thought out and written, and they make a strong case. The essays in the present book were prepared in more piecemeal fashion and provide glimpses into the kinds of wide-ranging studies that Dawson undertook as he was thinking through his more extended works. Dawson moves effortlessly from complex philosophical and theological ideas to large-scale historical currents and specialized subjects like Islamic poetry. Anyone familiar with Dawson will not be surprised by the overall perspective of the present collection. On Easter Day 1909, when he was only nineteen and not yet a Catholic, Dawson sat overlooking the Roman Forum on the same spot where, more than a century and a quarter earlier, Edward Gibbon had conceived the idea of writing *The Decline and Fall of the Roman Empire*. He felt moved to undertake an equally ambitious project: a comprehensive history of culture. In a later journal entry, he described his plan as, in fact, "a vow made at Easter in *Ara Coeli*," and added that, since the initial inspiration, he had received "great light on the way it should be carried out. However unfit I may be, I believe it is God's will I should attempt it."[1]

Whatever a reader might make of this story—Rome often induces dreams in Romantic temperaments—the sequel, though slow in developing, was impressive. It took almost two decades, including fourteen years of quiet but intense reading and preparation, for the author to publish his first book, *The Age of the Gods* (1928), as he was nearing forty. But once he began publishing, he was immediately recognized as a major cultural voice. T.S. Eliot thought him "the most powerful intellectual influence in England" and invited him to become a regular contributor to his *Criterion*, as did the editors of other prestigious journals.[2] By the time Dawson's 1948–49 Gifford lectures were published under the title of *Religion and the Rise of Western Culture,* the praise was universal. The *Saturday Review* called the author "the most exciting writer of our day" and "unequaled as a historian of culture." The *New York Times* characterized him as having few rivals "for breadth of knowledge and lucidity of style." In England, the reaction was, if anything, even more effusive. The *Spectator* found it "one of the most noteworthy books produced in this generation." The author's old tutor at Oxford, the eminent student of classical political philosophy Sir Ernest Barker, referred to him as "a man and a scholar of the same sort of quality as Acton and von Hugel."[3]

Actually, Dawson's work is at the same level of intellectual excellence as the work of these great figures but has a scope, tone, and continued relevance that theirs does not. Few historians—Arnold Toynbee is one of a handful of names that might come to mind—have attempted as

---

1. Christina Scott, *A Historian and His World* (New York: Sheed & Ward, 1984), 49.
2. Ibid., 210.
3. Ibid., 110.

Dawson did a history of human culture, including religious culture, from its earliest appearance into the modern age. There is no mystery why he has so few competitors. Scholars have devoted their entire lives to the study of, say, aboriginal religion and not produced the insights into the thing itself and its continuity with modern culture and worship that Dawson did in *The Age of the Gods*. But his mastery of material and ease of exposition, as is evident everywhere in the present collection, extends to Hinduism, Buddhism, Confucianism, the various syncretisms of the Middle East and the Greco-Roman world, as well as the whole sacred history of the main Abrahamic faiths: Judaism, Christianity, and Islam. A modern reader may remain less than convinced by the periodization in essays such as "Cycles of Civilization" than were readers in the first glow of modern efforts at world history by titans like Spengler and Toynbee. But it is uncanny how Dawson's sympathetic reading of the world's cultures gives us a sense of their specific textures and complexities, and of a common and intelligible human heritage.

Dawson's aim in carrying out this history of culture was always animated by a profound sense of the crisis in the West caused by our weakening attachment, in many instances amounting to a complete break, with our own cultural roots. He often repeats that a civilization cannot survive when it has lost its connection with its vital energies, particularly the spiritual vision that must inspire and order civilization's more mechanical parts. In his view, a new culture began to emerge in the nineteenth century, but it was not the one that century thought it was creating. Instead of liberalism leading to individual freedom, the very forces that "liberated" people from older religious and social restrictions delivered them up to an increasingly impersonal system of industrialization and naked political and economic interests. The middle classes, who came to take the place of the older nobility in setting the cultural tone of society, had no substantial intellectual culture of their own and therefore tended to confuse cultural progress with material well-being. Though Dawson was well aware of the imperfections of earlier periods in the West, he astutely notices: "There is something honourable about a king, a noble, or a knight, which the banker, the stockbroker, or the democratic politician does not possess." Decades after that sentence was written, the immense worldwide popularity of stories like J.R.R. Tolkien's *The Lord of the Rings* suggests that Dawson was profoundly right. We possess many things in the modern world that other ages could hardly dream of, and more of us share in that abundance than ever before. But we sense that we lack something fundamental that no amount of wealth can replace.

Dawson may exaggerate somewhat the bourgeois element in modern life; he certainly misread America, at least at the early stage of his thinking represented here, as the most thoroughly bourgeois nation in the West (America is unique in combining modern pursuit of comforts with a stubborn adherence to ancient religious and cultural traditions). But he was right that the loss of cultural roots and pursuit of wealth had produced in every Western society a skepticism about—and weak commitment to—the value of Western culture that make us vulnerable to all sorts of attacks. In the period between the two world wars, communism and fascism were the main threats, and logically so, says Dawson. Both are poor social philosophies, but, "The lesson of Bolshevism is that any philosophy is better than no philosophy, and that a *régime* which possesses a principle of authority, however ill conceived it may be, will be stronger than a system that rests on the shifting basis of private interests and private opinions." Happily, the West was able to gather up enough of its vital forces to defeat both fascism and communism, but the problem continues, with seemingly weaker resources, in today's confrontation with militant *jihadism* and other threats.

Some of the most powerful material of the present volume appears in the book's second half. In "Civilization and Morals: Or, the Ethical Basis of Social Progress," for example, Dawson makes his usual case for vibrant religious conviction as the true cultural energy behind a healthy social order. But contrary to what many people might assume, he points out that this is in no way a cautious conservatism, as we can see from the earliest dawn of human civilization:

Could Aurignacian man divine the coming of civilization? Could the men of the Mycenaean age foresee Hellenism? When the people of Israel came riding into Canaan, could they look forward to the future of Judaism? . . . If they had limited themselves to the observance of a purely rational social ethic based on the immediate advantage of the community, they might have been more prosperous, but they would not have been culturally creative. They would have had no importance for the future. The highest moral ideal either for a people or for an individual is to be true to its destiny, to sacrifice the bird in the hand for the vision in the bush, to leave the Known for the Unknown, like Abram going out from Harran and from his own people, obedient to the call of Yahweh, or the Aeneas of Vergil's great religious epic.

There is a high imaginative grasp in this passage of the kinds of things that really move individuals and societies. In modern democracies, we tend to think that material improvement and comfort are the mainsprings of social life—and they are in an immediate, but limited, way. What really moves history in its large lines, however, are the great visions that only the most far-seeing figures are able to capture for us. As Dawson formulates it later in the same essay, there is always a difference between "the age-long racial and spiritual communion which is a civilization and the association for practical ends which is an actual political society." Few historians, especially among those who possess great learning, are able to lift their gaze to such wide horizons.

Dawson regarded this deep division as a key to our current circumstances, in which we have very extensive and detailed knowledge of nature and, as a consequence, power over the world as never before, but have a very weak and fragmented sense of cosmic order, moral standards, and human purpose. People with minds not as capacious as Dawson's have enlisted in the practical scientific, technological, and economic camp or have sought remedies for our troubles in a sincere but shallow humanism. Some of the most knowledgeable or practical of people put themselves at odds with the deepest aspirations of the West, while those who would defend characteristically Western values like freedom, human dignity, and the rights of conscience have no foundations on which to mount that defense. Such divisions do not bode well for any community.

The situation has probably worsened since Dawson wrote. Postmodern developments have exploded the notion of a transparent scientific rationality, which earlier regarded itself as unassailable truth as opposed to the mere sentiment and mysticism of religion. Progress, many of us now see, was not so simple a human thing as that. The two world wars in particular called into question the previous technological optimism and shook the foundation of all civilization's claims. Postmodern developments, however, have taken things too far in the other direction, and it is not difficult to imagine Dawson objecting that while progress as it was understood in the nineteenth century was an illusion, there is true progress of a particular sort that should not be overlooked. Almost everyone will agree that a society that has abolished slavery is superior in that respect to societies that have not. All anthropological considerations aside, similarly, it is simply a better state of things when all human beings enjoy the same dignity and rights in a society. A society in which women are fully respected as human persons, for instance, is on its face better in that respect than one in which women are little better than chattel or beasts of burden. The list could easily be expanded. There is no progress in history except toward a fuller humanity. We cannot know that path fully; only discrete improvements are available to our sight.

It is characteristic of Dawson's responsiveness to the modern predicament that he includes here an extensive essay on "Christianity and Sex," even though he was in personal matters a reticent man. Curiously, he saw the Soviet Union and America in the 1930s as pursuing a similar goal by different means: abolishing the old religious sanctions on divorce and sexual activity outside of marriage in favor of the needs of modern economics and social structures. In retrospect, this seems to have been a partly mistaken moral equivalence. But several of his observations of nearly a century ago have proved true. For example, he excoriates the philosopher Bertrand Russell, then and for long after a prominent radical, for his Romantic notion of sex and his opposition to the restrictions that marriage places on a free man's emotional life. Dawson understood, however, that changes in attitudes toward marriage would not have merely personal effects. They would reverberate throughout entire societies. Referring to Pope Leo XIII, Dawson asserts that "the alteration by the state of the fundamental laws that govern marriage and family life will ultimately lead to the ruin of society itself. No doubt the state will gain in power and prestige as the family declines, but state and society are not identical. In fact, the state is often most omnipotent and universal in its claims at the moment when society is dying, as we see in the last age of the Roman Empire." This comparison of modern Western civilization with the late Roman Empire has often been made by others, but Dawson has at his fingertips a precise knowledge of the late Greek city states and late Roman Empire (see the long essay "St. Augustine and His Age") that few others have. In particular, refusal to marry and decline in birth rates were associated in the ancient world, as they may be in ours, with a decline in the whole civilization.

Many today view these problems through the lens of women's emancipation. But Dawson distinguishes two different types of Christian families. In the one that has most predominated over two millennia, women had a far higher status than they had in either Greek or oriental societies. Dawson connects this fact with the way Christianity preached chastity and asceticism for both men and women, a uniform standard that was rare outside Christian influence. He sees the relatively stronger position of women in Catholic families as stemming from this history. The Protestant Reformation, by contrast, returned to older patriarchal tendencies. In addition, says Dawson, industrialism—which he constantly criticizes, perhaps overlooking some of its undeniable benefits—grew in the remote regions of Europe where dissenters had little use for the social heritage of Christian history, and demonstrated that disdain by a radical withdrawal from social networks that had been common in the past.

In spite of the strength and perspicacity of this analysis in social terms, for us there are also limits to Dawson's views on industrialization and urbanization. His own childhood in rural England gave him a deep appreciation for nature and the kind of life that could be lived by a well-ordered family on the land.[4] In fact, some of Dawson's most personal and touching writing in this volume appears in that context. Many of us today living in cities and suburbs find his experiences and vision particularly attractive. Our separation from nature and the order it expresses throughout the seasons is a painful loss alongside many gains in developed nations. But Dawson advocated a return to families living on the land at a time when the human population was much smaller than it is today. If city dwellers were to move back to the land now, it would make what some environmental advocates call "urban sprawl" seem a minor annoyance and would have incalculably bad effects on the overall global environment.

4. "The World Crisis and the English Tradition."

It remains true, however, that in other respects the decline in the traditional family has had several unfortunate results, not least, as Dawson predicted, that "the functions which were formerly fulfilled by the head of the family are now being taken over by the state, which educates the children and takes responsibility for their maintenance and health."

The problem goes beyond questions of the size and scope of the state to the very survival of Western civilization. State schools and the whole apparatus of government agencies convey a very different set of values than did the old Christian family. The modern state does not teach chastity, fidelity, or the good of children. Wedded to an allegedly realistic approach to such matters, it has chosen technocratic responses and become the purveyor of contraception, no-fault divorce, and population control. Even worse, the modern state asserts that these are practical, value-neutral policies despite an epidemic of illegitimacy, sexually transmitted diseases, and broken families—all of which in a self-reinforcing downward spiral seem to call for even more state intervention into the family. Paradoxically, the very freedom of divorce and sex has made women feel more vulnerable than in earlier ages, when religious and secular laws encouraged men to stay with and provide for wives and children. We have fulfilled the sad prediction Dawson made: "The energy of youth will be devoted to contraceptive love and only when men and women have become prosperous and middle-aged will they think seriously of settling down to rear a strictly limited family."

We may be well on the way toward another outcome that Dawson forecast: "The suppression of the family means not progress, but the death of society, the end of our age, and the passing of European civilization." Dawson predicted that this would lead to a rapid decline of civilization, far more rapid than what occurred in the ancient world. Further, in an uncanny anticipation of what is today happening in low-birth Europe, he says, "The peoples who allow the natural bases of society to be destroyed by the artificial conditions of the new urban civilisation will gradually disappear and their place will be taken by those populations which live under simpler conditions and preserve the traditional forms of the family." He predicted that Eastern Europeans would have to replace missing Western births, as is the case in much of Western Europe today. The large Muslim immigration into

Europe and its rapid birth rates were still not visible. Dawson urged both a change in cultural attitudes and legal measures to shore up the family, but no combination of analysis and social disorder to date has really reversed the theoretical and practical decline of the family.

Against the advocates of a freed sexuality along the lines of D. H. Lawrence and the Romantic notion of people as being truer and purer in their defiance of social "convention" and legal restrictions, he writes:

> Now it is true that natural sexuality is good, and that it is the highest and, as it were, the most religious activity of which the animal is capable. But in man this natural purity of sex is no longer possible, it is inevitably contaminated by egotism and conscious emotion. It passes beyond its natural function and becomes an outlet for all the unsatisfied cravings of the psychic life. It ceases to be a natural physical appetite and becomes a quasi-spiritual passion which absorbs the whole man and drags his nature away.

For this and many other reasons, sex, like the rest of modern life, has to be spiritualized, something we have actually seen happen earlier in Western history. Instead of this successful sublimation, however, modern tendencies are to rationalize sex, which Dawson regards as an utter impossibility. Only the great world religions have shown themselves capable of this large spiritualizing task, which has to confront untutored human impulses that are quite powerful. Among the world religions, some such as Buddhism and certain Christian heresies that first appeared with the Gnostic Gospels, seek to eliminate all bodily desire. By contrast, Judaism, Christianity, and Islam—the Abrahamic faiths that look upon Creation as a good willed by God— affirm the goodness of sexuality, while recognizing the need to master it lest it become a master itself. From the Song of Songs to the nuptial mysticism of Christian and Islamic poets, marriage and sexual passion are contextualized as an image of Divine Love. Love as we think of it in everyday terms only comes into its full meaning when it acknowledges the claims of what Dante called "The Love that moves the sun and other stars."

In this as in many other particulars, Dawson made the case for what he calls the "desecularization" of modern societies. As a prelude to what seemed an almost hopeless task at the beginning of the twentieth century, he recommends and practices the desecularizing of intellectual life. One element in this process that he did not anticipate, however, was the popular reaction around the world to the sheer unliveability of strictly secular societies. In the past century, there has been a worldwide upsurge in religious renewal movements among Christians, Jews, Muslims, Hindus, and other traditions. Since September 11, 2001, most people have become aware of Muslim fundamentalism in its militant *jihadist* form. But there is a vast return to religious tradition in nonviolent forms across the globe. Traditional Christian groups in the United States are often characterized as fundamentalist when in fact they are just popular reactions to the quite pointed secularist challenges to historical faith. In much of the rest of the globe, Christianity—particularly in its charismatic and Pentecostalist forms that straddle Protestant and Catholic divisions—is a fast-growing segment of the world population. As Philip Jenkins has shown in his remarkable study *The Next Christendom: The Coming of Global Christianity*, those forms of Christianity are growing faster even than Islam, though few in America and Europe know about it.

Though these developments are encouraging, Dawson's question about the recovery of a Christianity that will shape our whole civilization remains a vital one. Europe, of course, remains the heartland of secularist social organization. And America, though blessed with a more steadily believing population, has largely ceded its universities, media, and major cultural institutions to secularist modes of thought. The sociologist Peter Berger, who has documented the desecularization that has occurred in many parts of the world, has rightly pointed out that Americans are a people with the religious fervor of Indians presided over by an elite with the secularist outlook of Swedes. Whether the new upsurge in popular religiosity will also produce the intellectual, cultural, and social renaissance needed is difficult to say. But there are signs that in both America and Europe younger thinkers who come out of the renewal movements and immigration from the global South may provide just such a ferment in thought. This large process of social renewal will be immensely helped if its leaders become familiar with and deeply internalize the multifaceted wisdom of one of the modern age's greatest geniuses, Christopher Dawson.

Introduction

The present volume contains a number of essays that I have written on many different subjects during the last fifteen years. But in spite of their diversity I believe that they all possess a certain community of aim and deal in one way or another with a common problem. All genuine thought is rooted in personal needs, and my own thought since the war, and indeed for some years previously, is due to the need that so many of us feel to-day for social readjustment and for the recovery of a vital contact between the spiritual life of the individual and the social and economic organisation of modern culture. Social detachment is a necessary condition for the scientific study of society, but is a difficult and dangerous state; for the man who is separated from the organic life of his culture is in little better case than the oyster that has been extracted from its shell. Happy is the people that is without a history, and thrice happy is the people without a sociology, for as long as we possess a living culture we are unconscious of it, and it is only when we are in danger of losing it or when it is already dead that we begin to realise its existence and to study it scientifically.

But this process is not a uniform one. It is plainly perceptible to those who are concerned with the spiritual functions of culture—the poets and artists, philosophers and religious thinkers—as well as to those who are socially unsuccessful and in a state of spiritual revolt, while all those who live on the surface of society—the politicians and the men of business, and the socially successful—are still unconscious of it. And thus men to-day are divided between those who have kept their spiritual roots and lost their contact with the existing order of society, and those who have preserved their social contacts and lost their spiritual roots. Such a state of things has not been unknown in the past, but whenever it has occurred it has marked the dissolution or the weakening of a culture. The central conviction which has dominated my mind ever since I began to write, and which has increased in intensity during the last twenty years, is the conviction that the society or culture which has lost its spiritual roots is a dying culture, however prosperous it may appear externally. Consequently the problem of social survival is not only a political or economic one; it is above all things religious, since it is in religion that the ultimate spiritual roots both of society and of the individual are to be found. When a man has found his roots, he has found his religion, and the irreligious man is precisely the man without roots who lives on the surface of existence and recognises no ultimate spiritual allegiance.

This view is, of course, diametrically opposed to the dominant social philosophy of the modern world, whether individualist or socialist. The liberal thinkers and statesmen who were the makers of nineteenth-century civilisation regarded religion and culture as entirely independent phenomena. Religion was entirely a matter for the individual conscience and it had nothing to do with social and economic life. But the resultant secularisation of culture which took place throughout Western Europe in the nineteenth century brought its own nemesis. It led to the discredit of a religion that had no power over social life and of a culture that had no spiritual sanctions. It found at once its logical conclusion and its refutation in the yet more radical secularisation of life which characterised the Marxian philosophy. While Liberalism had pushed religion on one side, Communism eliminated it altogether and thus prepared the way for the complete re-absorption of the individual in the social organism, while at the same time it transformed the social organism into an economic mechanism. Thus Communism reduces the whole social process to the economic factor and treats the spiritual element in culture as something altogether secondary and derivative. In the words of Marx, "the mode of production in material life determines the social character of the social, political and spiritual processes of life. It is not the consciousness of men that determines their existence, but their existence that determines their consciousness."[1]

Now the error of this materialistic interpretation of history does not consist in the view that the spiritual aspects of culture are conditioned

---

1. Marx *Zur Kritik der Politischen Oekonomie.* Introduction.

by its material elements, but in the assertion of an absolute causal dependence of the former on the latter and in the identification of the economic and the sociological categories. In the passage that I have just quoted Marx speaks of "economic production" as though it was conterminous with "existence," and this illegitimate substitution reveals the fundamental weakness of the Marxian theory. Because economic production explains *some* social phenomena, therefore it is supposed to explain them all and the creative spiritual element in culture drops out through the hole in the argument. Actually, however, Communism supplies its own refutation, for while its philosophy is materialistic, the driving force in its historical development has been essentially religious. It owes its success not to the impersonal evolution of capitalist society, but to the religious fervour of its disciples, their spiritual revolt against the practical materialism of modern culture and their apocalyptic hopes in the realisation of a Messianic reign of social justice on earth. How far this quasi-religious element in Communism will stand the test of time, it is impossible to say. It seems to me to be inseparable from the revolutionary phase of Communism and to be destined to pass away in proportion as Communism becomes an established order. In any case, it must be recognised by the Communists themselves as an illegitimate element that is alien to the true spirit of scientific socialism, and this disharmony between socialist theory and socialist practice itself shows the inadequacy of the Marxian philosophy, when it is applied to the complex realities of social life, which refuse to be reduced to purely economic terms. A genuinely scientific sociology must reject all such arbitrary simplifications of the problem by the elimination of an essential factor. Religion can no more be reduced to economics than economics can be reduced to religion. Each is an independent factor with its own formal principle and it is the business of the sociologist to accept this as part of his data.

Unfortunately the majority of sociologists, while recognising the fundamental social importance of religion, have been loath to admit its autonomous character. They have been misled by the false analogy of the physical sciences into an attempt to create a science of society which will reduce all social phenomena to a single principle and will provide an absolute causal explanation for the many-sided activities of social life. And thus they have aimed at the complete elimination of philosophy and theology, and the incorporation of religion and the whole realm of spiritual values in general into the domain of sociology. Such an attempt, however, results not in the "sociologising" of religion, but in the "theologising" of sociology. From the time of Comte onwards sociology has been discredited by the tendency of sociologists to usurp the role of theologians and religious reformers, and the result has been to create not a scientific religion of society, but a series of hybrid monstrosities which are neither scientific nor religious. The sociologist has no more right to lay down the law on theology or metaphysics than on physics or biology. The spiritual factors which affect the life of society possess their own formal principles, no less than the material ones. They are not mere functions of society, but have their own ends which in a real sense transcend the social category and can be studied as autonomous principles. It is the business of the sociologist to study how religious beliefs, for example, affect social development, but he has no right to go beyond this and to pronounce on the objective intellectual validity or the ultimate spiritual value of these beliefs; those are questions for the philosopher and the theologian.

Hitherto the lust for simplification has been the bane of sociology. As Pareto has shown, the fundamental condition for a scientific sociology is the abandonment of all attempts to reduce the social process to a single factor. It is the result of a complex series of interdependent factors and it is fatal to conceive the relation between them as one of causal dependence. Social phenomena are conditioned by both material and spiritual factors, and we can neither explain the social process by one of them alone, nor exalt one factor into the source and cause of the other.

But if sociology cannot understand the spiritual elements in the social process without the help of theology and philosophy, the latter also need the help of sociology. There is a false spiritualism, just as there is a false materialism and a false "sociologism." We cannot understand a religion or even a philosophy unless we understand how it has been conditioned by social and historical factors. Ideas and beliefs ally themselves with social forces and become fused with them in such a way that it is often difficult to disentangle them. The trained theologian may often fail to recognise the social and economic elements in religious changes, with the result that a confusion between religious and sociological values takes place and a racial or economic opposition becomes transformed into a religious conflict. This is fairly obvious in the case of the Wars of Religion in the sixteenth and seventeenth centuries, but it has also contributed in a more obscure and subtle way to the rise of practically every religious controversy and ecclesiastical schism.

I give an example of this process in one of the later essays in this volume where I deal with the rise of the Donatist schism in Africa and it would be easy to multiply instances of it. And consequently wherever the theologian or the student of comparative religion has to face the problem of religious unity and to deal with the clash of creeds, it is essential for him to possess an adequate knowledge of the sociological factors which affect the problem and to make a complete sociological analysis of the situation. As a rule it is not a genuine *odium theologicum,* but some hidden sociological conflict which infuses bitterness into religious questions. This was recognised by Roger Bacon in the thirteenth century, when he pointed out that the real obstacle to the conversion of the heathen Prussians and Lithuanians was not their devotion to paganism but their fear of losing their land and their freedom, and if theologians had realised the importance of the sociological factors in religious dissent, it is probable that the history of Christendom would have been a very different one.

Consequently sociology and theology ought not to be either hostile or indifferent to one another. Each can help the other so long as it observes its own limits and respects the autonomy of the other in its own field. The history of European civilisation in the past shows the failure of the attempt of theology to establish a dictatorship over sociology and the natural sciences, and to-day we are witnessing the bankruptcy of the secularist culture which sought to subjugate the whole of life to natural science and regarded theology and every higher form of knowledge as empty and useless. It is no more possible for society to live by bread alone than it is for the individual. Technology and material organisation are not enough. If our civilisation is to recover its vitality, or even to survive, it must cease to neglect its spiritual roots and must realise that religion is not a matter of personal sentiment which has nothing to do with the objective realities of society, but is, on the contrary, the very heart of social life and the root of every living culture. The desecularisation of modern civilisation is no easy matter; at first sight it may seem a hopeless task. But we can at least prepare the way for it by desecularising our intellectual outlook and opening our eyes to the existence of the spiritual forces that create and transform civilisation.

✺

I have to thank the Editor of the *Sociological Review* for permission to include *The Passing of Industrialism, Cycles of Civilisation, Civilisation and Morals,* and *The Mystery of China;* The Editor of the Dublin Review and Messrs. Burns, Oates & Washbourne Ltd. for *The New Leviathan, Islamic Mysticism, On Spiritual Intuition in Christian Philosophy* and *Religion and Life;* the Editor of the English Review and Messrs. Eyre and Spottiswoode for *The Significance of Bolshevism* and *The World Crisis and the English Tradition;* Messrs. Faber & Faber for *Christianity and Sex;* Messrs. Gerald Duckworth & Co. Ltd. for *Religion and the Life of Civilisation;* Messrs. Longmans, Green & Co. for *The Nature and Destiny of Man.*

I

I

The New Leviathan

The great fact of the twentieth century is the definite emergence of
a new type of civilisation different from anything that the world has
known hitherto. All through the nineteenth century the new forces
which were to transform human life were already at work, but their real
tendency was to a great extent veiled by current modes of thought and
preconceived ideas which had their origin in political and philosophical
doctrines. The mind of the nineteenth century was dominated by the
ideals of Nationalism and Liberalism, and the actual process of social
and economic change was interpreted in terms of these doctrines. In
reality, however, the forces that were at work were only partially ame-
nable to such theories; in many respects they were actually moving in a
contrary direction.

Thus, while the peoples of Europe were consciously accentuating
their national idiosyncrasies and their political independence, they were
at the same time becoming more and more alike in their customs, their
ideas, and their whole apparatus of material culture. At the same time,
they were losing their economic self-sufficiency and being drawn into
the meshes of a super-national industrial and commercial system, which
transcends political frontiers and renders each people dependent on the
rest for the very necessities of material existence.

In the same way, while Liberalism was destroying the old restrictions which interfered with the liberty of the individual and was basing
political life anew on free representative institutions, the individual was
losing all control over the circumstances of his daily life and becoming, more than ever before, the servant of impersonal economic forces,
which absorbed all his time and energies. Human life was becoming

mechanized, and man was losing his spontaneity under the vast pressure of the new material organisation.

The new civilisation is not the civilisation which the nineteenth century believed that it was creating. It is a new social organism which cannot be understood unless we set aside all preconceived ideas and study it with strict scientific impartiality. This is what M. Lucien Romier has attempted to do in the series of works which he has devoted to "The Explanation of our Times," and he has succeeded better perhaps than any of the multitude of writers on the subject, because he combines in such a remarkable way the actuality of the journalist and the man of affairs with the sympathetic imagination of a true historian.[1]

To M. Romier the distinguishing note of the new order is that it is a "mass-civilisation," by which he means a civilisation not so much of the masses in the ordinary sense of the word, as of economic aggregates which arise from the grouping of masses of population and capital round particular economic interests.

"In a hundred years," he writes, "the population of the world has doubled, that of Europe has tripled, and that of North America has multiplied thirty or forty times. This new humanity, actually created by the new sources of wealth, lives in masses and can only live in masses. If you alter one of the facts which contribute to the life of the mass, if you suppress the wealth that is being exploited, the aggregation or the unity of the individuals who together exploit this, if you take away their outlet or their profit from the collective activity, everything crumbles, the mass falls in ruins, the surplus population dies off, the children who were to be born fail to see the light of day."[2]

The old divisions which have determined the historic life of Europe break down or vanish into insignificance by the side of these impersonal economic forces. An economic unit may come into existence on either side of a political frontier, as in Belgium and the North of France, or in Prussian and Polish Silesia, and all the forces of national antagonism and official red tape are powerless to prevent its development. The population itself changes not only its social character, but its racial

1. M. Romier established his reputation as an historian by his numerous works on the history of France in the sixteenth century.
2. L. Romier: *Who will be Master: Europe or America ?* pp. 19–20.

composition in obedience to the vital needs of the mass. It brings Berbers from North Africa and Poles from Eastern Europe to work side by side in the automobile factories of Paris; it has poured a whole population of Chinese workers and merchants into the Malay Peninsula, and it creates new centres of wealth and population in regions which were up to yesterday barbarous or deserted, like Katonga or the Persian oil fields or the Chilean nitrate deposits.

These, however, are only the external consequences of mass-civilisation. Far more important are the effects that it produces on the internal organisation of society and the very form of culture itself. Hitherto the tradition of European civilisation has been governed mainly by non-economic standards. The economic functions were almost excessively depreciated, in comparison with the aristocratic and humanist ideals of the leisured class, which had their origin in the Renaissance culture. These ideals were handed on from the courtiers and nobles of the old *régime* to the nineteenth-century middle class. In both periods the ideal of culture was placed in an intensive intellectual culture of the individual, and the acquisition of wealth was regarded as an opportunity of escaping from the servitude of business to the freedom of the non-economic life.

To-day all this is changed. The end of civilisation is no longer found in intellectual culture, but in material well-being, and it is no longer limited to a single class, but is the common aim of every member of the society. The economic functions are no longer despised; in fact, it is the non-economic functions that are in danger of being neglected, since they offer no material rewards and are no longer surrounded by a halo of social prestige. It is true that for the ordinary man life has become more enjoyable and richer in opportunities than it ever was before. He owns his wireless set and his motor-bicycle, palatial cinemas and dancing halls are built for his amusement, and he has much the same standard of education and intellectual culture as his employer. But against this we must set a loss of spiritual independence, of which the average man himself is probably unconscious. However harsh and narrow was the existence of the European peasant, he still possessed the liberty to be himself—a liberty which flowered in a rich diversity and an intense vitality of character and personality. But to-day, if a man is to enjoy the material benefits of the new mass-civilisation, he must put off his individuality and conform himself to standardised types of thought and conduct. And this extends also to the details of taste and personal habits. As M. Romier writes: "Such and such a way of dressing, furnishing the home, feeding, amusing oneself, once advertised to the public and successfully 'launched,' becomes entrenched and defended through the solidarity of manufacturers, workers, wholesalers, shopkeepers, salesmen, all banded together in quest of profits they will share in common."[3]

For an individual to escape the pressure of this mass-movement is almost impossible. For "he who would escape from the fixed morals or modes set by standardisation must pay a fearful price; he must undergo a kind of penance." And, consequently, the springs of creative originality are stopped at the source. The artist and the thinker are no longer the leaders of culture; they have become exiles and outlaws from the general body of society, which is governed more and more by purely external forces. Humanity has become the servant of the economic mass.

It is in the United States that this new type of civilisation has reached its fullest development. For the conditions of American life allowed full play to the new forces, which were here unfettered by social traditions and political complications. In M. Romier's words: "This enormous social organism, in which under an iron-handed police the most novel as well as the most traditional forms of human activity are carried on at amazing speed and on a colossal scale, has been built up as if at one stroke and without any serious attention to either political ideals or theories of civil administration."

In Europe, on the other hand, the new forces have been checked and deflected by the social and political traditions of an ancient civilisation. Neither the political framework of independent national states, nor the social organisation, nor, above all, the European cultural tradition was entirely compatible with the new type of civilisation. Nevertheless, the same tendencies are at work, and the industrial development of the European nations has been hardly less rapid and less intense than that of

3. *Op. cit.*, p. 91.

the United States. The same trend towards the growth of economic masses and the material standardisation of culture is observable in the Old World as in the New, but here it is complicated by national rivalry and class antagonism and threatens to disrupt the old societies into which it has been introduced.

This is most evident in the case of the European system of political organisation. Europe taken as a whole — even apart from Russia and the Balkans — is superior to the United States in population, in wealth, and in political and military power, but whereas the States of North America are United and are consequently able to devote their undivided energies to the economic organisation of a continent, the states of Europe, divided from one another by national traditions, political frontiers, and artificial tariff walls, are forced to construct a number of independent and often antagonistic economic systems. Hence the new mass-economy is cramped and unbalanced. Each nation is forced to scramble for the largest possible share in the restricted markets and supplies of raw material, and this leads to over-protection, over-production, and over-population. So long as this state of things continues, no purely juridical methods can prevent national competition in armaments and the perpetual danger of war. And yet it is impossible to solve the problem in the obvious way by the abolition of nationality and the creation of a United States of Europe, since all that is strongest in the life of Europe has its source in the national tradition, and to destroy nationality would be to cut the roots of our social vitality. We are forced by the whole trend of our past development to seek some less facile solution which will do justice at once to historic and economic realities.

No less pressing are the internal problems of our culture. The new standardised type of mass-civilisation found ready acceptance in the United States. It was regarded as an original American creation, and it harmonised well with the needs of an expanding people in the new colonial environment. But in Europe the situation is entirely different. Society is still deeply imbued with the intellectual and artistic traditions of the Renaissance culture. The ideals of the leisured class still preserve their prestige, and the Americanisation of European life is regarded by the majority of European writers and thinkers as a wave of barbarism which threatens all that makes life worth living. Nevertheless, the new material culture has the same attraction for the European man in the street as for his comrade in America. No amount of literary denunciation will avail to check the tentacular advance of the civilisation of the cinema, the motor-car, and the bungalow. The new civilisation may be, as Count Keyserling thinks, a civilisation of the taxi-driver, but it offers the ordinary man opportunities of a richer and more enjoyable life than he ever knew before. Moreover, it is not wholly materialistic. As M. Romier points out, one of the most striking features of the new American society is its idealism—its enthusiasm for every cause which seems to promise social or ethical progress. "The modern masses," he writes, "are not closed to ideas, but they want them and understand them only within the limits of their own experience or of their most constant and vital preoccupations." The great problem of modern culture is to bring these vast potentialities of spiritual development into contact with the higher forms of cultural activity which the older European tradition possessed. And since in Europe we have in a higher degree than in America all the elements of such a synthesis, it would seem that it is from Europe that the solution of the problem must come.

It is not, however, possible to reach this goal by a mere popularisation of the cultural and political ideals of the middle classes, as the nineteenth century believed. The decline of the social and political influence of the middle classes, which is a striking feature of the post-war period in every European country, does not stand alone. It has brought with it the decline of Liberalism and a general loss of prestige for parliamentarianism and representative institutions.

Everywhere, save in the most stable and conservative societies of Western Europe, parliamentary government has been giving way before the dictatorships of the left or the right and the revival of authoritarian forms of government. And this is not merely the result of the temporary unsettlement produced by the war, it is due, above all, to the fact that the presuppositions of the old Liberal *régime* are no longer valid. The parliamentary system can only function properly in a stable society, in which all the active political elements are in agreement on fundamental matters. It invokes not only the opposition of parties, but also their co-operation. For the conflict of parties is not a fight to the death: it is a game that can only be played by a strict adhesion to the rules. It is no accident that the system was created by the same people which invented the game of cricket. They are, as Spengler would say, parallel expressions of the same psychic principle.

But as soon as the new economic factors come to dominate society, all this is changed. Parliament is no longer a debating society; it becomes a battlefield of impersonal forces. Either the political parties become the organs of class interests, in which case the state is threatened with social disruption and revolution, or they are dominated by economic mass-interests and the politician becomes the agent of industrial and financial powers, who dictate his policy from behind the scenes. In either case, the centre of gravity has shifted from the political to the economic sphere, and the old Liberal democratic principles have become empty forms which no longer correspond to social realities. The new polity is a kind of mass-dictatorship which leaves little room for free discussion and for the expression of individual opinion.

And as it is with the Liberal middle-class polity, so is it also with the Liberal humanist culture. It is essentially the culture of a leisured class, and it cannot thrive in the atmosphere of the new mass-civilisation. Its supreme achievements were always due to the adventurous freedom of the individual mind, which revolted alike against the authority of tradition and the received opinions of the multitude. This spirit of individualism is equally characteristic of the two great currents of modern culture which in other respects are so dissimilar—the movement of rationalist criticism, on the one hand, and that of sentimental or imaginative romanticism, on the other; for Rousseau and Voltaire, Shelley and Bentham, Ruskin and Herbert Spencer, in spite of their mutual contradictions, were all of them great individualists in revolt against intellectual orthodoxy and the pressure of social conformity.

But in the new mass-civilisation which is growing up in America and Europe it is no longer possible for the individual to isolate himself from his social milieu. The pressure of economic necessity forces him to conform. Moreover, the thought of the masses, as we see in America to-day, is essentially simple and uncritical. It is humble and receptive, so that it is often in danger of accepting the quack or the demagogue at, his own valuation. For the masses demand above all a creed and a leader. Any criticism which goes beyond matters of detail, and which tends to shake their confidence in the existing order of life and thought, is abhorrent to them, and they are apt to regard the critic as a traitor to his society.

Hence it seems that modern democracy is breaking away from the Liberal tradition which nursed its infancy and is tending both in the political and the cultural sphere in the direction of collectivism.

At first sight this appears to justify the claims of Socialism, for the latter since the days of Marx has preached the supersession of the parliamentary *régime* by a mass-dictatorship and the coming of a new proletarian civilisation which will take the place of the old humanistic culture with its ideals of individual freedom and the liberty of opinion. Certainly in Russia, where the Marxian programme has been ruthlessly carried out, we have the most complete example of a collectivist dictatorship that the world has ever seen. The inner life of the individual is sacrificed to the needs of the mass in their crudest and most brutal form. Herr Füllop-Miller has shown in his interesting book, *The Mind and Face of Bolshevism,* how the Soviet Government has taken as a deliberate policy the mechanisation of social life, and how the cult of the machine has acquired almost the character of a religion.

But it would be a mistake to regard the Russian development as a typical example of the mass-civilisation of the future. Russia was the one country in Europe where the new civilisation possessed no natural roots. It was a society of semi-mediaeval type governed not by the economic forces of industrial capitalism, but by a rigid official hierarchy and a pre-industrial agrarian system. The Russian Revolution was not so much the proletarian revolution of Marx's theory, as a servile insurrection of the type of a mediaeval Jacquerie. Consequently, the attempt to create a new economic mass-civilisation in Russia by the application of Marxian principles was an artificial experiment and not, like the new American mass-civilisation, the spontaneous product of existing economic forces.

Indeed, while it must be admitted that Marxian Socialism was a remarkable advance on the contemporary political and economic Liberalism in its realisation of the new economic tendencies that were about to transform our civilisation, it may be questioned whether it is not to-day a reactionary and retrograde force in European life. The principle of state ownership of the means of production was intended by Marx to secure the subordination of political forms to economic realities. Actually it means the sacrifice of economic efficiency to political requirements and the accentuation of those very factors which even to-day hinder the full development of economic organisation. As we have seen, the wonderful economic expansion of the United States has been largely due to the fact that it has been unfettered by political restrictions, and it is the hypertrophy of political units that is mainly responsible for the difficulties of the economic situation of Europe.

Moreover, as M. Romier points out, the other main principle of Marxian economics, the class conflict, is equally discordant with modern economic realities. The essential condition of the life of economic masses is not conflict, but co-operation. In each mass, workers, capitalists, scientific specialists, salesmen, and directors form a block with common interests, and their respective rewards depend not on the sharing out of a fixed amount of money, but on their successful co-operation in creating new sources of wealth. The important thing is not who controls the capital, but how it is controlled; and a millionaire, like Henry Ford, who makes the industrial-commercial machine function smoothly is a truer collectivist than a Government department which allows the engine to run down or the wheels to become clogged. Class conflict is a phenomenon which flourishes only in societies, such as Russia, where the class system is antiquated and no longer represents social and economic realities, or in those industrial societies which are undergoing an economic crisis and are no longer creating new wealth. In either case it is a morbid symptom, which must be eliminated by any society which aims at prosperity and efficiency.

But Socialism is not the only alternative to the Liberal *régime*. The last ten years have seen the appearance of a new force in European life which is equally opposed to the class-dictatorship of Marxian Socialism and to the party government of Liberal democracy. The rise of Fascism in Italy was a protest alike against the anti-social tendencies of Socialism and the anti-national tendencies of Liberalism, which had between them reduced Italy to a state of political and social chaos. Its ideal was the union of all the creative forces of the nation in the service of a constructive policy. The Fascist state was to be not the state of a class or a party, but *totalitarian* and universal. In place of the parliamentary *régime* with its chaos of warring parties in which the Government represented no permanent social reality, but a shifting coalition of opinions, it has attempted to substitute a "corporative state" which should represent the living economic and social forces of the national life. And so, too, in the economic sphere it has striven to eliminate class conflict and to unite labour and capital in a co-operative effort towards increased economic efficiency and productivity.

Thus Fascism has attempted to face the problems and adapt itself to the needs of the new situation in a more realist and objective spirit than that of Socialism. It has accepted the conditions of the new mass-civilisation even in their harshest and most brutal consequences. It has not hesitated to employ ruthless methods of intimidation, the proscription of individual opponents, and the destruction of those guarantees of the liberty of the individual which were the Ark of the Covenant of Liberalism. And, consequently, there are many who see in Fascism nothing but the tyranny of the bludgeon and the castor-oil bottle. Nevertheless, the strength of Fascism is due as much to its idealism as to material force. It has realised that the new social discipline must have a moral foundation and that mass-civilisation is impossible without mass-ideals. Consequently, it has striven to unite all the moral and intellectual forces of the nation, and, to this end, has broken with the continental Liberal tradition of "laicism," and has put an end to the schism in the national life caused by the separation of Church and state.

Thus from every point of view the Fascist development is a most striking example of the new forces that are at work in Europe. Can we go further and look to Fascism for a definitive solution of the European problem? This is what Mr. Barnes claims in his interesting essay on *The Universal Aspects of Fascism*. He believes that the appearance of Fascism marks a turning-point in European history—the end of the centrifugal and individualistic tendencies which have dominated Europe since the Renaissance and the reawakening of that older tradition of European unity which expressed itself in mediaeval Christendom. "For Europe," he writes, "Fascism stands at the cross-roads looking back towards the two Romes, Imperial and Catholic, that made her civilisation, and pointing to its straight continuation as the only road by which to advance. Thus its historical function and mission is simply this: to prepare the ground for a new European political and social synthesis, founded on the race-traditions of the past when Europe was yet one."[4]

Now it is easy enough for Mr. Barnes to prove his case with regard to the authoritarian and anti-individualist character of Fascism. From that point of view it is certain that the movement is a reaction from the whole Liberal tradition which reaches back to the eighteenth century and beyond it to the Renaissance.

But the other part of Mr. Barnes thesis is not so easily demonstrable. Indeed, at first sight it seems a sheer paradox to assert that Fascism marks a return to European unity and to the mediaeval ideal of society. For if Mussolini is unsparing in his denunciations of what he terms "Demo-Liberalism," he has, on the other hand, never attempted to disguise his adhesion to the Nationalist doctrine of the state in its most uncompromising form. He is the disciple of Machiavelli rather than of St. Thomas, and, though he is willing to accept the Church as an ally, he will be satisfied with nothing less than the undivided allegiance of every citizen at every moment of his life. The policy of Fascism is definitely an imperialistic one, and it is an imperialism which looks back, not to the romantic idealism of Gioberti and the mediaeval Empire with its head of paper and its feet of clay, but to the blood and iron of the authentic Rome. It is the aim of Fascism to fit the new generation for the winning of empire by an education which will train them to arms and inspire them with "the spirit of conquest," and, as the Pope himself has recently had reason to point out, this consorts ill with a policy of European peace and co-operation.

Mr. Barnes believes that the adoption of Fascist principles and ideals by the other European nations would prepare the way for a return to European unity, but we have only to study the *Survey of Fascism,* published by the International Centre of Fascist Studies, of which Mr. Barnes is Secretary-General, to see the objections to such a view. Wherever the spirit of Fascism appears, it allies itself with the forces of militant Nationalism. In Germany, as Herr von Binzer shows, it finds its affinity in the great national associations of semi-military character

4. p. 63.

such as the Stahlhelm, the Jungdeutsche Orden and the Werewolves, organisations which reject the new German State as a "republic of hucksters and grave-diggers," and place their hopes in a violent resurgence of national patriotic feeling.

In France, it is true, there is no organised party which can be compared to the Fascisti, but if a French Fascism should come into existence, we can hardly imagine that it would show much sympathy to its opposite numbers in Germany or even in Italy.

So, too, in Austria the Fascists are at present fully occupied with their Socialist and Communist fellow-countrymen, but if they should ever hold the reins of power it is probable that they would have something to say about the policy of the Italian Fascists in Southern Tyrol. While as for the Balkans, it is probable that Fascism as interpreted by a Macedonian komitadji would be something of which it is better not to think.

Thus the great danger of Fascism is its tendency towards militant nationalism, for if Fascism involves the exacerbation of our national rivalries, it cannot help Europe in its present need. But on the other hand it must be remembered that there is another side to Fascism. In theory the organic corporate idea of the state corresponds to an organic conception of our culture as a whole, and the Fascist ideal of order within the state demands a similar principle of international order. The success or failure of Fascism as a European movement depends above all on the question whether it is able to develop these latent principles of international order and of co-operation between the historic national units of Western culture, or whether it relapses into an anarchy of competitive national imperialisms. The regeneration of Europe must come from within by the unification of the creative forces in its life and a gradual reformation of political and social institutions which will bring them into line with the requirements of the new type of culture. But everything depends on the ideal which inspires this reorganisation. We have to choose broadly between two alternatives. On the one hand, there is the ideal of secular cosmopolitanism, as preached by Mr. Wells and so many others in this country; on the other hand, there is the policy outlined by Mr. Barnes—a return to the historic traditions of European unity, based on a distinctively Christian and Catholic ideal of culture. And while this latter ideal can hardly be identified with that of Fascism, as Mr. Barnes would have it, there does exist a certain common ground between them, as against the other school of cosmopolitan idealism which has inherited the old Liberal bias in favour of secularism and anti-clericalism. The opposition of these ideals to that of the new spirit which is abroad in Europe has been expressed with remarkable clarity by the author of an article in *The Times Literary Supplement,*[5] which deals with the Youth Movement in Germany.

"In the last resort," he writes, "the *Jugendbewegung* is a religious movement. As such, it is not surprising to find it instinctively suspicious of what we call idealism. . . . All our modern English writers are idealists or sceptics; few are religious. Bernard Shaw, H. G. Wells, Bertrand Russell—men such as these apparently regard earthly life as a final state which it is man's duty and destiny to perfect. They call upon us to open conspiracies for the achievement of world order and the organisation of peace and equity with all the help that modern scientific discovery can lend. Not so the *Wandervögel.*[6] Something in him refuses to believe in this notion. For him the world is manifestly appearance, not reality, a condition of trial and testing, a state of passion, a place of striving and obedience to destiny. In fact, to the vision of the idealist he opposes the fatalism of religion. He is not concerned with the perfection of the machinery of living, but with a renewal of those faculties which connect man with the background of life, with an invisible reality."

This religious view of life is equally incompatible with the political rationalism of the Liberals and the economic materialism of the Socialists. It requires the subordination of both politics and economics to a principle of spiritual order which is the source alike of political authority and social function. Thus the refashioning of society must be accomplished not by political or economic revolution, but by the creation of new organs of social leadership and new human types. Just as the mediaeval knight had a different function and ideal from those leaders of the Viking pirate or the Roman centurion, so the leaders of the new order will be neither irresponsible capitalists nor Socialist bu-

5. *The Times Literary Supplement,* April 18th, 1929, p. xxii.
6. The writer is referring to the group of non-political Youth Associations, of which the Bund der Wandervögel is typical.

reaucrats, but members of a hierarchy dedicated to a life of voluntary responsibility and service. Herein it marks a breach with the secular and individualistic traditions of the Renaissance culture and a return to the hierarchic ideal of mediaeval Christendom. The realisation of this ideal must inevitably be a long and arduous process. Any attempt to impose it immediately and by force on the modern state involves a serious risk of ultimate failure. For the essential task is to create not a new state machine, but new men and a new spirit. Only on these conditions is it possible for Europe to accept the new forms of mass-civilisation without forfeiting its spiritual and cultural inheritance. An individualistic type of society can be secular and yet attain a high level of culture, but it seems impossible to conceive of a thoroughly secular mass-civilisation, whether of the American or the Russian type, which would not ultimately be destructive of the human personality and consequently of all the higher cultural values. Mass-civilisation can only be made spiritually tolerable if subordinated to a principle of the religious order which the individual can serve freely and wholeheartedly without becoming either a slave or an automaton.

II

The Significance of Bolshevism

The economic crisis of the last two years has proved a godsend to the Bolsheviks. The years of the New Economic Policy in Russia and of the post-war boom in the West were a time of disappointment and trial for the leaders of the communist party. Fortunately for them the launching of the second communist offensive in Russia—the Five-Year Plan— has coincided with the apparent collapse of the capitalist system in the West and has revived the hopes of world revolution which for a time had been abandoned. Above all, these hopes are concentrated on the approaching dissolution of the British Empire, which the Bolsheviks regard not without reason as the chief element of cohesion in the divided ranks of their enemies. To-day Trotsky writes: "Only a blind man could fail to see that Great Britain is headed for gigantic revolutionary earthquake shocks in which the last fragments of her conservatism, her world domination, her present state machine, will go down without a trace."[1]

These hopes are encouraged by the mood of fatalism and despair that is so common in Western countries. Professed communists may be few enough, but everywhere we find intellectuals who are fascinated by the grandiose projects of communist state planning and who feel that the social and economic system of Western Europe neither deserves nor is able to surmount its present crisis.

What is the reason for the success—even though it be only a relative success—of Bolshevism; for the way in which it has maintained itself essentially unchanged through all the vicissitudes of the Revolution and the Civil War, the New Economic Policy and the Five-Year

1. *The History of the Russian Revolution,* Vol. I, p. 117, translated by Max Eastman. (Gollancz 18*s.*)

Plan; above all, for the attraction that it seems to exercise not only for the discontented and the disinherited proletarian, but also for the disinterested idealist? This is the question that a young German sociologist, Dr. Waldemar Gurian, has attempted to answer in an important book that has just been translated into English[2] and he has succeeded better than any other writer that I know in getting to the root of the matter and revealing the essential nature of the Bolshevik *régime*. For Bolshevism is not a political movement that can be judged by its practical aims and achievements, nor is it an abstract theory that can be understood apart from its historical context. It differs from other contemporary movements above all by its organic unity, its fusion of theory and practice, and by the way in which its practical policy is bound up with its philosophy. In a world of relativity and scepticism it stands for absolute principles; for a creed that is incarnate in a social order and for an authority that demands the entire allegiance of the whole man. The Bolshevik ideology, writes Dr. Gurian, "has been transformed from a philosophy consciously learned and imposed on life from without into a concrete living force, a national outlook, which unconsciously, implicitly, and spontaneously determines and moulds all men's judgments and opinions." "These revolutionaries are not simply politicians satisfied with the possession of power. They regard themselves as bearers of a gospel which shall bring to humanity the true redemption from its sufferings, the imperfections of its earthly existence.

"It is precisely in this respect that Bolshevism is superior to the sceptical, relativist and purely opportunist political and social attitude so common in the outside world. It claims to represent immutable principles. Though it regards earthly existence, the economic and social organisation, as the final end of human life, it follows this belief with a zeal and a devotion that give it the appearance of a religion, in comparison with which the frequent panegyrics of man's spiritual freedom and dignity which carry with them no practical obligation appear worthless and hollow. It is therefore impossible to combat Bolshevism with arguments of a purely opportunist kind."[3]

And, in the same way, the communist party has little resemblance to

2. *Bolshevism: Theory and Practice,* translated by E. I. Watkin. (Sheed & Ward)
3. *Op.cit.* p. 4.

a political party in the ordinary sense of the word. It is a voluntary organisation only in the same sense as is a religious order. Its members are
bound by a rigid and impersonal discipline, but they are not the servants
of the state, for the state itself is their instrument. It is true that they regard themselves as the representatives and trustees of the proletariat, but
it would be a great mistake to suppose that they think it is their business
to obey the wishes of the working class, as the democratic politician fulfils the mandate of his electors. The proletariat that they serve is a mystical entity—the universal church of the Marxian believer—and the actual
populace is an unregenerate mass which it is their duty to guide and
organise according to the principles of the true faith. The communist is
not a representative of the people: he is the priest of an idea.

Consequently the triumph of Bolshevism was not a triumph of the
popular will over Tsarist tyranny, or of revolutionary enthusiasm over
conservative order. It was the victory of authority and discipline over
democratic idealism and individualism. As we see clearly enough in the
first volume of Trotsky's *History of the Russian Revolution,* it was the victory of a few men who knew what they wanted and allowed nothing
to stand in their way over a vast majority that was driven to and fro by
the uncertainty of the politicians and the passions of the mob. It was,
above all, the victory of one man—Lenin—the most remarkable personality that the age produced.

The age of the Great War was an age of iron, but it gave birth to no
military genius and no great statesman; its political leaders were men
of paper. The one man of iron that the age produced arose from the
most unlikely quarter that it is possible to conceive—from among the
fanatics and revolutionary agitators who wandered about the watering
places of Switzerland and Germany conspiring ineffectually and arguing with one another. To the practical politicians, even those of the Socialist party, Lenin was nothing but an ineffective visionary. Kerensky
himself at first seems to have regarded him with condescending toler-
ance as a man who "knew nothing, who had lived apart from the world
and viewed everything through the glasses of his fanaticism."

Certainly Lenin was a fanatic, but he was a fanatic who had no illusions
about himself or others and who was as ready to learn from experience as
the most opportunist of practical politicians. Nothing could be more un-

like the popular idea of a revolutionary leader than this simple and even common-place man who derided idealism and hated fine phrases, and who, in his own words, "always kept a stone in his pockets" in dealing with his fellow-men. He was the complete antithesis of Trotsky, the man of words, and it shows his power of self-suppression that he should have worked so long with a man whose nature was so utterly alien to his own, because he was a useful asset to the revolutionary cause.

But Lenin's cynicism and hatred of "idealism" must not lead us to suppose that he undervalued ideas. He was above all a man of theory and he differed from the average Socialist leader, both among the Bolsheviks and outside the party, in his insistence on the philosophical absolutism of the communist creed. "We must realise," he wrote in 1922, "that neither the natural sciences nor even a materialism that lacks solid philosophical foundations is capable of carrying on the struggle against the onslaught of bourgeois ideas and preventing the re-establishment of the bourgeois *Weltanschauung*. If this contest is to be waged victoriously, the scientist must be a materialist of our time, that is to say, a conscious adherent of the materialism represented by Marx: in other words, a dialectical materialist."[4] And even Marx by himself was not enough, since he held that without Hegel Marx's *Kapital* is unintelligible. Hegel and Marx are the Old and New Testaments of the Bolshevik dispensation, and neither of them can stand without the other. No amount of practical success can justify the sacrifice of a jot or a tittle of this revelation, and it is better to postpone the immediate realisation of communism as a working system (as Lenin actually did by the New Economic Policy), rather than imperil the orthodoxy of the picked minority that forms the spiritual foundation of the whole system.

Thus the communist system, as planned and largely created by Lenin, was a kind of *atheocracy,* a spiritual order of the most rigid and exclusive type, rather than a political order. The state was not an end in itself, it was an instrument, or, as Lenin himself puts it, "simply the weapon with which the proletariat wages its class war—*a special sort of bludgeon, nothing more.*"[5]

4. Gurian, *op. cit.,* p. 306.
5. From the notes for a monograph on the dictatorship of the proletariat drafted by Lenin in 1920 and printed in Vol. 25 of his collected works. (Gurian, p. 300.)

Nothing could be more characteristic of Lenin's inhuman simplicity and directness than this sentence: for, unlike his Western admirers, Lenin was never afraid to call a bludgeon a bludgeon.

To the Western mind such an attitude may seem shocking or even inconceivable, just as does the Bolshevik conception of law and the judiciary system as a weapon to be wielded by the dictatorship for political ends. But it must be recognised that it has roots deep in Russian character and in Russian history. Ivan the Terrible and Peter the Great also regarded the state as a bludgeon and dealt with the Boyars and the Old Believers as mercilessly as Lenin dealt with the bourgeois and the Kulaks. It seems as though it were the fate of the vast, slow-moving masses of the Russian people to be periodically bludgeoned into activity by the ruthless energy of their rulers. Trotsky himself fully recognises this feature of the Russian development. "A backward culture," he writes, "is forced to make sudden leaps under the whips of external necessity"; and the whole of his first chapter is a commentary on those words of Vico: "The Tsar of Muscovy, although a Christian, rules over a lazy-minded people."

But all this does nothing to explain the attraction of the Bolshevik experiment for certain elements in the West. If it were simply a question of *catching up* with capitalist Europe, as Trotsky almost seems to suggest, Western Europe has no more reason to disturb itself than it had in the past. After all, nobody in the West thought of idealising Ivan the Terrible or even Peter the Great. The fact is that while Bolshevism is in the concrete a Russian phenomenon, its theoretic basis and its absolute claims have given it a much wider significance than any purely national revolution could have. It reflects in the distorted and exaggerated medium of Russian society a crisis that is common to the whole of the modern world. As primitive peoples succumb more easily than white men to the diseases of civilisation, so the spiritual maladies of European civilisation become more deadly in a simpler social environment. The influence of revolutionary ideas, the loss of spiritual order, the substitution of private interests for public authority and of individual opinions for social beliefs are factors common to the modern world, but the Western peoples have been in some degree immunised by two centuries of experience and they have hitherto been able to preserve their social stability in spite of the prevalence of subversive ideas. In Russia, however, this was not the case. The Russian bourgeoisie possessed in an exaggerated form all the weaknesses of their Western counterparts. They were a source of weakness rather than of strength to the social order, which they undermined spiritually at the same time that they exploited it economically. They showed a platonic sympathy for every kind of subversive ideal, and even the Bolsheviks themselves received financial support from prominent industrialists, such as Sava Morosov. Above all, it is in Russia that we can study in its purest form the phenomenon of an intelligentsia—that is to say, an educated class— that is entirely detached from social responsibilities and provides a seed bed for the propagation of revolutionary ideas. It was not from the peasants or the industrial proletariat, but from the ranks of the lesser nobility and the bourgeois intelligentsia that the leaders of the revolutionary and terrorist movement arose from the time of Herzen and Bakunin to that of Lenin himself.

Hence it is not surprising that the same society that has seen the most extreme development of the subversive elements in bourgeois culture should also produce the most extreme type of reaction against that culture. The disintegration of bourgeois society has worked itself out to its logical conclusion and has given place to a movement in the reverse direction. The futility and emptiness of Russian bourgeois existence as described, for instance, by Chekhov, or still earlier in Goncharov's *Oblomov*, is such that any *régime* which offers a positive and objective end of life becomes attractive. Man cannot live in a spiritual void; he needs some fixed social standards and some absolute intellectual principles. Bolshevism at least replaces the spiritual anarchy of bourgeois society by a rigid order and substitutes for the doubt and scepticism of an irresponsible intelligentsia the certitude of an absolute authority embodied in social institutions. It is true that the Bolshevik philosophy is a poor thing at best. It is philosophy reduced to its very lowest terms, a philosophy with a minimum of spiritual and intellectual content. It impoverishes life instead of enriching it, and confines the mind in a narrow and arid circle of ideas. Nevertheless, it is enough of a philosophy to provide society with a theoretical basis, and therein lies the secret of its strength. The lesson of Bolshevism is that any philosophy is better than no philosophy, and that a *régime* which possesses a principle of authority, however misconceived it may be, will be stronger than a system that rests on the shifting basis of private interests and private opinions.

And this is the reason why Bolshevism with all its crudity constitutes a real menace to Western society. For although our civilisation is stronger and more coherent than that of pre-war Russia, it suffers from the same internal weakness. It needs some principle of social and economic order and yet it has lost all vital relation to the spiritual traditions on which the old order of European culture was based. As Dr. Gurian writes, "Marxism, and therefore Bolshevism, does but voice the secret and unavowed philosophy of the bourgeois society when it regards society and economics as the absolute. It is faithful, likewise, to its morality when it seeks to order this absolute, the economic society, in such a way that justice, equality and freedom, the original war cries of the bourgeois advance, may be the lot of all. The rise of the bourgeoisie and the evolution of the bourgeois society have made economics the centre of public life."[6] And thus: "Bolshevism is at once the product of the bourgeois society and the judgment upon it. It reveals the goal to which the secret philosophy of that society leads, if accepted with unflinching logic."[7] At first sight this criticism of the bourgeois society seems unjust, in view of the great services that it has rendered to civilisation during the last two centuries. It may be plausibly argued that the faults of the bourgeois are no greater than those of the leading classes in other ages, while his virtues are all his own. But the fact remains that the typical leaders of bourgeois society do not arouse the same respect as that which is felt for the corresponding figures in the old *régime*. We instinctively feel that there is something honourable about a king, a noble, or a knight which the banker, the stockbroker or the democratic politician does not possess. A king may be a bad king, but our very condemnation of him is a tribute to the prestige of his office. Nobody speaks of a "bad bourgeois"; the Socialist may indeed call him a "bloody bourgeois," but that is a set formula that has nothing to do with his personal vices or virtues.

This distrust of the bourgeois is no modern phenomenon. It has its

6. *Op. cit.*, p. 237.   7. *Op. cit.*, p. 242.

roots in a much older tradition than that of Socialism. It is equally typical of the mediaeval noble and peasant, the romantic Bohemian and the modern proletarian. The fact is that the bourgeoisie has always stood somewhat apart from the main structure of European society, save in Italy and the Low Countries. While the temporal power was in the hands of the kings and the nobles and the spiritual power was in the hands of the Church, the bourgeoisie, the Third Estate, occupied a position of privileged inferiority which allowed them to amass wealth and to develop considerable intellectual culture and freedom of thought without acquiring direct responsibility or power.[8] Consequently, when the French Revolution and the fall of the old *régime* made the bourgeoisie the ruling class in the West, it retained its inherited characteristics, its attitude of hostile criticism towards the traditional order and its enlightened selfishness in the pursuit of its own interests. But although the bourgeois now possessed the substance of power, he never really accepted social responsibility as the old rulers had done. He remained a private individual—an *idiot* in the Greek sense—with a strong sense of social conventions and personal rights, but with little sense of social solidarity and no recognition of his responsibility as the servant and representative of a super-personal order. In fact, he did not realise the necessity of such an order, since it had always been provided for him by others, and he had taken it for granted.

This, I think, is the fundamental reason for the unpopularity and lack of prestige of bourgeois civilisation. It lacks the vital human relationship which the older order with all its faults never denied. To the bourgeois politician the electorate is an accidental collection of voters; to the bourgeois industrialist his employees are an accidental collection of wage earners. The king and the priest, on the other hand, were united to their people by a bond of organic solidarity. They were not individuals standing over against other individuals, but parts of a common social organism and representatives of a common spiritual order.

The bourgeoisie upset the throne and the altar, but they put in their

8. The same conditions obtained in a highly accentuated form in the case of the Jews, who are, so to speak, bourgeois *par excellence,* and this explains how it is that the East European Jew can adapt himself so much more rapidly and successfully than his Christian neighbour to modern bourgeois civilisation.

place nothing but themselves. Hence their *régime* cannot appeal to any higher sanction than that of self interest. It is continually in a state of disintegration and flux. It is not a permanent form of social organisation, but a transitional phase between two orders.

This does not, of course, mean that Western society is inevitably doomed to go the way of Russia, or that it can find salvation in the Bolshevik ideal of class dictatorship and economic mass civilisation. The Bolshevik philosophy is simply the *reductio ad absurdum* of the principles implicit in bourgeois culture and consequently it provides no real answer to the weaknesses and deficiencies of the latter. It takes the nadir of European spiritual development for the zenith of a new order.

The bourgeois culture in spite of its temporary importance is nothing but an episode in European history. This is why the current Socialist opposition of communist and bourgeois society is in reality a false dilemma. Western civilisation is not merely the civilisation of the bourgeois; it is the old civilisation of Western Christendom that is undergoing a temporary phase of disorganisation and change. It owes its strength not to its bourgeois politics and economics, but to the older and more permanent elements of its social and spiritual tradition. In no country, save perhaps in the United States, does the bourgeois culture exist in the pure state as a self-subsistent whole. England, above all, which seems at first sight to be the most thoroughly bourgeois society of all, has in reality never possessed a bourgeoisie in the true sense. Its ruling class down to modern times was agrarian in character and incorporated considerable elements of the older aristocratic tradition. Ever since Tudor times it was the aim of the successful merchant to "found a family" and leave the city for the country, and even the city man remained to a great extent a countryman at heart, as we see as late as the Victorian period in Surtees Jorrocks. The English Nonconformists did indeed possess a tradition of cultural separatism analogous to that of the continental bourgeoisie; but even they were not pure bourgeois, since their basis of social unity was a religious and not an economic one.

In the same way the government in England has never been completely transformed by the bourgeois revolution, but still preserves the monarchical principle as the centre of national solidarity and order.

And the same state of things exists in varying degrees in every Western state. Even France, which politically is an almost pure type of bourgeois culture, is sociologically far from simple and owes it strength to the delicate equilibrium that it has established between two different social types—the peasant and the bourgeois—and two opposite spiritual traditions—that of the Catholic Church and that of the Liberal Enlightenment.

Consequently, it is impossible to solve the problem of Western society by disregarding the social and spiritual complexity of European civilisation. Bourgeois civilisation is not the only European tradition, and Rousseau and Marx are not the only European thinkers. The new order must be conceived not in terms of bourgeois exploiter and exploited proletarian, but as a unity that incorporates every element in European culture and that does justice to the spiritual and social as well as to the economic needs of human nature. In Russia such a solution was impossible owing to the profound gulf that divided the bourgeoisie and the intelligentsia with their imported Western culture from the governmental tradition of Byzantine autocracy and Orthodoxy and from the peasant culture of a semi-barbaric peasantry. But Western civilisation is still fundamentally homogeneous. Our intelligentsia has not entirely lost its roots in a common spiritual order, and our bourgeoisie is not entirely divorced from social responsibility. It is still not too late to restore the integrity of European culture on the basis of a comprehensive and Catholic order. We must go back to an older and more fundamental social tradition and to a wider and more perennial philosophy, which recognise the depth and complexity of human nature and the existence of a moral order that must govern political and economic relations no less than private behaviour. As Dr. Gurian says, Bolshevism itself is an unintentional and therefore most impressive witness to the existence of such an order, since its attempt to treat society as a closed and self-sufficient order has led not to Utopia but to tyranny. Man is first mutilated by being deprived of some of his most essential activities, and this maimed and crippled human nature is made the standard by which civilisation and life itself are judged.

III

The World Crisis and the English Tradition

The crisis that has arisen in the modern world during the post-war period is not merely an economic one. It involves the future of Western culture as a whole, and, consequently, the fate of humanity. But it is not a simple or uniform phenomenon. It is not confined to any one state or any one continent. It is world-wide in its incidence and shows itself in a different form in every different society. The problem of Russia is essentially different from that of America, and that of Germany from that of England. And yet all are inextricably interwoven in an immense and complicated tangle which politicians and economists are vainly struggling to unravel.

Hence it is useless to hope to find the solution of the world crisis in some simple remedy that can be applied to every society indifferently. The problem is a real one, and it cannot be solved by the manipulation of credit and currency. It is a question of how to adjust the traditional forms of social and political order which are the result of a long and gradual process of historical evolution to the new economic forces that have transformed the world during the last century, and above all during the last forty years.

Thus each people has to find the individual solution that is in conformity with its own sociological and historical structure. And nowhere is this more necessary than in England, for while the English situation is one of the key positions of the world crisis, it has no exact analogy with anything that exists in any other country. It shows a peculiarly abrupt contrast between a highly individual national culture and an ex-

27

ceptionally highly developed system of world trade and finance. Of all countries England is at once the most national and insular in its cultural tradition and the most cosmopolitan in its economic and imperial position. In this it resembles Rome, the peasant state that became the organiser of a world empire and the centre of a cosmopolitan civilisation.

And as the development of Roman culture was late and backward in comparison with the Hellenic world, so was it with the English national culture as compared with that of continental Europe. The development of a native English culture was checked by the Norman Conquest, and during the best part of the Middle Ages England was under the dominion of an alien culture that had its roots across the channel. England first began to become herself in the fourteenth century, when the mediaeval unity was passing away, and it was only in the three centuries that followed the Renaissance and the Reformation that the English national culture acquired its characteristic form.

At that time civilisation on the Continent was following in a remarkable way in the footsteps of the great Mediterranean civilisation of the past. Renaissance Italy inherited the traditions of Hellenism, while Spain and Baroque Austria and the France of Louis XIV inherited the Roman Byzantine tradition of state absolutism and sacred monarchy. But in England there is no room for such comparisons. Partly, though not entirely, as a result of the Reformation, she remained apart from the main current of European life, following her own path and jealously guarding against any influence from outside, somewhat after the fashion of Japan in the Far East during this very period. Her development was, in fact, the exact opposite to that of Germany during the seventeenth and eighteenth centuries, open as the latter was to all the cultural and political currents in Europe, receiving French influence from across the Rhine, Italian influence through Austria, and Swedish influence from the Baltic.

It was this accentuation of her island position which was the essential condition of England's achievement. She was a little world, secure behind the guardian barrier of the narrow seas, the most peaceful land in Europe, almost the only spot in the world that was free from the constant menace of war and invasion. Hence there was a general relaxation of tension in the social organism. There was no need for the rigid centralisation, the standing armies, the bureaucratic organisation, which on the Continent were absolutely necessary for national survival. And so, while in other countries culture concentrated itself in cities and in the courts of kings, in England it spread itself abroad over the open country. A new type of civilisation grew up that was not urban or courtly, but essentially rural and based upon the life of the family.

It was this characteristic that was the source of the exceptional stability and strength of the English social organism which so impressed continental observers in the eighteenth and nineteenth centuries. On the Continent ever since the time of the Roman Empire every people and every state was divided within itself by a duality of culture. On the one hand there were the traditions of the court and the city which, finally, after the Renaissance, fused with one another; on the other the peasant tradition, which to a greater or less extent preserved an older and more primitive culture and possessed its own art, its own costume, its own social customs, almost its own laws. We have an extreme instance of this in Russia during the last two centuries, where the contrast of the French-speaking official or courtier of Petersburg, living by the culture of modern Europe, and the patriarchal peasant, living in a half-Slavonic, half-Byzantine, wholly mediaeval world, was so intense as to be unbearable, and ultimately caused the dissolution of Russian society. But in England, at least since the close of the Middle Ages, there has been no such contrast. Our society and culture have been single and homogeneous. We have not had a special peasant art and costume because our whole culture has been a rural culture. That characteristic figure, the eighteenth century squire, was not the member of a noble class as was even the smallest German baron or French count, he was a glorified yeoman. No doubt he, too, was sometimes an oppressor, but he was never a stranger, and when he was most high-handed, as in the enclosure of the commons, he was fighting the last stage of the peasant's long battle for the Plough against the Waste. Like Tennyson's Lincolnshire Farmer, he thought that a few moral deficiencies would be overlooked in the man who "stubbed Thurnaby Waste."

Thus the English culture and the social discipline that went with it were not a civilisation imposed from above, but grew up from below out of the very soil of England. When all the great states of the Continent were shaken by revolution and disorder, England alone stood firm and preserved an unbroken continuity with her past. Her constitution was not a paper document, based on the most admirable abstract principles and entirely altered every few years, it was herself; she could not throw it aside any more than a man can discard his own personality.

One of the most original Catholic sociologists of the nineteenth century, Frederic Leplay, devoted a work to the study of English society. He had been impressed when first he visited England in 1836 by the stability of the social organism and by the weakness of the forces of irreligion and disorder which were then in the ascendant throughout Western Europe; and he found the source of England's greatness in the characteristics that we have just described. It was not simply the strength of family life and the home, but the way in which a whole culture and social order had been built up on these foundations. Elsewhere in those households that he studied so devotedly in the six volumes of his *Ouvriers Européens,* he had seen family life that was as strong or stronger, from a moral and economic point of view, but nowhere else was it the centre of the national culture and polity to the same extent as it was in England.

This development had its roots far back in the Middle Ages. Long before the Reformation English society had begun to acquire its characteristic rural aspect. The English village, with its pacific manor-house and its richly adorned parish church, was already far different from those of the war-harried castle-studded countrysides of France and Germany. But it was only in the centuries which followed the Renaissance that this English society began to bear fruit in an equally distinctive style and culture. How incomparably English are the typical Tudor and Jacobean manor and farmhouse, and how rich is their social content. They make us understand how it was possible for England to produce men like Herrick and Herbert and Henry Vaughan, poets who lived out of the world, far from the possibilities of the city and its culture, but whose art had a purity and freshness as far from that of the poets of the same period in Italy and France as an English meadow from a Neapolitan street.

And with the following century the contrast between English and continental culture becomes even stronger. It is true that the hard brilliance and rationalism of the French eighteenth century had its parallel here in Pope and Bolingbroke, and later in Chesterfield and Gibbon, but the victory was not with them. More and more their spirit was felt to be alien, their spiritual home was at Paris and Lausanne. The heart of England was with the solid traditionalism of Dr. Johnson or the intense pietism of Cowper and the Wesleys. Moreover, the coming of the house of Hanover, so far from introducing continental influences, served rather to weaken the prestige of the court and to make the country more obstinately English than ever. Neither our society nor our art served the court and the capital, both alike centred in the family, in the country houses or in the homes of the merchants. And this is true of both the chief manifestations of English art during this period, the great portrait painters and the late Georgian school of architecture and decoration, of which the typical representatives are the brothers Adam.

In the latter the English tradition has reached maturity. It is no longer purely rural it has begun to impress its image on the town and on urban life. The ordinary London house of this type, with the reserved severity of its exterior and the intimate refinement and grace of the interior, is a true type of the society that produced it. A society whose civilisation was essentially private, bound up with the family and the home, and which brings with it even into the city and its suburbs something of the quiet and retirement of the countryside. It is the complete antithesis of the Latin social ideal, which is communal and public, which finds its artistic expression in the baroque town square, with its fountains and statuary and monumental façades, a fitting background to the open-air life of a many-coloured voluble crowd.

So if one compares the London of a hundred years ago, when this English culture was still practically intact, with the great cities of the Continent with their ancient tradition of a splendid civic life, the comparison is at first all in their favour. In England there was a rustic individualism and a boorishness which sink at times to downright callousness and brutality, as in the penal code and the treatment of the poor. But as soon as we leave public life and look behind the severe and sometimes dingy façade, what treasures does the interior life of that late Georgian London reveal! The harvest of Renaissance Florence was greater, may be, but there the resources of a brilliant court called together the talent of all Italy. In London it was a spontaneous flowering from the poorest and most unpromising soil. Blake, Keats, Charles Lamb, Thomas Girtin, and the Varleys, Turner and Dickens, were all of them poor men, for the most part completely without any of the advantages of birth or education. Yet each of them is unique, each of them is a voice of England, and some of their work possesses the same unearthly beauty and spirituality which marked English poetry in the seventeenth century.

But with the close of the Georgian period a profound change begins to pass over English society. England ceases to be an agrarian state, and the new industry, which had been developing for more than half a century, becomes the dominant element in. the life of the nation. The centre of gravity shifts from the village and the country house to the industrial town, the mine and the factory.

This change was not a gradual, modification of the older non-industrial civilisation, it was an independent growth. For the new industry developed in just those districts of England that were most backward and furthest removed from the centres of the old culture. Great masses of population began to settle on the wild moorlands of north-western England and in the valleys of the Welsh hills, and new cities grew up, like mushrooms, without plan and forethought, without corporate responsibility or civic tradition. Thus two Englands stood over against one another without social contact. As long as the Georgian era lasted the old England still ruled, and the new nation of industrial workers lived a disenfranchised existence as a mere wealth-producing caste. Then came the ferment of the years after the Napoleonic War, the rise of Liberalism and the passing of the Reform Bill. Finally, with the repeal of the Corn Laws, the old rural England passed into the background, and a new financial industrial state took its place.

Thus the nineteenth century and the Victorian age can be looked on from two points of view: as the last phase of the old rural domestic culture—the culmination of the English tradition; or as the revolt against it—the growth of a new urban-industrial civilisation with its centre in the group-work of the mine and the factory, bringing with it the disintegration of the family into a number of independent wage earners and the degeneration of the home into a workers' dormitory.

Yet, in spite of all, the English were faithful to their old ideal. The clerk and the workman clung to their rural tradition of a separate home, and the English industrial town to this day stands apart from its fellows on the Continent as a separate type by reason of its square miles of little brick boxes—each the home of a single family—in which it houses its workers. But a tree cannot continue to bear fruit, even of this stunted and unbeautiful kind, when the roots are gone. With the twentieth century we see the coming of a new urban civilisation, which has no contact with the English tradition. The old ideals have grown discredited, and the Englishman no longer disdains to dwell in flats. And with the flat comes a corresponding new anti-domestic ethos; divorce, birth control, the turning to outer society for all vital needs.

England, in fact, has been going through the same social crisis as ancient Rome experienced at the end of the Republic.

Rome, too, had been founded on the life of the family and the rural community, and the loss of the agrarian foundations of Roman society caused a profound revolution in Roman culture and in the Roman polity. The national Roman tradition was only saved by an immense effort for social regeneration which was indeed but partially successful. And the parallel is all the more instructive, because in both cases the essential problem was the same—namely, how to reconcile the national tradition of an agrarian state with the imperial responsibilities of a world empire.

For in modern England, no less than in ancient Rome, the disintegration of the agrarian foundations of the old national culture was accompanied by the formation of a great imperial state. As Rome unified the Mediterranean world by her work of military conquest and organisation, so England by her maritime and commercial expansion became the great organiser of the new cosmopolitan economic unity. Everywhere in the nineteenth century the English financiers, engineers, colonists, explorers, seamen and administrators were breaking down the geographical, social and economic barriers that separated continents and civilisations, and were binding the world together by an intricate structure of world trade and world finance on the summit of which the new English industrial society was poised. We have a classical example of this in the Lancashire cotton industry, depending as it did on the three-fold relation of American raw material, English industry and Oriental markets, bound together by English shipping and financial organisation, and secured by English sea power and imperial administration. Nevertheless, this new economic imperialism was not the result of the unaided enterprise of the new industrial society. Its foundations had already been laid in the eighteenth century by the old agrarian state. The British Empire owes its creation not to the England of the millowners, but to the England of the squires, the England of Walpole and the Pitts, which also produced the merchants and the seamen who created the East India Company and the mercantile marine. The spirit of the new society is to be seen in the cosmopolitan Free Trade ideals of the Manchester school, which disavowed the old mercantile imperialism, even though it actually owed to it the possibility of its own existence. And, consequently, these ideals never dominated English policy. The prosperity of nineteenth-century England was due to a working compromise between the two societies and the two traditions which is represented by the Free Trade imperialism of Palmerston and Disraeli, a compromise which was essentially unstable since it concealed latent contradictions.

To-day these contradictions have worked themselves out, and the instability of the nineteenth-century compromise is patent to all. It is no longer possible to reconcile Free Trade and imperialism or to combine the old national agrarian tradition with that of a completely industrialised society. The English achievement is threatened both within and without: within, by the almost complete dissolution of the rural life from which our national culture derived its inner vitality; and without, by the crumbling of the whole edifice of world trade and world finance on which the economic prosperity of English industrialism was based. Consequently, we seem faced by a dilemma between two alternatives, each of which promises to be equally disastrous. Either we can attempt to restore the agrarian foundations of our culture by a return to agricultural self-sufficiency, in which case we destroy the economic foundation of the urban industrialism by which the vast majority of our population lives; or we can sacrifice everything to maintaining the cosmopolitan mechanism of world industry and trade, which would mean the final destruction not only of our agriculture, but of our national tradition and our social vitality.

While the spread of industrialism and its growing perfection of technique are steadily increasing the volume of actual and potential production, the world market is being increasingly restricted by economic nationalism and the political control of trade. England is faced with the prospect of being the workshop of a world that does not need her services. At the very moment when the existence of the world market is being threatened, our whole population is becoming dependent on the world market for. its very existence. English agriculture is at its last gasp, and any serious effort to revive it would be opposed by the united forces of capital and labour as involving either a rise in the costs of labour or a decline in the standard of living.

But if we cannot afford the economic cost of preserving our agricultural population, can we afford the social cost of destroying it? It is impossible to decide the question by purely economic considerations. A landlord might find it more profitable to clear his estate of its farming population and to let it to a game syndicate, but that does not mean that it would be in the national interest for him to do so. And in the same way our present abundant supplies of cheap food may be bought too dear, if they involve the sacrifice of the agrarian foundation of our national culture. The land of England is not just a food factory that can be dismantled at will, it is a part of ourselves, and if it becomes derelict, our whole social life is maimed. The first consideration for a society is not to maintain the volume of its industrial production or even "the standard of life" in the current sense of the expression, but the quality of its population, and that cannot be secured by the mere expenditure of money on the so-called "social services," but only by the preservation of the natural foundations of society: the family and the land.

It is, of course, obvious that we cannot disregard economic factors, and that a society which cannot pay its way cannot exist. Nevertheless, the system that produces the largest profits is not necessarily the most efficient in the long run, even from the economic point of view. A purely urban industrialism is at its best a wasteful system, for it destroys the natural mechanism of social life, and is forced to construct at immense cost an artificial mechanism to take its place. For example, under the old order the land-owning class was also the ruling class, and provided the permanent *cadres* from which the administrators and the servants of the state were recruited. But in an industrial state the wealthy class is a plutocracy that possesses no definite social function, and a separate governing class of paid bureaucrats has to be created and trained at the expense of the state. And thus the plutocracy of the industrialist order actually costs the country more than did the old ruling class, while it is decidedly inferior to the latter, from the non-economic point of view, as an organ of national culture.

Such considerations as these, however, have no influence on modern politics, which invariably sacrifice sociology to economics, and which even in economics prefer immediate profit to ultimate advantage. Socialism alone possesses any kind of a sociology, and it derives considerable advantage from the fact. But it is a naïve and rudimentary sociology which shuts its eyes to the existence of any but economic values, and seeks national salvation in the complete subordination of the social organism to the economic machine. In fact, socialism and industrial capitalism both share the same economic fallacy and the same urbanist and mechanical ideals: both alike lead to the disintegration of the social organism and to the destruction of its agrarian foundation.

If England is to be saved, it is necessary to abandon the economic fatalism that has dominated our thought for a hundred years and to base our national policy on sound sociological principles. We must recognise that our national culture is our greatest asset, and the true foundations of society are to be found neither in commerce nor in financial and industrial mechanism, but in nature.

Instead of exploiting nature for financial profit and forcing society into the straight waistcoat of a mechanical order, we must adapt our economic mechanism to the needs of the social organism and the safeguarding of its vital functions. Science and technology can be used in the service of rural life as well as of urban industry, and the recovery of some measure of equilibrium between the agrarian and the urban elements in our national life would strengthen the whole structure of the social organism. It is true that we cannot transform England into a self-sufficient peasant state, but it is possible to restore the life of the English countryside if we seriously wished to do so. The obstacles to recovery are not merely economic, they are also and in an even greater degree political and social. If in the England of the eighteenth century the towns were governed in the interests of the country, to-day the country is governed in the interests of the towns, and rural society is forced to adapt itself to the educational and social legislation that is a product of the utterly different social environment of urban industrialism. And at the same time the rural society is being deprived of social leadership. The old land-owning class filled so large a place in rural society that its disappearance leaves an immense gap in the social and cultural life of the countryside, and nothing is being done to fill it, owing to the concentration of all the vital forces of the nation in the great cities. Here again there is a pressing need for the restoration of social equilibrium by a measure of cultural decentralisation and by a more even distribution of the non-economic resources of the nation between city and countryside. And all these changes are not merely desirable: they are absolutely necessary if England is to survive.

No civilisation hitherto has been able to resist the destructive effects of urban and bureaucratic centralisation. It has been well said that the great city is the grave of a culture, and in the same way the substitution of a centralised bureaucratic control for the spontaneous activity of normal social life involves a process of ossification and the senile decay of the whole social organism.

The only question is whether the process has already gone too far to be checked in this country. There is no *a priori* reason why a society should not recover its health-and social stability by reversing the drift towards centralisation and deliberately strengthening its foundations in the life of the family and the country. But such a movement of social regeneration requires a vigorous moral effort and a consciousness of our responsibility. We cannot do anything so long as we are hypnotised by economic fatalism and so long as we cannot free ourselves from the decaying remains of nineteenth-century philosophy. It is necessary for us to revise our whole scheme of social values and to educate the nation in the ideas that have some relation to the realities of the modern situation. The work of social restoration must be preceded and accompanied by the reconstitution of our intellectual and spiritual traditions.

IV

The Passing of Industrialism

The war presumably marks the end of an age no less decisively than did the wars of the French Revolution. In this case, however, it is not a venerable and moribund society like the *ancien régime* that is passing away, but a transitional order, which was essentially a compromise and which never attained to a mature and consistent development.

Will the new age be a continuation of the main tendencies of the nineteenth century or a reaction against them? Will the world continue to "progress" in the old Liberal sense, or shall we witness a return to older principles which have been falling into discredit for the last few centuries? Those who incline to the latter view are already numerous in England; but the popular belief in the infallibility of "progressive" principles is still hardly touched.

The last age was essentially a time of violent and destructive change. It seems to resemble, on a far larger scale, the hundred years of disorganisation and expansion in the Ancient World which preceded the establishment of the Roman Empire. And like that period it was necessarily transitory. It can only be explained as the transition state between one relatively stable order of society and another; in the one case from the city-state to the Roman Empire, in the other from mediaeval society to what we may hope is a new world order.

The last age was an age of exploitation and therefore its duration was limited; it was not simply a case of the exploitation of the weak by the strong as in the last age of the Roman Republic; it was the exploitation of the world and of its resources by man. The natural riches lying unused for ages were spent recklessly for the sake of immediate advantage without thought of the future. It was the case of a pigmy, with the mind and aims of a pigmy, suddenly endowed with the power of a giant. In England the whole powers of the nation were thrown recklessly into the struggle for exploitation. The welfare of the people, the moral law, were thrown aside in order that the newly discovered riches could be made profitable; that the iron and coal and cotton could be put on the world market, and the riches of the exploiters increased. Thus there was not only no spiritual purpose in the process—here was not even a worthy human end. On the immense suffering and labour of the people was built up the hideous edifice of Victorian industrial society.

The men of that age did not realise that this process could not last. They accepted the industrialisation of England and the wealth that sprang from it as a natural consequence of the freedom of society and trade. England was in the nature of things fitted to be the workshop of the world, though other nations might follow her progress at a distance, and there could be no question but that the new order was desirable and permanent. In reality the note of the time was not freedom, but conquest and exploitation. England had gained an advantage over the rest of the world by the evolution of the new industry and capitalism and of the new *entrepreneur* class, while the rest of Europe was absorbed in war and politics, and also by her naval and colonial supremacy, and for many years the whole world was economically at her mercy. Lancashire and Birmingham obtained an artificial and temporary command of the markets of the East, and the New World became a great plantation from which the British factories drew their raw material.

The industrialisation of England was completed in the latter part of the nineteenth century, when her dependence on the home food supply was eliminated by the development of steam transport. Henceforward she was truly cosmopolitan, existing for and supported by the world market, and agriculture ceased to be of national importance either socially or economically. But by the time this had happened England was no longer the one great workshop of the world. The nations of the Continent and the U.S.A. had revolted against the economic supremacy of England, and had organised themselves afresh so as to gain a share in the new industry and in the world trade that had made her rich. The industrialisation of the Continent, however, was not built up on the optimistic free-trade individualism which had established itself in Great Britain half a century earlier. Protective tariffs, organised educations, and labour legislation were all co-ordinated by the State to one end. The economic powers of the nation were concentrated so as to give one another mutual support; and the race between the nations for industrial efficiency and commercial supremacy went hand in hand with the increase in armaments and the struggle for military power. The world was too small for the gigantic development of the new industrial powers, and in every market they jostled and undercut one another for an opening. No country was too small or too backward to join in the race, and even the oriental nations began to take their part. The old distinction between manufacturing and agricultural lands tended to disappear, and even in the new countries of North America and Australasia industrialisation outstripped agrarian development. Almost every nation became obsessed by the idea of using the resources of its own territory solely for its own enrichment. So that while industrialism is becoming ever more universal, the international markets are becoming relatively more restricted.

The economic supremacy, first of nineteenth-century England, then of Western Europe, was based on a monopoly of industrial skill and capital and on an unlimited supply of cheap raw material. Prairie farming—i.e., the cheap and wasteful cultivation of great spaces of fertile virgin soil—rendered possible the cheap food supply, which in turn permitted low wages and cheap labour. But already this state of things is coming to an end. So rapid has been the process of development, so quickly has the increase of population answered the stimulus of the new conditions that extensive agriculture even before the war was becoming out of date. Even in the prairies of the Western states land was becoming sufficiently valuable to repay careful cultivation, and the price of corn and meat was rising steadily.

The vacant spaces of the earth are not yet filled, but they are already limited, and the end of the process is in sight. The new world of five continents is becoming a closed and settled area like the old world of Southern Europe and Southern Asia; and once again there begins the severe pressure of great nations on territory and food supply. The limitation of the future is not one of industrial skill and capital, but one of raw materials. As population advances, the price of raw materials must increase, while, owing to the growing perfection of organisation and machinery, there is practically no limit to the reduction in costs of manufacture. In the long run the valuable capital will not be machinery or the labour which can work it, for these can be found everywhere, thanks to the spread of industrialism, but the produce of the soil, the amount of which is essentially limited. Thus there will be a tendency for agriculture to recover the place that it lost in the nineteenth century and to become once more the basis of national prosperity. The need for intensive cultivation will involve the concentration of more money, more labour and more thought on agriculture. The peasant, who was in nineteenth-century England an unimportant and neglected member of society, will tend to become influential, and will demand a larger share in the produce of his labour. No land will be poor enough to be neglected, or rich enough to be cultivated wastefully. The aim of the agriculture of the future will be the maximum produce rather than the maximum net profit, and every productive possibility will have to be developed to the full. This will involve the increase of the agricultural population in all the regions of the New and Old World where intensive cultivation is not already the rule, and points ultimately to the growth of a new territorial self-sufficiency. This process is already at work in the U.S.A., and there is a tendency in some districts for the old large-scale pioneer wheat farming to yield place to the small holdings and intensive culture of the Italians and Portuguese.

At the same time the causes which led to the formation of great centres of industrial population have begun to diminish. The growing importance of water power favours a new type of industrial settlement, and the transmission of power by electricity makes it no longer necessary for the great factory towns to be huddled together at the mouths of the coal pits.

It is obvious that these two factors which make for an equal distribution of population cannot easily or quickly take effect on so highly industrialised a country as England. They act first on the new countries where conditions are more plastic. Nevertheless, it is difficult to exaggerate the importance of the economic world-change that they foreshadow.

The third factor which is making for a new social order is the human one, and nowhere is it more insistent than in England. The disaffection of the wage labourer, on whom the industrialist system rests, endangers the solidity of the whole edifice; and this disaffection is not simply discontent with hard conditions or low wages, it is an intellectual and spiritual dissatisfaction with the present social system, and a demand for a new life. This spirit is a necessary product of the transitional state of society which characterised the nineteenth century. Industrialism involved the destruction of the economic and social hierarchy of the old *régime,* and it was therefore forced to ally itself with the political liberal movement which preached the rights of the individual and the abolition of privilege. It was inevitable that the worker, who had been fed on democratic political theories, should come in time to demand a corresponding adjustment of economic and social conditions. He demanded full citizenship.

Hitherto every form of society has limited the true citizen class to a minority. Civilisation has been built up on the foundation of a slave or helot class, which did not exist for itself but was the instrument of the dominant race or class.

In the Middle Ages, it is true, the real slave class disappeared, and even the peasant came to have a half citizenship. The craftsmen of many of the free towns and the peasants of certain exceptional regions attained integral political and economic freedom. Taking West Europe as a whole, however, the true citizen under the old *régime* was the noble or the "gentleman" *(generosus).*

The period of revolution produced the anomaly of political advance and economic retrogression. The new industrial society was constituted once more on a basis in effect, servile. The function of the wage labourer, like that of the slave, was instrumental. He possessed control neither over his work nor its fruit, but remained a human tool in the hands of the *entrepreneur* and the middleman. This state of things was felt instinctively by the worker and held consciously by the reformer to be unnatural in that it meant the subordination of the higher to the lower.

If we look on the present labour movement simply from the point of view of class war, the prospect is hopeless enough. The victory of capitalism and the reign of blind repression, or the triumph of anarchy and confiscation, or the alternate dominance of either tendency, would each be equally possible and equally disastrous.

But the modern revolt of the worker is not simply a case of the struggle between the "Haves" and the "Have Nots," the Rich and the Poor; it is rather an attempt to reverse the subordination of the human to the mechanical and the creative to the commercial function; and however stormy may be the period of change, we may be sure that a permanent social order can only be attained by the recognition of the human end and the reorganisation of the economic process on that basis.

The ideal of the new order will (let us assume) be the substitution of co-operation for competition. Avoiding the sacrifice and exploitation of men, or the waste of natural resources, in the race for wealth, the economic organisation will be directed towards the all-round development of the resources of the society. The tendency of the industrial age was to consider reward rather than work, to judge everything in terms of money. Men worked in order to get rich, and the state of being rich was an absolute end which need not serve any other social purpose—a kind of Nirvana. In this, as in other things, that age subordinated the human to the material.

On the other hand, in the Middle Ages, and in many other periods of a more stable social order, social status was inseparable from function. The knight's land and the merchant's money existed like the endowments of the abbeys and colleges, in order to enable them to fulfill their office. A man who had great wealth and no function was an anomaly, and so also to a lesser degree was the man who had a function and no means with which to fulfill it.

Will not the new age be marked by a return to these principles? A man's position will be determined by his function rather than by his possessions, and wealth will be subordinate and instrumental to work. Thus capital will be regarded not as an abstract entity but as so much apparatus, and, unless state socialism should succeed in nationalising the means of production, the apparatus would normally be owned by the men who use it, while the higher non-economic functions would be provided for, as in the Middle Ages, by endowment.

But the acceptance of such a social and economic reorganisation, however, involves a further problem—will it proceed directly from the state, or from the free association of individuals, *i.e.,* will the ideal of state socialism or that of voluntary co-operation prevail?

The former ideal was essentially a product of the industrial age. It was based on a belief in the superiority of the industrial centralisation of the large-scale business, and presupposed an industrial type of society in which agriculture was of little relative importance. It was an answer to the question, How can the lives of the workers be made tolerable if the economic conditions of the nineteenth-century industrial state are to continue? And it made no attempt to restore true economic freedom and self-determination to the individual. The exaggerations of the *laissez faire* school had caused a profound distrust of all individualism, popular faith in Parliamentarism was still unexploded, and there was as yet no realisation of the dangers of a pseudo-democratic servile state.

The last generation, however, has seen the growth of bureaucracy and the extension of government control in all departments of life and an increasing distrust of politics and politicians among the people, and there is a general recognition of the necessity for a different type of guidance and direction if democracy and freedom are to be anything but a sham. Moreover, though the centralised socialist state may make for efficiency, it could hardly make for harmonious world development, unless the dream of a single world state were realised. The existence of a number of socialist centralised states, each perfectly organised internally, and independent with regard to one another, would of itself do nothing to obviate the present state of national rivalries and war.

Is not the co-operative ideal that which best meets the needs of the new order? The substitution of all-round world development for the exploitation of the world by the industrial powers, the gradual equalisation of conditions between the old world and the new, and between the industrial and agricultural countries, as well as the dominance of the new humanist-democratic ideal, all make in the direction of decentralisation and free association rather than of the unitary state and bureaucratic control.

The co-operative theory conceives the state, not as a mechanico-political unit under the control of the sovereign, whether autocratic or democratic, but as a living organism in which each part has its own function and develops according to its own laws.

Thus citizenship is a manifold thing. The individual is not simply a member of the state; he belongs to other corporate unions according to the function which he performs and the locality in which he dwells; and as the guild or union of which he is a free partner is bound to respect his rights, so also is the state bound to respect the rights of the corporate entities of which it consists.

Functional unions, *i.e.,* the associations of members of a particular trade or profession, are not the only corporate bodies which make up the state. The territorial and inter-functional units are of even greater importance, since they possess the capacity for a political and social life of their own.

During the past age the centralised state and centralised industry tended to absorb all local life into the great urban conglomerations, and brought about a separation between the town and the country which paralysed rural life and gave an unhealthy and one-sided development to the city. On the other hand, the general economic tendencies of the new age, which we have discussed, all point towards a revival of local life. The more equal distribution of population and industrial development together with the revived importance of agriculture will restore the connection between the city and the agricultural districts which surround it, and the city will tend to become again what it was before the industrial revolution—the centre and head of a natural region rather than the offshoot of a cosmopolitan organisation which has little in common with the country life which environs it.

The co-operation and mutual interpenetration of town and country would benefit both the countryman and the town worker, and would help to produce a new local patriotism and civic life.

There is, to be sure, a certain competition between the federation of unions for the same function in different regions, and the federation of the different functional unions in one region and city. But adjustment has to be sought in the principle that the local citizenship should come before membership of the general functional union, and that the primary functional unions should consider themselves as members of the regional society even more than of the national or international federation of the unions of their own trade. Thus the co-operative state, like the Roman Empire, would be a federation of local organisms, each possessing a civic life of its own, but it would begin where the Roman Empire left off, with a common citizenship and equal rights of development for all its members. Moreover, from the co-operative point of view the national state is not, as the last age believed, the one absolute society, its position and powers are interdependent and related to the other corporate unions. As there are societies with rights below it, so there are societies with rights above it, though these are as yet unrealised. As the national culture existed to a great extent before the national state, so the international culture exists before the international state.

In modern times the claims of international society have been represented by a somewhat thin and narrow cosmopolitanism. The strength of the Nationalist movement of the nineteenth century was due to its being based on a sense of the past and on a deep and rich conception of the national tradition, while the typical internationalist too often tended to despise the spiritual heritage of the past and concentrated his attention too much on the mechanical adjustments of the industrial and scientific movement, and in general on the material progress which was transforming the world. His conception of the new age was, so to speak, apocalyptic. He looked for the coming of a new culture which would be absolutely a new departure—a break in spiritual tradition. As there was an unbridgeable gulf between the steam engine and the horse, so it seemed to him there could be nothing in common between the old civilisations based on religious ideals and the new material rationalist culture. The Englishman and the Hindu, putting off the old man and his superstitions, were to enter, new born, on equal terms, into the Kingdom prepared for them by Adam Smith and Herbert Spencer.

This habit of mind, though it still survives, is not characteristic of the present age. The most sceptical and the least traditionalist begin to realise that the new mechanism of our civilisation has to make adjustment with the more perennial spiritual forces which have created every culture since the world began. That the great spiritual traditions of the past, in religion, philosophy and art, are not only still alive, but stand out as the dominant realities of life, is becoming increasingly realised. And with that perception comes the problem of developing and applying these living realities with the greater powers and further knowledge we now have.

Any attempt to substitute an artificial cosmopolitan civilisation for the cultural traditions which have moulded the thoughts and the lives of peoples for ages, not only makes for spiritual impoverishment and superficiality, but even reacts on the physical existence of a people. European civilisation of the nineteenth-century type has proved a more deadly enemy to the native races, which have been fully exposed to its influence, than famine, disease or war, and it has had a profoundly depressing effect even on races of high civilisation, such as the Burmese or the Egyptians.

On this account it is seen that missionary activity must work from within by grafting a new spirit onto the traditional culture. Any attempt to convert people of a different race by dressing them in trousers and teaching them the phraseology of British Liberalism is to create a being false to its own instincts, which must be either a monstrosity or a hypocrite. It is true that whole peoples have received a new religion imposed upon them from without, but this, it would seem, is only possible in the case of a really theocratic society, like Islam.

The true internationalism, like the true nationalism, bases itself on real social entities, which have been evolved in the course of ages. Everywhere we find local and national societies bound together by spiritual and cultural conditions which form them into a single civilisation. Such civilisations are real societies which demand real loyalty from their members; and the relations of the nations towards them are similar to those of the counties and provinces to the national states of the Middle Ages. Underlying them there is usually a religion, as in the case of the great church-state, Islam, which is the most typical of all, but sometimes their basis is predominantly secular, as in the case of China.

These civilisations are the ultimate social realities and in the past they were like closed worlds which were hardly conscious of each other's existence. In the present age, however, the most complex of all these civilisations—that which was developed in the Mediterranean world and Western Europe—has attained to a world hegemony, and the other world cultures are more or less submitted to its influence.

It thus occupies a somewhat similar position to that which Hellenism attained among the cultures of the ancient world, and it may become in the future, as Hellenism did, the parent of a world civilisation.

Its first duty, however, lies towards itself. The international anarchy, which has been growing worse since the Renaissance and during the very centuries in which the organisation of the national societies has been perfected, needs bringing to an end, and the society of nations of European civilisation, in the old world and the new, calls for the fullest recognition.

This, however, is not a simple problem. It is true that our civilisation is the direct descendant of both the Roman Empire and mediaeval Christendom, and consequently has a religious as well as a political unity behind it, but this unity has been rent in pieces by racial and religious schism. The great divisions of Europe, the Latin, the Germanic and the Slavonic or East Slav peoples, each possess a different spiritual tradition, and are only united by the secular culture of modern Europe. The great question of the immediate future is how far the international spirit can overcome these greater divisions as well as national and local particularism.

The heaviest responsibility to the new age lies, it would seem, upon Great Britain. The peculiar intermediate position historically and geographically which she occupies between the Latin and the Germanic peoples and between the Old World and the New, allocates to her a high rôle in the building up of an international order. As we have seen, the future of the world rests very largely on the great agricultural territories of North and South America and Australasia. And of these the greater parts are being filled up rapidly by English-speaking people, moulded by British institutions. If England were to conceive her mission in a narrow nationalistic sense, and were to attempt to organise her empire as a self-sufficient whole over against other national empires, the result could in the end hardly be other than disastrous. She is a trustee for Europe—at least for that part of Europe which cannot reproduce its culture in South America or Siberia, and it is her duty to prepare the new lands to receive the full European heritage through the contribution of the different national cultures.

This does not, of course, imply the creation of a cosmopolitan population in the colonies. The indiscriminate mixture of different races and nationalities brings with it the loss of social personality and only the worst elements are apt to survive. While English, Irish and Scandinavians can unite fruitfully in a new environment, the immigration of peoples of widely different race or civilisation, *e.g.,* the Polish Jews or the Armenians, causes acute social indigestion. The United States, which are, *par excellence,* the creation of the Exploitation period, are a remarkable example of the dangers of this state of things, and the problem of the assimilation of the Slav, the Levantine and the Jew is hardly less acute than that of the Negro in the Southern States.

Instead of immigrants from every corner of Europe being poured pell-mell into the great cities and industrial districts of the New World, each region should be settled deliberately, on the basis of its natural possibilities and the character of its actual population.

These are among the great problems that lie before the new age; but one fundamental question remains to be discussed on which the whole possibility of the co-operative ideal depends. If guidance, direction, control are to be distributed so that each part and organ of society performs its function freely as a living thing, and not part of a machine, there must be a living union of mind and will between the society and its members, such as we can hardly conceive at present.

Under the old régime society was based on religion, and the unquestioning acceptance by all of one spiritual tradition and one moral ideal was a stronger uniting force than any political authority or organisation.

In the modern state the mind of the average citizen is moulded by the government school and the popular press, and these afford no genuine substitute for the more profound spiritual guidance that was provided by the teaching of the old religious traditions.

Religion still claims the right to direct men's lives, but it is to a great extent precluded from direct action on the secular world and is no longer a dominant social force. The ordinary life of the farm and the factory has little contact either with church or school, and so the daily work of mankind has been materialised and rendered both selfish and servile. Education in any real sense should be the nervous system of society, by which the whole organism is guided and kept in union with the spirit. It should be in touch on the one hand with the actual daily life of every citizen, on the other with the higher spiritual ideals which are the end and justification of every civilisation.

Many movements in this direction have already been begun by schools of social reform, which collectively may be called the new humanism, but a profound revolution will have to take place if the present system is to be genuinely transformed.

The idea of a standardised state education, centring round the examinations system, has entered deeply into men's minds, and the blasphemous conception of two educations—the liberal or ornamental, and the mechanical or utilitarian—still largely dominant in England.

In a truly co-operative state, the school would be vitally and systematically connected first with the social unit that it serves, whether that be an agricultural village or an industrial guild; and secondly with the larger regional unit or city with its richer many sided social life, itself equipped with the completer educational institution we call the university. If the one aim of education were the complete and harmonious culture of the whole man, then the intellectual faculty would not as at present be favoured at the expense of either physical, artistic or moral development. And for the full enrichment of personality and community together is needed above all an education based on a spiritual tradition. Under the present system religious instruction seems to the average man a singularly dead thing, and the question of religious education has come to be treated as a dry bone of sectarian controversy. But the fundamental problem is a very vital one. The spiritual faith and ideals of a man or a society—their ultimate attitude towards life—colour all their thought and action and make them what they are. It is true that the multiple sects of the English-speaking peoples are largely historical relics, and no longer represent a fundamental religious attitude. Nevertheless, different spiritual traditions do exist, and it is unjust to deprive them of free expression in education and social life. The adherent of the secular tradition, which is now perhaps the dominant spiritual force in our civilisation, naturally claims that education should harmonise with his view of life, and his interpretation of man's history, but only a bigot can demand that the mind of every man should be forced into the same mould, irrespective of the spiritual tradition to which he belongs. In the long run, the idea of uniform state education is inseparable from a state religion and the penalisation of religious dissent.

A free co-operative order which gives full liberty for the development of man in both his individual and his corporate life must likewise give free play to the spiritual forces by which alone humanity can realise its highest possibilities. The great hope for the future lies, after all, not so much in changes of social organisation as in a spiritual renascence. The curbing of the brutal economic struggle of the industrial age finds its justification not in the equal diffusion of material prosperity, which was the goal of the philosophers of the industrial age, but in the opportunity it gives for every member of society to take an active share in the life of the mind and the spirit.

※

Note.—This essay was written during the war and first printed in 1920. The crisis of modern industrialism has taken a very different form to that which I then predicted. Nevertheless and partly for this very reason, I think the essay still retains sufficient interest and actuality to justify its inclusion in the present volume.

—C.D.

II

V

Cycles of Civilisation

SUMMARY

At the present time the world is divided between four great cultures, respectively European, Islamic, Indian and Chinese. Although the first of these has attained a kind of world hegemony, it has not eliminated the other three, nor has it succeeded in penetrating them internally. Any general theory of progress must take account of the organic development of these cultures, no less than of the material and scientific advance of modern civilisation during the last four centuries, for they are the ultimate social entities in history, and on this foundation all the racial and national strands are woven.

Each of these cultures possesses a spiritual tradition of its own, which gives it an internal unity. This is most obvious in the case of Islam, where the civilisation is also a religion, but it is no less true of the others, and in each case this tradition rests on some synthesis which gives a common view of life and a common scale of values to the entire civilisation that it dominates. As long as a spiritual tradition of this kind controls a civilisation, the latter possesses an inner unity such as we see in Europe during the mediaeval period, or in India during the age of the Guptas. But as soon as it begins to decline, the civilisation itself undergoes a process of rapid social change, and this continues until a new synthesis reintegrates civilisation on a new plane. Thus we have a double movement of synthesis and disintegration, and it is the aim of

This paper, which was read to the Sociological Society on December 20th, 1922, owes its interest largely to the fact that it was written before I was acquainted with Spengler's *Decline of the West.*

the following paper to show that it is this movement which determines the normal life-cycle of any civilisation.

When a civilisation is young, as in the Dark Ages and the mediaeval period of Western Europe, it finds its unity in the synthesis which it has inherited from the mature period of the previous civilisation.

When external and internal influences have weakened the hold of this synthesis on society, and the young civilisation rejects traditional guidance and seeks to rediscover the world anew, we have a period at once of progress and of disintegration such as Western Europe has passed through during the four centuries following the Renaissance and such as the Greek world experienced from the fifth century to the Christian era. Finally, the last phase of the cycle, which I have named the period of maturity, witnesses the gradual reconsolidation of the civilisation on a new basis and the dominance of a new synthesis.

Thus the cycle runs as follows:

A. Period of Growth. Dominance of the old synthesis in the young civilisation.

B. Period of Progress. Disintegration of the old synthesis in the progressive civilisation.

C. Period of Maturity. Rise of the new synthesis in the mature civilisation.

Thus the progressive movement which lies behind the history of civilisations is due to two rhythmic movements, one of which produces the physical renewal of a civilisation, the other its psychical renewal, and these movements alternate with one another. There is, therefore, no period in the life of civilisations which is a time of death or of a complete arrest of growth, but even while the outer body of a civilisation decays, its inner life is renewed, and by its transmission to a daughter-culture becomes the fertilising principle of a new age.

In the four culture-areas of the Mediterranean, Persia with Babylonia, India and China, we see the almost simultaneous flowering of a new synthesis in the early centuries of the Christian era. This was the period of the conversion of the Roman Empire to Christianity, of the Sassanian revival in Persia, of the revival of Indian culture under the Guptas, and of the rise of Buddhism in China. And about the sixth century A.D. each of these movements expressed itself in the creation of a great religious art.

Again, about the sixth century B.C., we can trace an almost simultaneous process of intellectual awakening and change which marks the beginning of a new period of progress. It was the time of the early Greek philosophers, of Buddha and the writers of the Upanishads, of Confucius and Laotze.

These synchronisms are studied more fully in the following paper, in which there is an attempt to trace in outline the course of the four successive ages of civilisation which history seems to reveal.

In another paper[1] I try to show that the true basis for a history of world progress is to be found in the organic development of the great historic world-cultures of Europe and the East. For while the progress of material civilisation is discontinuous, the great cultural traditions possess an internal unity which includes the "Dark Ages" and the periods of decline, as well as the ages of social and material achievement. These are the ultimate social entities in world history, and they form the foundation into which all the racial and national strands are woven.

Every great world-culture has its geographical unity no less than the great nationalities. This is obvious enough in the case of India and China, and fairly clear also with regard to Europe. Islam at first sight is less homogeneous, since it occupies a broad band of territory running across two continents from the west coast of Africa to the frontiers of China. Yet, although that great region is nameless, it is perhaps the most remarkable unity of all. From Timbuktu to Kashgar we are everywhere in the presence of similar conditions, and practically all the great cities of Islam, except Constantinople, are oasis cities, ports of the desert, hardly out of sight of the lands of the nomad tribesman.

Nevertheless, the geographical factor is not the essential cause of the unity of civilisation. We have seen lands crossing from one civilisation to another, as Tunis and Sicily and Spain have done in the West. We have seen a civilisation, which seemed to be inseparable from the dry desert plateaux, stretching itself out to embrace the steaming tropical islands of the East Indies and the Zanzibar coast, the lowlands of Ben-

---

1. *Religion and the Life of Civilisation.*

gal and the rainy valleys of south-west China. And the same thing is true of the racial factor, since the modern Berber is further in point of civilisation from his neighbour across the straits of Gibraltar than is the Frenchman from the Finn, or the Englishman from the Magyar. Philip the Arabian was probably an ordinary Roman officer whose thoughts and behaviour were not very different from those of his Gallic or Illyrian contemporaries. When their respective descendants met again a thousand years later in the Crusades, they were worlds apart; not because of any racial change, but because the currents of two different civilisations had swept them apart.

The essential unity of a civilisation consists in a common consciousness, which makes of it a social entity no less real than those of the lesser civic and political units. The ultimate barriers are not the racial or geographical ones, but those of cultural tradition which are expressed in the contrast of Hellene and Barbarian, of Moslem and Unbeliever, and which were seen in their full intensity in China during the European penetration of the last century. In all such cases there is a different view of reality, different moral and aesthetic values, which make a different world.

Consequently, the historian of civilisation must look above all for the great spiritual movements which give unity and continuity to the world-cultures, movements which are to be traced in the development of art and philosophy and religion even more than in the political and economic movements which tend to absorb the attention of historians. For the spirit of a civilisation which imprints its character on all its products, social, political and intellectual, finds its most intimate expression in religion, philosophy and art. These are not accidental to the general development, the work of independent individuals, they are the very essence and centre of the social activity.

Behind the cultural unity of every great civilisation there lies a spiritual unity, due to some synthesis which harmonises the inner world of spiritual aspiration with the outer world of social activity. Such a synthesis expresses itself in what we may call a Religion-Culture, such as that which dominated Western Europe during the Middle Ages, when civilisation in all its manifestations was indissolubly wedded to a great social religion. In these cultures, so opposed to our own, we feel that life is internally unified and that the same spirit finds expression in the instinctive work of the uneducated craftsman as in the deliberate achievement of the artist and the writer. When once a synthesis of this kind has been attained, it dominates civilisation for centuries and its comprehension affords the key to the history of a whole world age. Thus there are the Religion-Cultures of Islam, of Confucian China and ancient India, each of them with its own view of reality, its own harmony of knowledge and aspiration, which it expresses in the external development of its civilisation. Even when the synthesis on which the Religion-Culture is based no longer expresses a living relation between the inner and the outer worlds—between the individual consciousness and reality, society still struggles to retain it, and to force the new and rebellious conditions into the categories of the old Religion-Culture. Nevertheless, any great change in men's knowledge and in their relation with the external world makes this effort increasingly difficult. There is a painful sense of strain in the maintenance of the social faith, and individuals are tempted to break away from the traditional order and to realise for themselves the new opportunities that they see for knowledge and action. Eventually the breaking point may be reached, the new forces burst the barriers of tradition, and there is a period of progress with its brilliant individualism, its irreverence for the past and its sense of new life and new achievements everywhere. The two classical examples of this period are the intellectual awakening of the Greek world about the fifth century B.C. and the European Renaissance of the fifteenth and sixteenth centuries. In the Eastern civilisations the progressive period is much less brilliant, and much less marked, but it is present there, nevertheless. But the spiritual anarchy which springs from the dissolution of the traditional order is a heavy price to pay for the new gains. Hence the tendency both in fifth-century Greece and in sixteenth-century Europe to look back towards the past—to hold up the men who fought at Marathon as examples to the contemporaries of Alcibiades. One sees this tendency in the Platonic admiration for Sparta and the Roman literary cult of the early Republic, or in the reaction from Machiavelli to the idealist chivalry of Tasso.

In spite of these premature reactions, the progressive movement continues. Only after centuries of social and intellectual change can we see the real beginnings of a new social synthesis, which is often only attained on the eve of the material decline of the civilisation. Yet the power of a Religion-Culture based on a mature synthesis of this kind is out of all relation to the material prosperity of the civilisation that has achieved it. Even when the latter undergoes complete dissolution, as was the case with the Roman-Hellenistic culture in the West, the synthesis that it has created is handed on to the new peoples that take its place, and dominates in its turn the first period (which we may call the mediaeval stage) of the new civilisation

Thus we have a series of cycles, of three phases each, in which the movement of history consists:

A. First there is the period of growth, in which the young civilisation is dominated by the synthesis which was the work of its predecessor; its culture is the daughter of the Religion-Culture of the previous age, as the culture of mediaeval Europe was the daughter of the Religion-Culture of the Christian Empire of the fourth to the sixth centuries.

B. Secondly there is the period of progress, when the young civilisation begins to outgrow the heritage of the parent culture, and strikes out new paths for itself.

C. Thirdly there is the period of maturity during which the achievements of B (the period of progress) are co-ordinated, and civilisation enters on a new period of social and intellectual unification.

The ancient Hellenic world passed through the first of these stages (A) between 1100 and 500 B.C., when society was dominated by what I may call the civic Religion-Culture. The second of these stages (B) embraces the period from Pericles to Augustus, the great age of Greek Science and discovery. The third stage (C) reaches from the age of Augustus to that of Justinian, and witnesses the rise of the Religion-Culture of the Christian Empire with its new art and its new social principles.

Every historic culture period can be classified under one of these types. Thus under type A comes the civilisation of Islam, the Rajput culture in India, Homeric Greece and mediaeval Japan, and under C Egypt of the Ramasside period, India under the Guptas, and Sassanian Persia. If one of these stages is lacking to a civilisation, that civilisation stagnates or becomes ossified, like China and Islam in recent centuries, until the domination of the ancient synthesis which holds it back is forcibly broken by foreign conquest and exploitation. It might seem that when a civilisation has attained its mature synthesis, it will thenceforward remain stationary; and, in fact, the historic civilisations have usually been renewed, not from within, but by the irruption of less-civilised peoples who have taken over and modified the synthesis of the mature culture, thus initiating a new cycle. Nevertheless, the history of Egypt and China shows that it is possible for the same people to pass through successive civilisations without any very important infusion of new blood. In the Nile Valley the successive cycles of civilisation are more clearly traceable than anywhere else, and here we can see three successive civilisations rise and decline in historic times before the Arab conquest, which marks the beginning of a fourth age, wrought fundamental changes in the Egyptian people.

The progressive element in history is most strongly marked when a new racial stock comes forward, as in the case of the Achæans and Dorians in the ancient Ægean world, and the Teutons in the Roman Empire, but the rise of new civilisations is not dependent on the racial factor, but is a general process common to the East and the West, and alike to the old and the young culture areas. This cyclic movement in history was clearly recognised by Vico at the beginning of the eighteenth century. He taught that history consists of a succession of cycles, each of which consists of three phases, which he named the Age of the Gods, the Age of the Heroes and the Age of Men. Each of these ages has its distinctive ways of thought and modes of expression, and Vico devotes one of the most brilliant parts of his book to showing how the Homeric poems are not the creation of an individual poet, but the voice of the heroic age of Greek society. Similarly, he showed how the Middle Ages were the heroic period of our civilisation, and he attempts to draw out the parallel between mediaeval Europe and Homeric Greece. His work met with little recognition either in his own days or afterwards. Indeed, his only disciple so far as I am aware was the French thinker Ballanche, the author of *La Palingénésie Sociale,* though no doubt he also had a considerable influence on the St. Simonians.

But though Vico recognised the part played by religion in the growth of civilisations and saw that the appearance of Christianity marked the beginning of a new world age in Europe, he did not realise the central importance of the Religion-Culture which is evolved in the period of maturity (C). Vico's *Age of the Gods* is merely the first part of the mediaeval development—when the beginnings of civilisation were sheltered under the shadow of the great abbeys and at the shrines of famous saints—not the Byzantine or patristic period which is the true foundation of the mediaeval culture. In this he was no doubt misled by the false perspective of Renaissance scholarship which judged ancient civilisations from an exclusively literary standpoint, and saw nothing but barbarism and decadence outside the limits of the strictly classical tradition. It is true that he himself largely contributed to overthrow this tradition by his *Discovery of the True Homer,* but the men of the Renaissance loved and studied Homer, even though they did not understand him. The art and culture of the Byzantine world they held in no less contempt than the Gothic barbarism of the Western Middle Ages. Their point of view finds typical expression in Gibbon's *Decline and Fall of the Roman Empire,* and it is still not unknown. For while the old contempt for the Middle Ages is a thing of the past, the unjust depreciation of Byzantine culture has persisted almost to our own days.

However, it may be admitted that there is a certain degree of justification for this. The civilisations of the West during the last. 3,000 years stand out from those of the East by reason of the extraordinary brilliance of their Progressive Periods—the intellectual achievements of their Renaissance and the material achievements of their post-Renaissance period. And this moment of expansion has met with a correspondingly marked reaction when the civilisation has come to maturity. At least that was the case in the Græco-Roman world, and it is not impossible that it may be the same with modern Europe.

To see a Mature Period at its best, we must turn to a civilisation like that of India, in which the elements of a material and economic expansion have been small, and where the period of progress has been mainly negative and passive, marked rather by the assimilation of external influences than by any creative activity. Thus, for example, in the India of the Gupta period (fourth and fifth centuries) we see the rise of the new Religion-Culture showing itself in a many sided flowering, which includes not only art and religion, but also science and philosophy and literature. It was the age of Kalidasa and of the wonderful frescoes of Ajanta and Sigiriya; and at the same time the classical texts of the six Hindu schools of philosophy were being composed and the great Buddhist doctors were giving final expression to both the Hinayana and the Mahayana systems. Indeed, the creative activity of this period moulded the art and thought of all Eastern Asia during the ensuing centuries— centuries of rich culture and high achievement.

The civilisation of the Byzantine Age had a similar importance for the Western world. The period that produced St. Sophia and the churches of Ravenna and Parenzo was assuredly no contemptible one, and modern scholarship is only just beginning to appreciate the wide intellectual synthesis on which the culture of the patristic period was based. In fact, the scientific achievements of the ancient world were being synthetised by such men as Ptolemy and Galen, Pappus and Diophantus, Simplicius and John Philoponus, at the same time as the eclectic philosophers and the Christian Fathers were elaborating their metaphysical and religious syntheses. Yet in many respects it was undoubtedly a time of decadence; literature was in a state of decline, and the political and economic energies of society were concentrated in a desperate struggle for conservation. These unfavourable conditions in the parent culture were reflected in the comparative barbarism of the early mediaeval period in Western Europe right up to the eleventh century, during the very time in which Mesopotamia and China, not to mention lesser civilisations such as Cambodia and Java, were enjoying a period of extraordinary brilliancy. From the twelfth century onwards the civilisation of the West makes rapid progress, whilst those of the East begin to decline.

It almost seems as though the occidental element in civilisation goes to sleep during the periods that are dominated by a Religion-Culture, while the oriental element does the same during the periods of progress. The beginning of the one period is marked by a reawakening of the East, such as took place, for example, in the third century A.D., while the beginning of the other is marked by a reawakening of the West. Thus world civilisation and true progress require the concurrences of both types, the Oriental and the Occidental. It was at once the strength and weakness of the Roman Hellenistic culture that it came to include a strong oriental element; our civilisation, on the other hand, has hitherto been exclusively occidental, and that too is a source both of weakness and of strength. If during the last centuries the civilisation of Western Europe has taken to itself whole continents and has attained to a military and economic hegemony over the rest of the world, it nevertheless remains but one amongst several units, and any theory which seeks to explain the progress of mankind by the development of that one civilisation alone is partial and unsatisfactory. Such theories were comprehensible enough at a time when the East was passive under European exploitation, but that is rapidly ceasing to be the case, and if the coming age should attain to any kind of world order and world citizenship, it is obvious that the oriental civilisations will bring a growing contribution to the common stock, just as they did under the Roman Empire, even though the political guidance and organising power should still remain in the hands of the Western peoples. The great social syntheses are in fact not confined to a single civilisation, but are part of a world movement, the reality of which it is impossible to doubt, although its causes are still obscure. Thus, in the present state of historical knowledge, it is possible to distinguish clearly four successive world ages, each of which, except the last, which is still in being, culminates in a great Religion-Culture.

AGE I

The first of these (c. 4500–2700 B.C.) is the age of the closed valley civilisations of Egypt and Babylonia, and culminates in Egypt in the age of the Pyramid builders.

AGE II

During the following age (c. 2700–1100) the isolation of the civilisations—at least in the Near East—passes away and intercultural influences are wide and deep. In Egypt this age falls naturally into three divisions: A. The period of feudal anarchy: Seventh to Eleventh Dynasties. B. The period of the Middle Kingdom: Eleventh to Thirteenth Dynasties. C. The Empire: Eighteenth to Twentieth Dynasties.

The contemporary civilisation of the Ægean passes through similar stages, and comes to maturity in the late Minoan and Mycenaean periods, c., 1500–1200.

During these two earlier ages, our knowledge is so limited that it is impossible to judge how far the different civilisations passed through a similar course of development. We can see that the civilisations of Egypt and Babylonia about 3000 B.C. were both of them theocratic in character—in both alike the power of the god was literally the ruling power of the society; but our knowledge is external and vague, and we know nothing at all of the civilisations that undoubtedly existed in India and Northern China. During the following age the clouds begin to lift, but it is only in the third age, 1200 B.C. to 600 A.D., that all the great world civilisations emerge into the light of history, so that we can follow the rise and modifications of their ruling social and intellectual syntheses.

AGE III

In this period it is impossible for us to mistake the parallelism of the movement of the great world-cultures. In spite of differences of cultural type, all the great civilisations during this age undergo an internal change of closely similar character which finally results in the rise of the great World Religions and of the Religion-Cultures that are dependent upon them.

A. The Period of Growth

(1) *The Decline of the Ancient Civilizations and the Beginnings of a New Age, c. 1200–900 B.C.*

The Middle Ages of the Ancient World were preceded like our own Middle Ages by a time of barbarian invasions and of violent disruption and change. The whole of the Eastern Mediterranean was in a state of chaos. Egypt under Rameses III. succeeded in repelling the great invasions of the Libyans and the Sea Peoples in the first decade of the twelfth century, but her imperial power was broken, and thenceforward she sank into a more than Byzantine state of immobility, the chief power in the kingdom falling into the hands of the Priests of Amen. The same storm that had shaken Egypt utterly overwhelmed the Minoan and Hittite civilisations. It was the Viking Age of the ancient world, and the memory of it survives in the tradition of the Trojan War. The Semitic peoples were relatively fortunate. The Phoenician cities stepped into the place of the Cretan sea power, and the lesser kingdoms of Syria and Palestine enjoyed considerable prosperity in the interval between the decline of Egypt and the rise of the Assyrian Empire, which was destined to be the great imperial power of the period.

(2) The Flourishing of the Civic Religion-Culture, c. 900–500 B.C.

After the Dorian migration, which closes the period of barbarian invasions, Ægean civilisation gradually revived. The tribal organisation with its chieftain-king and its assembly of the free tribesmen began to give place, not as in our Middle Ages to a feudal society, but to the City State with its aristocratic magistrature. Only in Sparta and Crete and in the north-west of Greece did the old tribal society survive.

This is the formative period for all the characteristic social institutions of Hellenic civilisation, and it is in this period alone, as opposed to later times, that the classical Religion-Culture, which is described, for example, in Fustel de Coulanges' well-known study *La Cite Antique,* was truly dominant. It was the time of the Homeric poems, and of the first great wave of Hellenic expansion which colonised Sicily and the shores of the Black Sea. Throughout this period the Ionian cities were the focus of Hellenic civilisation. Their greatness ended only with the failure of the Ionian revolt against Persia, 499–494, and by that time they had already given birth to Greek art and Greek philosophy. Meanwhile, in the Near East, though Egypt was a prey to foreign adventurers, the civilisations of Syria and Mesopotamia were intensely alive. The Phoenician cities were founding their great trading colonies in the Western Mediterranean. Babylonia was still prosperous. Assyria was at the height of her power, and was advancing in culture and artistic development, but her pitiless militarism was gradually ruining the prosperity of Asia and prepared the way for a new series of barbarian invasions—Cimmerian, Scythian and Medic, which were ultimately fatal to her own power. The consequent exhaustion of Asia enabled the

Persians in the following century to establish their empire over all the East, somewhat in the same way as the Ottoman power conquered the exhausted Levant in the fifteenth and sixteenth centuries. Thus the close of this period coincides on the one hand with the final eclipse of the ancient civilisations of Egypt and Mesopotamia, and on the other with the dawn of that great intellectual awakening which is one of the vital moments in the history of Humanity.[2]

B. The Period of Progress

(1) The Intellectual Awakening

This intellectual awakening was not, like the modern scientific movement, the work of a single civilisation, it was a world-wide movement which extended from the Mediterranean to the Far East. It is represented not only by the Hebrew prophets and the Greek philosophers, but also by the Buddha and the writers of the Upanishads in India, and by Laotze and Confucius in China.

In the case of the Hebrew prophets, the spiritual crisis was no doubt precipitated by the breakdown of the traditional polity under the stress of foreign invasion, but in the Greek lands, and also, so far as we can see, in India and China, it resulted from a spontaneous movement by which the individual mind outgrew the traditional social and religious forms—positively by the new vision of the prophets and the philosophers, negatively by the rationalist criticism of the sophists. Nor is the latter exclusively Greek. The wandering philosopher who goes from court to court, seeking princely patrons and justifying by his sophistry the "impiety" of the successful tyrant, is a characteristic figure of the China of the fourth century, and in India Buddhism finds opponents not only among the traditionalists, but also in the sceptical rationalism of the Nastikas.

(2) The Expansion of the West: Fourth to First Centuries B.C.

This period is followed by a time of spiritual disorganisation and confusion, but also of great intellectual and material achievements. It was a period of triumphant expansion for the secular powers of the

---

2. Just as the end of our Middle Ages coincided on the one hand with the eclipse of the Arab and Byzantine cultures, on the other with the European Renaissance.

West—the Hellenistic monarchies and afterwards the Roman Republic—and of decline and stagnation for the Theocratic civilisations of the
Near East. Hellenistic art and culture in rather a low and commercial-
ised form began to influence the East. In China it is the age of the great
anti-traditionalist emperors of Ts'inn and Han—of Shih-Hwangti, the
Burner of the Books, and the builder of the Great Wall and the great
roads, and of Wuti, the conqueror of the outer barbarians and the
opener of the routes to India and Persia.

C. The Period of Maturity

(1) Rise of the World Religions: First Century B.C. to Third Century A.D.

This period witnessed the reawakening of the East, and at the same
time the process of cultural and religious syncretism attained its highest point of development. It was the age of the late Hellenistic art of
Palmyra and Petra and the Provincia Arabia, of the Græco-Buddhist art
of Gandhara and of the introduction of Indian art into China. It was
still an age of great secular empires, such as Rome, the Parthian power,
the Indo-Scythian Empire, which stretched from Bactria and the Tarim
to the Punjab, and the dynasty of the Later Han in China; but under
the surface there was an intense process of religious fermentation going
on, and the great world religions were being born or renewed.

In the Mediterranean world, the great fact was the rise of Christianity, the completest and most typical of all the world religions; but at
the same time the pagan cults were being remoulded in a spiritualist
and universalist sense, while the evolution of Greek philosophy finally
culminated in the semi-religious synthesis of Neoplatonism. In India
it was the time of the great Hindu revival, when the religion of India
was transformed by the fusion of philosophic Brahmanism and popular
paganism in theistic cults, like that of Krishna in the Bhagavad Gita—a
process which closely resembles the fusion of Greek philosophy with
the pagan cults of the Roman Empire, as we see it, for example, in the
writings of Julian the Apostate. At the same time Buddhism was being transformed from a moral discipline, analogous to Stoicism, into
a theology and even a mythology of salvation, and it was in this new

Mahayana form that it began to conquer China and the other lands of the Far East.

In Persia we have a great religious movement, which renewed, and in all probability radically transformed, the Mazdæan religion.

Finally, in China there is the introduction and gradual growth of Buddhism from 57 A.D., and at the same period the transformation of Taoism in a theistic direction.

It is noteworthy that in all four culture areas we find at this period a development closely resembling the Gnosticism of the Mediterranean world.

(2) Flowering of the Religion-Cultures: Third to Seventh Centuries A.D.

In this period the world religions have completely conquered the mind of society; culture becomes religious, and throughout the world there is an almost simultaneous flowering of great religious art. The Gupta period in India, A.D. 320–6th century, the Sassanian age in Persia, 220–637, the Period of North and South in China, 385–590, and the Early Byzantine Age in the Mediterranean, are all of them the Golden Ages of religious art in their respective areas. And this flowering of religious art is but the symptom of a great social synthesis by which civilisation once more attains the internal unity which finds expression in the complete Religion-Culture. Consequently, this period is of capital importance for our purpose, since it strikes the keynote on which the whole development of world civilisation during the next age was based. Undeniably this was a great age of incalculable importance in world history, but no less surely it was not an age of triumphant material progress. Rather it was the last effort of a dying order. In the Roman Empire, in Persia and in India, though material wealth was very great, the empires were faced with a steadily growing menace from the outer lands which eventually more or less overwhelmed them, while in China the empire had already gone to pieces, and the Golden Age of Buddhist art and religion was an age of political anarchy and material ruin.

AGE IV. THE MODERN WORLD

A. The Period of Growth or the Middle Ages

(1) Fertilisation of Daughter-Cultures: 500–750 A.D.

Nevertheless, when the crash came, and the material fabric of civilisation collapsed, or was at least half ruined, the synthesis of religion and culture which it had achieved did not die with it. The spiritual achievement was handed on to a new age and to new peoples. Thus, in Europe the Christian Empire, 323–645, was the foundation of that mediaeval order in which the Catholic Church carried over to the barbarian peoples the culture, the art and the *Weltanschauung* which had been created during the age of the Fathers.

In like manner the Indian Middle Ages, from the eighth to the fifteenth centuries, whether in the Rajput kingdoms of the north, or in Bengal and Orissa, or in the Dravidian kingdoms of the south, as also in Ceylon and in Java and Cambodia, embodied the Religion-Culture of the Gupta period, and carried on the tradition of that Golden Age in their art, their literature and their religion. In China, as in the Byzantine Empire, the continuity of civilisation was uninterrupted, but there also a daughter-culture came into being in the farthest East through the conversion of Japan and Korea to Buddhism and to Chinese civilisation at almost the same date as the conversion to Christianity of the new peoples of Western Europe; and the relation of the former countries to the parent civilisation of China is in many respects comparable to that of the Lombards and the Franks to the Byzantine world. There remains the most characteristic of all the mediaeval cultures—Islam. This is not a true daughter-culture, since it is not in the direct tradition of the earlier Religion-Cultures, but is of the nature of a new creation. The previous period had seen a great revival of cultural activity among the Semitic peoples from Syria to Mesopotamia, and the Islamic movement tore them away from the world civilisations—Byzantine and Persian—to which they had been subjected and reunited them under Arab leadership in a new culture-complex. Nevertheless, in spite of its independent character, Islam received the cultural traditions both of Byzantine Syria and Sassanian Persia, and to those it stands in very much the same relation as the true daughter-cultures do to their parent civilisation.

(2) The Flowering of the Daughter-Cultures: (a) Ninth Century; (b) Twelfth Century

This period saw the Religion-Cultures attain to full expression in these younger and more vigorous civilisations. The whole period has two main divisions—the first centering on the eighth to ninth centuries, the second on the eleventh to the twelfth or the thirteenth. Thus in the West we can distinguish the Byzantine-mediaeval phase from the Gothic-mediaeval phase, in which the predominant influence belonged to the Northern French. In this case the earlier or Carolingian culture is obviously much inferior to that of the thirteenth century, but in the case of the Eastern civilisations the two flowerings are almost equal in importance. Thus in Islam we have for the first the Golden Age of the Abbasid Caliphate, 750–850, for the second the period of the Almohads in the West, and of Saladin in Syria, the period of Averroes and Ibn Tufayl and Maimonides. In India the two periods are marked by the two great orthodox philosophers, Sankara, 788–850, and Ramanuja (d. 1137), and also by two great outbursts of art, the first represented by the best of the Ajanta frescoes and by the cave temples of Elura and Elephanta; the second by the great temples of Konarak and Mount Abu, and by the Golden Age of Rajput civilisation and art.

In Japan the two phases correspond (a) to the Nara and early Heian period, and (b) to the period of Kamakura.

In these instances the first flowering of mediaeval civilisation is in close touch spiritually and often geographically with the parent Religion-Culture, while the second flowering usually represents a more complete assimilation and a more individual expression on the part of the daughter-culture. This is especially evident in the cases of Western Europe and of Japan.

The relation of the two mediaeval phases to one another and to the parent culture is remarkably illustrated by the history of mediaeval philosophy. Thus, in the West we have first the philosophical revival of the Carolingian period, illustrated by the name of Scotus Erigena, and secondly the great scholastic movement of the thirteenth century which produced St. Thomas Aquinas. In Islam, Arabic philosophy makes its first appearance in the Abassid period, and attains its final development in the twelfth century with Averroes and Ibn Tufayl. Closely related to the Arabic development is that of the mediaeval Jewish philosophy, which also has its two great stages culminating respectively in Saadya (892–942) and Maimonides (1135–1204). In India the two classical exponents of the Vedanta are Sankara (ninth century) and Ramanuja (d. 1137), while in China the first phase is represented by Han Yu (768–804), and the second by Chu-Hi, the greatest philosopher of Confucianism. In all these cases philosophy is working at an identical problem—the creation of an intellectual synthesis between the philosophies produced by the intellectual awakening of the ancient world on the one hand—Plato and Aristotle, the Upanishads, Confucius— and the world religions of the mature period on the other—Patristic Catholicism, Islam, Talmudic Judaism, Neo-Hinduism and Mahayana Buddhism. But it is curious that in the case of China Chu-Hi has reversed the typical procedure, resorting to Confucius for moral principles, and to Buddhism only for metaphysics.

(3) The Ruin of the Ancient Culture Centres: Thirteenth to Fifteenth Centuries

The thirteenth century witnessed throughout the East a series of material catastrophes, which were more disastrous to the ancient cultures than anything that they had experienced in the time of the barbarian invasions. Between 1190 and 1206 the civilisation of Northern India collapsed before the attack of the Turkish and Afghan Moslems, and the next two centuries saw the gradual conquest of the Deccan and the South. Never probably in history has a conquest been accompanied by such vast and wholesale destruction of artistic monuments. In loss of life, however, it was no doubt far surpassed by the Mongol invasions of the thirteenth century, which ruined the great culture centres of Persia and Mesopotamia and subjected the eastern provinces of Islam to a heathen yoke. Islamic civilisation never recovered from the blow.

During the same period the Mongols were overrunning China, and in 1276 the Sung capital of Hangchow finally succumbed to them—a date almost as epoch-making for the Far East as was that of the sack of Bagdad (1258) for Islam.

The sack of Constantinople and the partition of the Greek Empire by the Latins (1204) was no less important for the Byzantine culture area. On the other hand, the daughter-culture of the European Middle Age was now attaining to perfection. Nevertheless, the fourteenth century saw a very swift decline here also; and though this was rather internal (*e.g.,* the decline of the Papacy, the great Schism) than external; catastrophes such as the Black Death and the devastation of France in the English Wars were not without their influence. The real close of the Middle Ages, however, comes in the fifteenth century with the Turkish conquest of the Levant. This was even more important for mediaeval Europe than was the Persian conquest of Ionia for ancient Greece, since it meant the destruction of the old Mediterranean culture-focus, and the closing of the roads to the East. Europe turned her face to the Western Ocean, and a northwesterly direction gradually became substituted for the south-eastern, whence for thousands of years the current of cultural and economic life had flowed. Thus the dawn of the "Atlantic Age," the discovery of America and the Cape Route and the intellectual awakening of the Renaissance ushered in a new world.

B. The Period of Progress

(1) The Intellectural Awakening: Fourteenth to Sixteenth Centuries A.D.

This period is analogous to III B. There is the same intellectual and artistic flowering, the same scientific curiosity and the same spirit of criticism. The same progress of disintegration also seems to be at work with respect to the world religion and the mediaeval order, as we saw in the first period with regard to the civic religion and social order. Only in this period the intellectual awakening seems to be confined to the European culture area, there is no world movement in the East such as we saw in the seventh to the fifth centuries B.C. The oriental Religion-Cultures are stagnating, but there is no sign of anything new to take their place.

(2) The Expansion of the West: Sixteenth to Nineteenth Centuries A.D.

Following, the intellectual awakening, we again see a great movement of expansion and conquest on the part of the West, but on a greater scale than any that the ancient world had seen. The discovery and colonisation of America, the beginning of the exploitation of Africa (gold and slave trades), the ocean trade with India, the discovery of the Pacific, and the opening of trade with China proceed rapidly in the years 1485–1550.

The oriental civilisations, so far from sharing in the movement, react somewhat violently against it. China, Japan and Korea are closed deliberately to European penetration. The Near East under the Ottoman power is more fully severed from Western Europe than ever before. On the whole, the seventeenth century represents a reaction in the direction of the old Religion-Culture. In Europe the Counter-Reformation; in India the revival of the Hindu tradition against the Moslem power, as exemplified in the rise of the Marathas and the Sikhs. Nevertheless, the European movement of intellectual criticism and scientific progress continues throughout. The secular national state more and more takes the place of the international order of mediaeval Christendom. Like the Hellenistic age, this is a time of great monarchies, but in the West there is growing up a great aristocratic semi-republic, which is destined to realise fully the potentialities of the new conditions of oceanic commerce, and naval and colonial power. One after the other, England defeats her great rivals, Spain, Holland and France. The Peace of Paris, 1763, leaves her supreme on the seas, in North America and in India.

(3) *The Economic World Revolution: Eighteenth to Nineteenth Centuries*

The eighteenth-century intellectual movements in France and England carried on the work of the Renaissance, and completed the victory of criticism and rationalism. The French Revolution and the ensuing wars swept away the decadent traditional social order, and completely secularised European civilisation. Meanwhile, in England the new economic world-power is being evolved. The concentration of ocean trade in her hands had made possible the rise of a strong and intelligent "entrepreneur" class: the new mechanical inventions provided the opportunity for the application of capital to wholesale industrial production, and the merchants again found markets across the seas for the new products. The process was helped forward by the absorption of the continent in the revolutionary wars, but it only found its completion after the discovery of the new means of transport had been developed. Now for the first time a really cosmopolitan economic system was possible: England became indeed the "workshop of the world," drawing her food and raw materials from five continents, and selling in the markets of all the world. Other peoples gradually followed her example. Consequently, the nineteenth century saw the most colossal advances in population and wealth made by the peoples of Western Europe and the eastern states of North America. The unoccupied areas of the world were settled and cultivated with extraordinary rapidity. Meanwhile, the East sank into passive dependence on the West. China and Japan were forcibly opened to Western commerce, India became the great market for Manchester and Birmingham. The lands of Islam were partitioned and administered by Europe, and Africa became exploited as a great tropical plantation. As a rule economic penetration was followed by political occupation, and last of all came Western knowledge and the predominance of European culture. Thus the period of which we are speaking produced a world revolution unparalleled in past history, since it was universal in extent, and in a sense irreversible in its methods.

The only other movement that in any way resembled it, the organisation of the ancient world by the Roman oligarchy in the first century B.C., was on an incomparably smaller scale, and the economic changes that accompanied it were of secondary importance as compared with the main factors, which were military and political.

(4) The Crisis of Industrialism: Nineteenth and Twentieth Centuries

In one respect, however, the economic expansion of the nineteenth century resembled that of the later Roman republic; it was a process of exploitation which, carried to its logical conclusion, was bound to destroy itself, and to make way for a new principle of organisation. It was essentially a transition period, during which the societies, which had been the first to adopt the new economic system, were able to use their monopoly in order to exploit the rest of the world, which remained passive under their economic hegemony. This monopoly could not last. As one by one fresh countries began to adopt the new methods, and manufactured for the world market, the original industrial societies began to feel the pressure of an increasingly keen international competition. The world became too small for the gigantic development of the new powers, and in every market they jostled and undercut one another for an opening. Even the new lands, which had at first acted simply as plantations and granaries for Western Europe, began to manufacture for themselves, and it is in these lands that the new economic methods have found their fullest development. Finally, the Asiatic peoples, notably Japan, began to emancipate themselves from their economic dependence on the West. Thus the nineteenth-century division of the world into manufacturing and agricultural peoples is passing away before the universalisation of industrialism, and at the same time the purely industrial peoples begin to feel the growing costs of raw materials and foodstuffs. The old nineteenth-century economic supremacy of England had rested on unlimited markets, cheap labour, cheap food and a monopoly of industrial skill. All these factors are now being altered; the world struggle of 1914–1918 has accelerated the change, and we are now beginning to witness a reaction from economic imperialism in the direction of economic self-sufficiency. Nor is this a retrograde step. It simply means that the new methods which were at first the monopoly of a few peoples have become the common conditions of economic life throughout the world. The last century was cosmopolitan in the sense that the economic life of the whole world was being controlled by a few highly organised societies; the present century, however, is cosmopolitan in a fuller sense, since the higher organisation and consequent economic self-control are becoming common to all societies. In other words, world citizenship in the nineteenth century was the monopoly of the great powers of Western Europe, now it is becoming general, and even the Asiatic peoples no longer live in a closed world. It is true that the process of transition is slow and difficult, and the internal economic problems of the industrial peoples seem to portend a ruinous social struggle. Moreover, the imperialist mentality continues to dominate the leading peoples; we are still in the habit of carrying over to the new world conditions the ideas and standards formed in the limited field of European state life. Nevertheless, the magnitude of modern war is itself a lesson in the new conditions. In the last age, a well-organised people of twenty or thirty millions could face the world without misgiving, but now no great power would be ready to embark on a war unless it had behind it a population of 100 millions and the resources of a continent. The scale of modern war and politics involves the necessity of a world settlement, if any settlement is to be made at all. The world is one now, whether we like it or not, and the successful states will be those which best adapt themselves to the realities of the new order. These external conditions of world unity are, however, but the necessary preparation for a new world synthesis, which shall bring to an end the spiritual disorder and social anarchy which has been growing in the midst of all the achievements of knowledge and material power of the period of progress. No civilisation has ever been more lacking in internal unity than our own; yet, unless it is to disintegrate entirely, it must attain some adequate synthesis. No civilisation continues indefinitely in a state of crisis, it either achieves its synthesis or it dies. We cannot foretell how the world problem will be solved. We can only see the general conditions of its solution. These are—firstly, the incorporation into the mind of society of the achievements of the past period of progress, so that these are no longer external appendages without organic relation to the social system, and, secondly, their reconciliation or combination with the fundamental achievements of the previous civilisations.

We cannot suppose that the ancient civilisations of the East will be ready to deny all that they have stood for in the past and to accept a ready made utilitarian culture—a shoddy imitation of Western Europe. On the contrary, the dominant tendency in the newly awakened East is an excessive depreciation of Western culture, and a revived faith in the social value of its own traditional Religion-Cultures. This is no doubt mainly a temporary reaction. History does not consist of a barren conflict between Occidentalism and Orientalism. Although the scientific and technical revolution of the modern world, unlike the spiritual revolution of the previous age, has been the work of Western Europe alone, not the common work of all the civilisations, yet its results are becoming more and more common to the whole world. The great task of the coming age is to promote that spiritual unity without which material unity and control over external nature become merely the organs of a world tyranny or a complication of machinery crushing out true life.

VI

Religion and the Life of Civilisation

Ever since the rise of the modern scientific movement in the eighteenth century there has been a tendency among sociologists and historians of culture to neglect the study of religion in its fundamental social aspects. The apostles of the eighteenth-century Enlightenment were, above all, intent on deducing the laws of social life and progress from a small number of simple rational principles. They hacked through the luxuriant and deep-rooted growth of traditional belief with the ruthlessness of pioneers in a tropical jungle. They felt no need to understand the development of the historic religions and their influence on the course of human history; for, to them, historic religion was essentially negative, it was the clogging and obscurantist power ever dragging back the human spirit in its path towards progress and enlightenment. With Condorcet, they traced religious origins no further than to the duplicity of the first knave and the simplicity of the first fool.

And in the nineteenth century, apart from the St. Simonian circle, the same attitude, expressed with less frankness and brutality, it is true, still dominated scientific thought, and found classical expression in England in the culture-history of Buckle and in the sociology of Herbert Spencer. Indeed, to-day, in spite of the reaction of the last thirty years, it has largely become a part of our intellectual heritage, and is taken for granted in much current sociology and anthropology. Religion was conceived of as a complex of ideas and speculations concerning the Unknowable, and thus belonged to a different world to that which was the province of sociology. The social progress which the latter science studies is the result of the direct response of man to his material environment and to the growth of positive knowledge concerning the material world. Thus social evolution is a unity which can be studied without reference to the numerous changing systems of religious belief and practice that have risen and fallen during its course. The latter may reflect, in some degree, the cultural circumstances under which they have arisen, but they are secondary, and in no sense a formative element in the production of culture.

And undoubtedly these ideas held good for the age in which they were formed. During the eighteenth and nineteenth centuries the world of secular culture was an autonomous kingdom, whose progress owed nothing to the beliefs and sanctions of the existing authoritative religion. But it is dangerous to argue back from the highly specialised conditions of an advanced and complicated civilisation to the elementary principles of social development. Indeed, it needs but a moment's thought to realise that that extraordinary age of intellectual political and economic revolution is comparable with no other period in the history of the world. It was at once creative and destructive, but essentially transitional and impermanent, and this instability was due to no other cause than to that very separation and dislocation of the inner and outer worlds of human experience, which the thinkers of the age accepted as a normal condition of existence.

RELIGION AND THE RISE OF ANCIENT CIVILISATION

For a social culture, even of the most primitive kind, is never simply a material unity. It involves not only a certain uniformity in social organisation and in the way of life, but also a continuous and conscious psychic discipline. Even a common language, one of the first requirements of civilised life, can only be produced by ages of co-operative effort—common thinking as well as common action. From the very dawn of primitive culture men have attempted, in however crude and symbolic a form, to understand the laws of life, and to adapt their social activity to their workings. Primitive man never looked on the world in the modern way, as a passive or, at most, mechanistic system, a background for human energies, mere matter for the human mind to mould. He saw the world as a living world of mysterious forces, greater than his own, in the placation and service of which his life consisted. And, the first need for a people, no less vital than food or weapons, was the psychic equipment or armament by which they fortified themselves against the powerful and mysterious forces that surrounded them. It is impossible for us to draw the line between religion and magic, between law and morals, so intimately is the whole social life of a primitive people bound up with its religion. And the same is true of the earliest civilisation. The first development of a higher culture in the Near East, the beginnings of agriculture and irrigation, and the rise of city life were profoundly religious in their conception. Men did not learn to control the forces of nature, to make the earth fruitful,. and to raise flocks and herds as a practical task of economic organisation in which they relied on their own enterprise and hard work. They viewed it rather as a religious rite by which they co-operated as priests or hierophants in the great cosmic mystery of the fertilisation and growth of nature. The mystical drama, annually renewed, of the Mother-Goddess and her dying and reviving son and spouse, was, at the same time, the economic cycle of ploughing and seed time and harvest by which the people lived. And the king was not so much the organising ruler of a political community, as the priest and religious head of his people, who represented the god himself and stood between the goddess and her people, interpreting to them the divine will, and. sometimes even offering up his own life for them in a solemn ritual ceremony.

Thus there was a profound sense that man lived not by his own strength and knowledge, but by his acting in harmony with the divine cosmic powers, and this harmony could only be attained by sacrifice and at the price of blood; whether the sacrifice of virility, as in Asia Minor, of the first-born children, as in Syria, or of the life of the king himself, as we seem to see dimly in the very dawn of history throughout the Near East.

It is even possible that agriculture and the domestication of animals were exclusively religious in their beginnings, and had their origin in the ritual observation and imitation of the processes of nature which is so characteristic of this type of religion. Certainly the mimicry of nature was carried to very great lengths, as we can see in the religion of Asia Minor in historic times. Sir William Ramsay has even suggested that the whole organisation of the shrine of the great goddess at Ephesus and at other places in Lydia and Phrygia was an elaborate imitation of the life of the bees and the hive; the priestesses being named *mellissae*—the working bees; the priests, or *essenes,* representing the drones; while the goddess herself was the queen-bee, whose behaviour to her temporary partner certainly bears a striking analogy to that of the goddess to Attis in the Phrygian legend.

But it is only in highly conservative regions like Asia Minor that we can see this primitive religion in comparative simplicity. In Babylonia at the very dawn of history, in the fourth millennium B.C., it had already developed a highly specialised theology and temple ritual. The god and goddess of each city had acquired special characteristics and personalities, and had taken their place in a Sumerian pantheon. But Sumerian civilisation still remained entirely religious in character. The god and the goddess were the acknowledged rulers of their city, the king was but their high-priest and steward. The temple, the house of the god, was the centre of the life of the community, for the god was the chief landowner, trader and banker, and kept a great staff of servants and administrators. The whole city territory was, moreover, the territory of the god, and the Sumerians spoke not of the boundaries of the city of Kish or the city of Lagash, but of the boundaries of the god Enlil or the god Ningirsu. All that the king did for his city was undertaken at the command of the god and for the god. Thus we read how Entemena, of Lagash, "made the mighty canal at the boundary of Enlil for Ningirsu, the king whom he loved." At the command of Enlil, Nina and Ningirsu he cut the great canal from the Tigris to the Euphrates—the Shatt el Hai—which was one of the greatest feats of ancient engineering. And the remains of the ancient literature that have come down to us prove that this is not merely the phraseology of the State religion; it represented a profound popular belief in the interdependence and communion of the city and its divinity.

And if we turn to Egypt, we find a no less intensely religious spirit impregnating the archaic culture.

Never, perhaps, before or since, has a high civilisation attained to the centralisation and unification that characterised the Egyptian state in the age of the pyramid-builders. It was more than state socialism, for it meant the entire absorption of the whole life of the individual, in a cause outside himself. The whole vast bureaucratic and economic organisation of the empire was directed to a single end, the glorification of the Sun-God and his child, the God-King.

> It is he [the sun-god] who has adorned thee [Egypt].
> It is he who has built thee.
> It is he who has founded thee.
> Thou dost for him everything that he says to thee
> In every place where he goes.
> Thou carriest to him every tree that is in thee.
> Thou carriest to him all food that is in thee.
> Thou carriest to him the gifts that are in thee.
> Thou carriest to him everything that is in thee.
> Thou carriest to him everything that shall be in thee.
> Thou bringest them to him
> To every place where his heart desires to be.[1]

It is indeed one of the most remarkable spectacles in history to see all the resources of a great culture and a powerful state organised, not for war and conquest, not for the enrichment of a dominant class, but simply to provide the sepulchre and to endow the chantries and tomb-temples of the dead kings. And yet it was this very concentration on death and the after-life that gave Egyptian civilisation its amazing stability. The sun and the Nile, Re and Osiris, the pyramid and the mummy, as long as these remained, it seemed that Egypt must stand fast, her life bound up in the unending round of prayer and ritual observance. All the great development of Egyptian art and learning—astronomy and mathematics and engineering—grew up in the service of this central religious idea, and when, in the age of final decadence, foreign powers took possession of the sacred kingdom, Libyans and Persians, Greeks and Romans all found it necessary to "take the gifts of Horus" and to disguise their upstart imperialism under the forms of the ancient solar theocracy, in order that the machinery of Egyptian civilisation should continue to function.

1. Breasted, *Development of Religion and Thought in Ancient Egypt*, pp. 13–14.

THE DECLINE OF THE ARCHAIC
RELIGION-CULTURE

Yet, both in Egypt and in Western Asia, the primitive theocratic culture had begun to decline by the second half of the third millennium B.C. The rise of the great states in Egypt and Babylonia had, on the one hand, made man less dependent on the forces of nature, and, on the other hand, had brought him face to face with a new series of problems—moral and intellectual—which appear in a striking form in the early Egyptian literature of the Middle Kingdom. The Song of King Intef, the Admonition of Ipuwer, the Complaint of Khekheperre-Sonbu, and, above all, the so-called Dialogue of One Weary of Life with his own Soul, all bear witness to a profound criticism of life, and an intense spiritual ferment. And at the same period in Babylonia we find a similar attitude expressed in the poem of the Righteous Sufferer, the so-called Babylonian Job. Man no longer accepted the world and the state as they were, as the manifestation of the divine powers. They compared the world they knew with the social and moral order that they believed in, and condemned the former. Consequently, for the first time we get a sense of dualism between what is and what ought to be, between the way of men and the way of the gods. The state and the kingship are no longer entirely religious in the kings of the new type— those Twelfth-Dynasty monarchs who are among the greatest and most virile rulers that have ever reigned. We are conscious of a clear realisation of human, personal power and responsibility, and at the same time of a profound disillusionment. We see this in the famous inscription which Senusret III set up at the southern boundary of Egypt, bidding his subjects not to worship his statue, but to fight for it; and yet more intimately in the warning that the founder of the dynasty, Amenemhet I, gave to his son and successor: "Fill not thy heart with a brother, know not a friend, make not for thyself intimates wherein there is no end, harden thyself against subordinates, that thou mayest be king of the earth, that: thou mayest be ruler of the lands, that thou mayest increase good."[2]

2. *Cambridge Ancient History,* I, 303; Breasted, *op. cit.,* p. 303, A.R.E., I, 474–83.

The same spirit of pride and self-reliance breathes in the fierce leonine faces of Senusret III and Amenemhet III, and distinguishes the sculpture of the Twelfth Dynasty from that of the Old Kingdom, which, for all its realism, was interpenetrated by a profoundly religious spirit. Hence, perhaps, the premature ending of this brilliant epoch, and the return, after the Hyksos invasions, to the traditional religiosity of the past, which was inseparable from the survival of the Egyptian state. That the new spirit of criticism and thought continued to be active is, however, proved by the appearance under the Eighteenth Dynasty, in the fourteenth century B.C., of Akhnaten's bold attempt to institute a new solar monotheism as the state religion of Egypt and Syria. Here already, in the fourteenth century B.C., we find the essentials of a world-religion—a religion that is universal in its claims, and which attempts to find the source and first principle which lies behind all the changing phenomena of nature. But the traditional theocratic religion-culture of the Nile Valley was too strong for any such innovation, and the author of the reform went down to history as "the criminal of Akhetaton."

THE COMING OF THE WORLD-RELIGIONS

But, in the course of the following millennium B.C., a spiritual change of the most profound significance passed over the world, a change which was not confined to any one people or culture, but which made itself felt from India to the Mediterranean and from China to Persia. And it brought with it a complete revolution in culture, since it involved the destruction of the old religious civilisation that was based on a co-operation with the divinised forces of nature, and the discovery of a new world of absolute and unchanging reality beside which the natural world—the world of appearances and of earthly life—paled into a shadow and became dream-like and illusory.

Alike in India and in Greece we can trace a striving towards the conception of an invisible underlying cosmic cause or essence—Atman, Logos, the One—and of the unreality of the continual flux which makes up the phenomenal world, but it was in India that the decisive step was first taken, and it was in India that the new view of reality was followed out unwaveringly in all its practical implications.

"He who, dwelling in the earth," says Yâjnavalkya, "is other than the earth, whom the earth knows not, whose body the earth is, who inwardly rules the earth, is thy Self [Atman], the Inward Ruler, the deathless. He who, dwelling in all beings, is other than all beings, whom all beings know not, whose body all beings are, who inwardly rules all beings, is thy Self, the Inward Ruler, the deathless. He who, dwelling in the mind, is other than the mind, whom the mind knows not, whose body the mind is, who inwardly rules the mind, is thy Self, the Inward Ruler, the deathless. He, unseen, sees; unheard, hears; unthought, thinks; uncomprehended, comprehends. There is no other than he who sees—hears—thinks—comprehends. He is thy Self, the Inward Ruler, the deathless. All else is fraught with sorrow."[3]

Hence the one end of life, the one task for the wise man, is deliverance—to cross the bridge, to pass the ford from death to life, from appearance to reality, from time to eternity—all the goods of human life in the family or the state are vanity compared with this. "Possessed by delusion, a man toils for wife and child; but, whether he fulfils his purpose or not, he must surrender the enjoyment thereof. When one is blessed with children and flocks and his heart is clinging to them, Death carries him away as doth a tiger a sleeping deer."[4]

How far removed is this attitude from the simple acquiescence in the good things of this world that is shown by the nature-religions and by the archaic culture that was founded on them! The whole spirit of the new teaching is ascetic, whether it is the intellectual asceticism of the Brahman purging his soul by a kind of Socratic discipline, or the bodily asceticism of the *sannyasi,* who seeks deliverance by the gate of *tapas*— bodily penance. And so there arose in India, especially in the fifth and sixth centuries B.C., a series of "disciplines of salvation"; that of the Jains, that of the Yoga and many more, culminating in the greatest of them all, the Way of Buddha. Buddhism is perhaps the most characteristic of all the religions of the new universalist and absolute type, since it seems to make the fewest metaphysical and theological assumptions, and yet to present the anti-natural, world-denying conception of life in its extremest form. Life is evil, the body is evil, matter is evil. All existence is

---

3. *Brihaddrânyaka Upanishad,* III, vii, trans. L. D. Barnett.
4. *Mahâbharata,* XII, chap. 175 and chap. 174, trans. L. D. Barnett.

bound to the wheel of birth and death, of suffering and desire. Not only is this human life an illusion, but the life of the gods is an illusion, too, and behind the whole cosmic process there is no underlying reality—neither Brahman nor Atman nor the Gunas. There is only the torture-wheel of sentient existence and the path of deliverance, the *via negativa* of the extinction of desire which leads to Nirvana—the Eternal Beatific Silence.

At first sight nothing could be further removed from the world-refusal of the Indian ascetic than the Hellenic attitude to life. Yet the Greeks of Ionia and Italy, during the sixth and fifth centuries B.C., were bent, no less than the Indians, on piercing the veil of appearances and reaching the underlying reality. It is true that the Greeks set out in their quest for the ultimate cosmic principle in a spirit of youthful curiosity and free rational inquiry, and thereby became the creators of natural science. But there was also the purely religious current of Orphic mysticism, with its doctrines of rebirth and immortality, and of the progressive enlightenment of the soul and its emancipation from the defilements of corporeal existence, which had a powerful influence on the Greek mind and even on Greek philosophy, until at last the vision of eternity, which had so long absorbed the mind of India, burst on the Greek world with dazzling power.

It was through the golden mouth of Plato that the vision of the two worlds—the world of appearance and shadows, and the world of timeless, changeless reality—found classic expression in the West. The Greek mind turned, with Plato, away from the many coloured, changing world of appearance and unreality to that other world of the eternal Forms, "where abides the very Being with which true knowledge is concerned, the colourless, formless, intangible essence, visible only to the mind, the pilot of the soul"; "a nature which is everlasting, not growing or decaying or waxing or waning, but Beauty only, absolute, separate, simple and everlasting, which, without diminution and without increase or any change in itself, is imparted to the ever-growing and perishing beauties of all other things." "What if man had eyes to see this true Beauty—pure and unalloyed, not clogged with the pollutions of mortality and all the colours and vanities of human life," would not all human and terrestrial things become mean and unimportant to such a one? And is not the true end of life to return whence we came, "to fly away from earth to heaven," to recover the divine and deific vision which once "we beheld shining in pure light, pure ourselves and not yet enshrined in that living tomb which once we carry about, now that we are imprisoned in the body, like the oyster in his shell." This note, so characteristic and so unforgettable, is never afterwards wholly lost in the ancient world, and it is renewed with redoubled emphasis in that final harvest of the Hellenic tradition, which is Neo-Platonism.

THE WORLD-RELIGIONS AND MATERIAL PROGRESS

It is easy for us to understand a few exceptional men, philosophers and mystics, adopting this attitude to life, but it is harder to realise how it could become the common possession of a whole society or civilisation. Yet, in the course of a few centuries, it became the common possession of practically all the great cultures of the ancient world. It is true that Confucian China was a partial exception, but even China was almost submerged, for a time, by the invasion of Indian mysticism and monasticism, for which the way had already been prepared by the native Taoist tradition.

And each of these cultures had to deal with essentially the same problems—how to reconcile the new attitude to life with the old civilisation that they had inherited, a civilisation that had been built up so laboriously by the worship and cultivation of the powers of nature. It is obvious that the new religions were not themselves productive of a new material civilisation; their whole tendency was away from the material and economic side of life towards the life of pure spirit. It is indeed difficult to see how the most extreme examples of this type of religion, such as Manichæanism, were reconcilable with any material social culture whatever. In other cases, however, especially in India, the archaic culture was able to maintain itself almost intact, in spite of the dominance of the new religions. As Professor Slater has well said, it is in the great temple cities of Dravidian India that we can still see before us to-day the vanished civilisations of Egypt and Babylonia.[5]

---

5. "In other parts of India, one feels oneself sometimes carried back into the Middle Ages . . . in such a temple as that of Menakshi and Siva in Madura one can only dream of

To the teacher or ascetic of the new religion the ancient rites have acquired an esoteric and symbolic significance, while the common people still find in them their ancient meaning, and seek contact through them with the beneficent or destructive powers of nature that rule the peasant's life. In yet other cases, above all in Islam, this dualism is impossible, and the whole of life is brought into direct relation with the new religious conception. Terrestrial life loses its intrinsic importance, it is but as "the beat of a gnat's wing" in comparison with the eternal. But it acquires importance as a preparation, a time of training and warfare, of which the discipline and suffering are repaid by the eternal joys of Paradise.

Thus the new religions in these three main types are, on the whole, not favourable to material progress. In some cases they are even retrograde. Sir William Ramsay has shown, in the case of Asia Minor, how the passing of the old nature-religions had a depressing effect on agriculture, on economic prosperity and even perhaps on hygiene; and the same thing is no doubt true, in some degree, of many different regions. The great achievements of the new culture lie in the domain of literature and art. But, from the material point of view, there is expansion rather than progress. The new culture simply gave a new form and a new spirit to the materials that it had received from the archaic civilisation. In all essentials Babylonia, in the time of Hammurabi, and even earlier, had reached a pitch of material civilisation which has never since been surpassed in Asia. After the artistic flowering of the early Middle Ages the great religion-cultures became stationary and even decadent. Eternity was changeless, and why should man, who lived for eternity, change?

This is the secret of the "Unchanging East," which has impressed so many Western observers, and which gives to a civilisation such as that of Burma its remarkable attractiveness and charm. But such societies are living on the past; they do not advance in power and knowledge, it even seems as though they are retreating step by step before the powers of primitive nature until at last they disappear, as the marvellous achievements of Ankhor and Anuradapura have been swallowed up by the jungle.

---

having revisited some great shrine of Isis and Osiris in Egypt, or of Marduk in Babylon."—
Slater, *The Dravidian Element in Indian Culture*, p. 167.

THE RISE OF THE MODERN
SCIENTIFIC CULTURE

But a ferment of change, a new principle of movement and progress has entered the world with the civilisation of modern Europe.

The development of the European culture was, of course, largely conditioned by religious traditions the consideration of which lies outside the limits of this inquiry. It was, however, not until the fifteenth and sixteenth centuries that the new principle, which characterised the rise of modern civilisation, made its appearance. It was then that there arose—first in Italy and afterwards throughout Western Europe—the new attitude to life that has been well named Humanism. It was, in fact, a reaction against the whole transcendent spiritualist view of existence, a return from the divine and the absolute to the human and the finite. Man turned away from the pure white light of eternity to the warmth and colour of the earth. He rediscovered nature, not, indeed, as the divine and mysterious power that men had served and worshipped in the first ages of civilisation, but as a reasonable order which he could know by science and art, and which he could use to serve his own purpose.

"Experiment," says Leonardo da Vinci, the great precursor, "is the true interpreter between nature and man." Experience is never at fault. What is at fault is man's laziness and ignorance. "Thou, O God, dost sell us all good things for the price of work."

This is the essential note of the new European movement; it was applied science, not abstract, speculative knowledge, as with the Greeks. "Mechanics," says Leonardo again, "are the Paradise of the mathematical sciences, for in them the fruits of the latter are reaped." And the same principles of realism and practical reason are applied in political life.

The state was no longer an ideal hierarchy that symbolised and reflected the order of the spiritual world. It was the embodiment of human power, whose only law was Necessity.

Yet no complete break was made with the past. The people remained faithful to the religious tradition. Here and there a Giordano Bruno in philosophy or a Machiavelli in statecraft gave their whole-hearted adhesion to Naturalism, but for the most part both statesmen and philosophers endeavoured to serve two masters, like Descartes or Richelieu.

They remained fervent Christians, but at the same time they separated the sphere of religion from the sphere of reason, and made the latter an independent autonomous kingdom in which the greater part of their lives was spent.

It was only in the eighteenth century that this compromise, which so long dominated European culture, broke down before the assaults of the new humanists, the Encyclopædists and the men of the Enlightenment in France, England and Germany. We have already described the attitude of that age to religion—its attempt to sweep away the old accumulation of tradition and to refound civilisation on a rational and naturalistic basis. And the negative side of this programme was, indeed, successfully carried out. European civilisation was thoroughly secularised. The traditional European polity, with its semi-divine royalty, its state Churches and its hereditary aristocratic hierarchy, was swept away and its place was taken by the liberal bourgeois state of the nineteenth century, which aimed, above all, at industrial prosperity and commercial expansion. But the positive side of the achievement was much less secure. It is true that Western Europe and the United States of America advanced enormously in wealth and population, and in control over the forces of nature; while the type of culture that they had developed spread itself victoriously over the old world of Asia and the new world of Africa and Oceania, first by material conquest, and later by its intellectual and scientific prestige, so that the great oriental religion-cultures began to lose their age-long, unquestioned dominance over the daily life and thought of the peoples of the East, at least, among the educated classes.

PROGRESS AND DISILLUSIONMENT THE MEANING OF MODERN SOCIAL UNREST

But there was not a corresponding progress in spiritual things. As Comte had foreseen, the progressive civilisation of the West, without any unifying spiritual force, and without an intellectual synthesis, tended to fall back into social anarchy. The abandonment of the old religious traditions did not bring humanity together in a natural and moral unity, as the eighteenth-century philosophers had hoped. On the contrary, it allowed the fundamental differences of race and nationality, of class and private interest, to appear in their naked antagonism. The progress in wealth and power did nothing to appease these rivalries; rather it added fuel to them, by accentuating the contrasts of wealth and poverty, and widening the field of international competition. The new economic imperialism, as it developed in the last generation of the nineteenth century, was as grasping, as unmoral, and as full of dangers of war, as any of the imperialisms of the old order. And, while under the old order the state had recognised its limits as against a spiritual power, and had only extended its claims over a part of human life, the modern state admitted no limitations, and embraced the whole life of the individual citizen in its economic and military organisation.

Hence the rise of a new type of social unrest. Political disturbances are as old as human nature; in every age misgovernment and oppression have been met by violence and disorder, but it is a new thing, and perhaps a phenomenon peculiar to our modern Western civilisation, that men should work and think and agitate for the complete remodelling of society according to some ideal of social perfection. It belongs to the order of religion, rather than to that of politics, as politics, were formerly understood. It finds its only parallel in the past in movements of the most extreme religious type, like that of the Anabaptists in sixteenth-century Germany, and the Levellers and Fifth-Monarchy Men of Puritan England. And when we study the lives of the founders of modern Socialism, the great Anarchists and even some of the apostles of nationalist Liberalism like Mazzini, we feel at once that we are in the presence of religious leaders, whether prophets or heresiarchs, saints or fanatics. Behind the hard rational surface of Karl Marx's materialist and socialist interpretation of history there burns the flame of an apocalyptic vision. For what was that social revolution in which he put his hope but a nineteenth-century version of the Day of the Lord, in which the rich and the powerful of the earth should be consumed, and the princes of the Gentiles brought low, and the poor and disinherited should reign in a regenerated universe? So, too, Marx, in spite of his professed atheism, looked for the realisation of this hope, not, like St. Simon and his fellow-idealist Socialists, to the conversion of the individual and to human efforts towards the attainment of a new social ideal, but to "the arm of the Lord," the necessary, ineluctable working-out of the Eternal Law, which human will and human effort are alike powerless to change or stay.

But the religious impulse behind these social movements is not a constructive one. It is as absolute in its demands as that of the old religions, and it admits of no compromise with reality. As soon as the victory is gained, and the phase of destruction and revolution is ended, the inspiration fades away before the tasks of practical realisation. We look in vain in the history of United Italy for the religious enthusiasm that sustained Mazzini and his fellows, and it took very few years to transform the Rousseauan idealism of revolutionary France, the Religion of Humanity, into Napoleonic and even Machiavellian realism.

The revolutionary attitude—and it is perhaps the characteristic religious attitude of modern Europe—is, in fact, but another symptom of the divorce between religion and social life. The nineteenth-century revolutionaries—the Anarchists, the Socialists and, to some extent, the Liberals—were driven to their destructive activities by the sense that actual European society was a mere embodiment of material force and fraud—*magnum latrocinium,* as St. Augustine says—that it was based on no principle of justice, and organised for no spiritual or ideal end; and the more the simpler and more obvious remedies—republicanism, universal suffrage, national self-determination—proved disappointing to the reformers, the deeper became their dissatisfaction with the whole structure of existing society. And, finally, when the process of disillusionment is complete, this religious impulse that lies behind the revolutionary attitude may turn itself against social life altogether, or at least against the whole system of civilisation that has been built up in the last two centuries. This attitude of mind seems endemic in Russia, partly, perhaps, as an inheritance of the Byzantine religious tradition. We see it appearing in different forms in Tolstoy, in Dostoievski and in the Nihilists, and it is present as a psychic undercurrent in most of the Russian revolutionary movements. It is the spirit which seeks not political reform, not the improvement of social conditions, but escape, liberation—Nirvana. In the words of a modern poet (Francis Adams), it is

> To wreck the great guilty temple,
> And give us Rest.

And in the years since the war, when the failure of the vast machinery of modern civilisation has seemed so imminent, this view of life has become more common even in the West. It has inspired the poetry of Albert Ehrenstein and many others.[6] Mr. D. H. Lawrence has well expressed it in Count Psanek's profession of faith, in *The Ladybird* (pp. 43–4).

I have found my God. The god of destruction. The god of anger, who throws down the steeples and factory chimneys.

Not the trees, these chestnuts, for example—not these—nor the chattering sorcerers, the squirrels—nor the hawk that comes. Not those.

What grudge have I against a world where even the hedges are full of berries, branches of black berries that hang down and red berries that thrust up? Never would I hate the world. But the world of man—*I hate it.*

I believe in the power of my dark red heart. God has put the hammer in my breast—the little eternal hammer. Hit—hit—hit. It hits on the world of man. It hits, it hits. And it hears the thin sound of cracking.

Oh, may I live long. May I live long, so that my hammer may strike and strike, and the cracks go deeper, deeper. Ah, the world of man. Ah, the joy, the passion in every heartbeat. Strike home, strike true, strike sure. Strike to destroy it. Strike. Strike. To destroy the world of man. Ah, God. Ah, God, prisoner of peace.

It may seem to some that these instances are negligible, mere morbid extravagances, but it is impossible to exaggerate the dangers that must inevitably arise when once social life has become separated from the religious impulse.

We have only to look at the history of the ancient world and we shall see how tremendous are these consequences. The Roman Empire, and the Hellenistic civilisation of which it was the vehicle, became separated in this way from any living religious basis, which all the efforts of Augustus and his helpers were powerless to restore; and thereby, in spite of its high material and intellectual culture, the dominant civilisa-

---

6. For instance, the following verse:

Ich beschwöre euch, zerstampfet die Städt.
Ich beschwöre euch, zertrümmert die Städte.
Ich beschwöre euch, zerstört die Maschine.
Ich beschwöre euch, zerstöret den Staat.

tion became hateful in the eyes of the subject oriental world. Rome was to them not the ideal world-city of Virgil's dream, but the incarnation of all that was anti-spiritual—Babylon the great, the Mother of Abominations, who bewitched and enslaved all the peoples of the earth, and on whom, at last, the slaughter of the saints and the oppression of the poor would be terribly avenged. And so all that was strongest and most living in the moral life of the time separated itself from the life of society and from the service of the state, as from something unworthy and even morally evil. And we see in Egypt in the fourth century, over against the great Hellenistic city of Alexandria, filled with art and learning and all that made life delightful, a new power growing up, the power of the men of the desert, the naked, fasting monks and ascetics, in whom, however, the new world recognised its masters. When, in the fifth century, the greatest of the late Latin writers summed up the history of the great Roman tradition, it is in a spirit of profound hostility and disillusionment: *Acceperunt mercedem suam,* says he, in an unforgettable sentence, *vani vanam.*

This spiritual alienation of its own greatest minds is the price that every civilisation has to pay when it loses its religious foundations, and is contented with a purely material success. We are only just beginning to understand how intimately and profoundly the vitality of a society is bound up with its religion. It is the religious impulse which supplies the cohesive force which unifies a society and a culture. The great civilisations of the world do not produce the great religions as a kind of cultural by-product; in a very real sense, the great religions are the foundations on which the great civilisations rest. A society which has lost its religion becomes sooner or later a society which has lost its culture.

What then is to be the fate of this great modern civilisation of ours? A civilisation which has gained an extension and a wealth of power and knowledge which the world has never known before. Is it to waste its forces in the pursuit of selfish and mutually destructive aims, and to perish for lack of vision? Or can we hope that society will once again become animated by a common faith and hope, which will have the power to order our material and intellectual achievements in an enduring spiritual unity?

VII

Civilisation and Morals

Or, the Ethical Basis of Social Progress

If we make a survey of human history and culture, we see clearly that every society has possessed a moral code, which is often clearly thought out and exactly defined. In practically every society in the past there has been an intimate relation between this moral code and the dominant religion. Often the code of ethics is conceived as the utterance of a divine law-giver, as in Judaism and Islam. In non-theistic religions, it may be viewed as a "discipline of salvation," a harmonising of human action with the cosmic process as in Taoism (and to some extent Confucianism) or else as the method by which the individual mind is freed from illusion, and led to Reality (Buddhism and Vedantism).

But it may be asked is it not possible to go behind these historic world-religions and find a simpler, purely social ethic? Certainly primitive morality is entirely customary, but it is also closely bound up with primitive religion or magic (if the two can be distinguished). A moral offence is not so much an offence against a man's fellow-tribesmen, as doing something which provokes the mysterious powers that surround man; the primitive "moralist" is the man who understands how to placate these powers and render them friendly. But if there is not much evidence for the existence of a pre-religious morality, there is no doubt about the existence of a post-religious one. In every advanced civilisation, as men become critical of the dominant religion, they tend to elaborate systems of philosophy, new interpretations of reality and corresponding codes of ethics. In every case the metaphysic and the ethic are inseparably connected, and in theory it is the metaphysic which is the foundation of the ethic. In reality, however, it may be questioned whether the reverse is not often the case, whether the ethical attitude is not taken over from the formerly dominant religion, and then justified by a philosophical construction.

Thus I believe Kant's ethic may be explained as a direct survival of the intensive moral culture of Protestantism, and many similar instances could be adduced. But, apart from these cases of direct inspiration, it is only to be expected there should be some relation between the dominant religion and the characteristic philosophies in the case of each particular culture.

The situation with regard to ethical codes, in a society in which a religion is no longer completely dominant, is somewhat as follows:

A. There is a minority which still adheres completely to the old faith and corresponding ethical system.

B. There is a still smaller minority which adheres consciously to a new rational interpretation of reality, and adopts new ideals of conduct and standards of moral behaviour.

C. The great majority follow a mixed "pragmatic" code of morality made up of (1) the striving for individual wealth and enjoyment; (2) an "actual" social ethic of group-egotism or "tribal" patriotism; (3) certain tabus left over from the old religion-culture. These are usually the great precepts of social morality, *e.g.,* against murder, theft, adultery, etc., but they may be purely ritual restrictions *e.g.,* the survival of the Scotch Sunday in spite of the disappearance of the religious substructure); (4) to a slight extent a top-dressing of the new moral ideals from B.

This situation is to a great extent characteristic of the modern world, but we must also take account of a great movement, neither a religion nor a philosophy in the ordinary sense of the words, which may be regarded as a reflection of the old religion-culture or else as the first stage of a new one. This is the Democratic or Liberal movement, which grew up in England and France in the eighteenth century, and which found classic expression in the Declaration of Independence, 1776, and the Declaration of the Rights of Men, 1789. It was based on the new naturalist philosophy and theology of the English Deists and the French Philosophes, and it owed much to the political and economic teaching of the Physiocrats and Adam Smith, but its great prophet and true founder was Rousseau. This movement continued to grow with the expansion of European civilisation in the nineteenth century. It is at present the established religion of the U.S.A. and Latin America, any deviation from it being regarded as heretical, and it is by no means a negligible force in Europe. It is doubtful, however, whether it can be regarded as a new culture-religion, since it seems simply to carry on, in a generalised and abstract form, the religious and ethical teaching of the previously dominant religion.

Supposing that we have correctly outlined above the general course of the development of moral conceptions, the chief problems to be solved are the following:

(1) Is the development of moral conceptions progressive, and, if so, in what direction does this progress tend?

(2) What is the cause of the changes in the dominant conception of Reality, on which the change of moral systems seems to depend?

(3) Is it possible to elaborate a rational system of ethics based on a modern scientific interpretation of Reality?

Now it seems clear that it is impossible to have a purely "practical" morality divorced from an interpretation of Reality. Such a morality would be mere social custom and essentially unprogressive. Progress springs very largely from the attempt to bring actual conditions and social habits into harmony with what are conceived as the laws or conditions of real life. The very conception of morality involves a duality or opposition between what "is" and what "ought to be." Moreover, from the very earliest conditions of primitive savagery up to the highest degree of intellectual culture, the ethical standard can be shown to be closely connected with some kind of world-view or conception of Reality, whether that is embodied in a mythology, or a philosophy, or is merely vaguely implicit in the customs and beliefs of the society.

Now the great obstacle to the attainment of a purely rational system of ethics is simply our lack of knowledge of Reality. If we can accept some metaphysic of Absolute Being, then we shall possess an absolute foundation for morality, as the Platonists did. But if we limit ourselves to positive and scientific knowledge of Reality, it is at once evident that we are limited to a little island of light in the middle of an ocean of darkness. Unfortunately, Herbert Spencer's attitude towards the Unknowable will not help us here, for the *machina mundi* is a dynamic unity, and the part of it that we know shares in the movement of the unknown whole. Most philosophies and religions have supposed that there is some kind of meaning or reason in the world process; though there are thinkers like Lucretius (and perhaps Bertrand Russell) who deny this, and yet try to fashion a kind of "island" morality for reasonable humanity shipwrecked amidst the chaos of an irrational universe. Nevertheless, the great majority of modern thinkers, and in fact modern men, believe profoundly in the existence of progress, and not merely a progress of succession, but a progress of improvement. "Life moves on to ever higher and richer forms. Here is an adequate goal for moral effort! Here is a justification of moral values! Here is the true foundation for a modern system of ethics!"

But from the purely rational point of view, what does all this amount to? So far from explaining the problems of human existence, it adds fresh difficulties. There is continual movement from the Known to the Unknown. Something that was not before, has come to be. Granted that the true morality is that which subserves Progress, how can we know what it is that will best serve the Unknown? Could Aurignacian man divine the coming of civilisation? Could the men of the Mycenean age foresee Hellenism? When the people of Israel came raiding into Canaan, could they look forward to the future of Judaism? And yet all these achievements were in some degree implicit in the beginnings of these people. They created what they could not understand. If they had limited themselves to the observance of a purely rational social ethic based on the immediate advantage of the community, they might have been more prosperous, but they would not have been culturally creative. They would have had no importance for the future. The highest moral ideal either for a people or for an individual is to be true to its destiny, to sacrifice the bird in the hand for the vision in the bush, to leave the Known for the Unknown, like Abram going out from Harran and from his own people, obedient to the call of Yahweh, or the Aeneas of Vergil's great religious epic.

This of course seems mere mysticism and the very contradiction of a reasonable ethical system. Nevertheless, it seems to be the fact that a new way of life or a new view of Reality is felt intuitively before it is comprehended intellectually, that a philosophy is the last product of a mature culture, the crown of a long process of social development, not its foundation. It is in Religion and Art that we can best see the vital intention of the living culture.

Ananda Coomaraswamy, writing of Indian Art, says: "The gods are the dreams of the race in whom its intentions are most perfectly fulfilled. From them we come to know its innermost desires and purposes. . . . He is no longer an Indian, whatever his birth, who can stand before the Trimurti at Elephanta, not saying 'But so did I will it! So shall I will it'."[1]

The modern psychologist of Art will probably object that this view of the meaning of Art is purely subjective and fanciful. A work of Art, he will say, represents simply the solution of a psychic tension, the satisfaction of a rather recondite and complicated impulse, which is of importance only for the psychic life of the individual. From the point of view of the psychologist this is no doubt justified, but then from the same point of view all cultural activities, nay the life process itself, may be explained in terms of psychic tensions and their solution. Yet this is merely an analysis of the psychic mechanism, and it takes little or no account of the underlying physical realities. For instance, when one eats one's dinner, one satisfies an impulse, and solves a psychic tension, viz., the hunger tension, but at the same time one builds up the physical organism, and the results of a persistent neglect to take food cannot be assessed simply in terms of a repression psychosis.

Consequently, in the case of Art, it is not enough to look at the psychic impulse of the individual artist. It is only in times of cultural decadence and social dissolution that Art is a "refuge from reality" for the individual mind. Normally it is an expression of mastery over life. The same purposeful fashioning of plastic material which is the very essence of a culture, expresses itself also in art. The Greek statue must be first conceived, then lived, then made, and last of all thought. There you have the whole cycle of creative Hellenic culture. First Religion, then

---

1. A. Coomaraswamy: *The Arts and Crafts of India and Ceylon,* p. 59.

Society, then Art, and finally Philosophy, Not that one of these is cause
and the others effects. They are all different aspects or functions of one
life.

Now it is obvious that if such a central purpose or life-intention exists in a society, the adhesion to it or the defection from it of the individual becomes the central fact in social morality. There remain, of
course, a certain number of obvious moral duties without which social
life is hardly conceivable and which must be much the same in every
age and society. But even these acquire very different meanings according to the ruling principle to which they are related. The offence of
murder, for example, cannot have the same meaning in a society such
as ancient Assyria, where religion and morality were essentially warlike,
as among the Jains, to whom taking of life, under any circumstances
and in respect to any creature, is the one unpardonable sin. Again, to
the modern European or American, social justice necessarily involves
an increasing measure of equality and fraternity; to the ancient Indian,
on the other hand, justice involves the strictest preservation of every
barrier between classes and occupations: to him the very type of law-
lessness is the man who oversteps the boundaries of his caste. If morality were purely social, and concerned entirely with the relation of
the individual to the group in which he lives, this difference of moral
standards would no doubt be less, though it would not be eliminated.
But actually men's views of social reality form but a part of their conception of cosmic reality, and morality involves a constant process of
adjustment not only between individual impulse and social reality, but
also between the actual life of society and the life of the whole, whether
that is conceived, cosmically or is limited to humanity. There is a tendency in every organism, whether individual or social, to stop at itself,
to turn in on itself, to make itself a goal instead of a bridge. Just as the
individual tends to follow his anti-social impulses, so the society also
tends to assert itself against the larger interests of humanity or the laws
of universal life. We see clearly enough that a dominant class is only too
apt to make society serve its own ends, instead of subordinating itself
to the functional service of society, and the same thing happens with
every actual society, in its relations towards other societies and towards
humanity at large.

This is why moral systems in the past have (except in China) so often shown a tendency of hostility to the actual social group, and have established themselves in a super-social sphere. Certainly the great moral reformers have usually found the greatest opposition not in the "immoral" and impulsive individual, but in the regularly constituted organs of social authority and law. And it is one of the greatest difficulties in the democratic system that the force of this actual social authority is so enormously strengthened by its identification with public opinion that the position of the individual whose moral standards and whose grasp of reality are in advance of his society is increasingly hard to maintain: instead of the triangle Government, People, Reformers, we have the sharp dualism Governing people, Reformers.

At first sight there may seem to be a contradiction between the conception of individuals in advance of the morality of their society and the conception of the existence of a central life-purpose in every civilisation. But it must be remembered that there is a great distinction between the age-long racial and spiritual communion which is a civilisation and the association for practical ends which is an actual political society. Not for thousands of years—perhaps not since the earliest kingdoms of Egypt and again excepting China—have the two coincided. There is always a dualism between the Hellenic state and Hellenism, the Christian state and Christendom, the Moslem state and Islam, the "modern" state and "modern civilisation," and the individual man has a double citizenship and a double allegiance. Certainly every actual society is moulded by the civilisation to which it belongs, and to which it always professes a certain loyalty, but the whole emphasis of its activity is on the present, the actual, the practical, and it tends to regard the civilisation as something fixed and achieved, as a static background to its own activities. Consequently, there are frequent conflicts between the spirit of the culture and that of the actual society, which become manifest in the opposition to the actual social will of those individuals whose minds are in closer contact with the wider movement of the whole civilisation. For a man's social contacts vary with the richness of his psychic life, and it is only in the mind of the man whom we call a genius that the creative movement in the living culture becomes explicit. The ordinary man is conscious only of the past, he may belong by his acts to the cultural present, by the part that he plays in the social life of his time, but his view of reality, his power of sight, is limited to what has been already perceived and formulated by others.

There remains a more serious objection in the difficulty of reconciling the dominance of an immanent group-instinct or purpose with any real moral or intellectual progress. For it might seem that if the highest products of a culture are the flowers of a social organism that has had its roots in particular geographical and ethnological circumstances, no permanent and objective progress will be achieved, and the greatest works of art and thought will simply reproduce in a more sophisticated form the results of the past experience of the organism. Certainly we must admit that every past condition will express itself in the life-impulses and life-concepts of a society, and that thus the cultural achievements of a people are largely determined by the past. But this does not occur mechanically. The existence of reason, thought, reflection, increases the range of possibilities in the fulfilment of instinctive purpose. An old impulse acting in a new environment, different from that to which it was originally adapted, may be not merely a decadent survival, but a stepping stone to the acquisition of new powers and to some new conception of reality. Thus there is a continual enlargement of the field of experience, and, thanks to Reason, the new does not simply replace the old, but is compared and combined with it. The history of mankind, and still more of civilised mankind, shows a continuous process of integration, which, even though it seems to work irregularly, never ceases. A modern writer has said, "The mind of man seems to be of a nature to assimilate itself to the universe; we belong to the world; the whole is mirrored in us. Therefore, when we bend our thought on a limited object, we concentrate faculties which are naturally endowed with infinite correspondences";[2] and, however fanciful this view may seem to be, we cannot shut our eyes to the significance of this steadily growing vision of Reality, which is at once the condition and the result of the life-purpose of human society.

And thus the great stages of world culture are linked with changes in this vision of Reality. The primitive condition of food-gathering and

2. *The Times Literary Supplement,* p. 330, 1923.

hunting peoples does not necessarily imply reasonable purpose or any reflective vision of Reality; consequently, it does not imply civilisation. The dawn of true civilisation came only with the discovery of natural laws, or rather of the possibility of man's fruitful co-operation with the powers of nature. This was the foundation of the primitive cultures of Elam and Babylonia and Egypt. To it belong the discovery of agriculture, irrigation, and the working of metals, with the institutions of kingship and priesthood, and it governed the progress of civilisation for millennia. It is remarkable that the most typical and perfect example of this civilisation grew up in Egypt just where natural conditions are most stable and the laws of nature most easily discernible.

(2) About 2,500 years ago civilisation underwent a great revolution owing to a change in men's conceptions of Reality. Throughout the ancient world from the Mediterranean to India and China, men came to realise the existence of a universal cosmic law to which both humanity and the powers of nature are subject. This was the foundation of the great religious civilisations, whether theistic or non-theistic, which have controlled the world for some 2,000 years. In some cases, especially in India and China, the old worship of the nature powers was carried over into the new culture, but even there, and still more in Islam and Christendom, there was a neglect of the material side of civilisation due to a concentration on ideal values and absolute existence, which in some cases, especially in Greece and Mesopotamia, led to a decline in material culture.

(3) Since the Renaissance there has been first in the West, and then increasingly throughout the world, a new comprehension of Reality, due to the turning of man's attention once more to the powers and processes of nature and resulting in the elaboration of scientific laws. On this new knowledge, and on the new power of control over nature that it gives, our modern Western civilisation is being built up. Thus it is in a sense a reaction against the second stage described above, and, since European and still more oriental culture has been based traditionally upon that stage, there is at present a conflict and a dualism existing within the culture itself. Moreover, the new third stage of culture, while far superior to the second in knowledge and power with regard to details, is far less unified and less morally sure of itself. It arose either

as an expansion or as a criticism of the second stage, and not as an independent self-sufficient culture As the recent history of Europe has shown, it may easily end in a suicidal process of exploitation and social self-aggrandisemeat, or it may lose itself in the particular. Therefore the great problem, both moral and intellectual of the present age lies in securing the fruits of the new knowledge of nature without sacrificing the achievements of the previous stage of culture, in reconciling the sovereignty of universal cosmic order, the eternal divine law with man's detailed knowledge of himself and the powers and processes of nature.

VIII

The Mystery of China

During recent years there has been a remarkable growth of interest in China and its civilisation among Western peoples. Chinese art and literature have at last come into their own and are being studied not as interesting curiosities, but as among the supreme achievements of the human spirit. Moreover, recent developments have caused the political and social situation in China to become a burning question of practical politics, so that the average man who knows and cares nothing about Chinese culture is forced to turn his attention to China whether he will or no.

Nevertheless, in spite of all this, the history of Chinese culture still remains a sealed book to the West. No other civilisation in the world is so fascinating and so impenetrable. The fact that Chinese poetry and Chinese art make so strong an appeal to the modern mind only throws into stronger relief our failure to understand Chinese society. The whole social life of China has been moulded to an even greater extent than that, of any other people in the world by the influence of a religion. The Confucian moral teaching and the influence of Confucian learning have so permeated society that they have become a second nature to the Chinese people, a psychic discipline that is no longer felt as something external, but which moulds every thought and feeling from within.

It may be said that each of the great civilisations of the world is dominated or has been dominated by its own religion, and this cannot be denied. But all the other world religions possess a common element which causes them to be mutually intelligible up to a certain point. They are all religions in the same sense, if one may put it so. All

of them possess a theology, all of them recognise the distinction between that which is religious and that which is secular. However hostile
they may be to one another, they share certain fundamental presuppositions. They are hostile, in fact, because they are competitors in the
same field.

But in the case of Confucianism all these characteristics are absent.
It is not a religion in the Western sense of the word at all. It is unintelligible to us by reason of its very rationality, of its absence of all supernatural claims and of any theological teaching. And yet it is stronger in
its hold upon society and upon the daily life of the people than any religion that we know. In other civilisations religion may control thought,
or the priesthood may possess a preponderant influence on society and
education, but there always remains a residuum of secular knowledge,
and the possibility of some resistance to priestly influence on the part
of other social elements or classes.

But in China thought *is* religion, and the only learning is Confucian
learning. The whole literary tradition of Chinese civilisation—and it is
the most ancient and continuous tradition in the world—has been in
the hands of the Confucian learned class, and outside this there is nothing save the scriptures of Buddhist monks and the fairy tales of Taoist
magicians.

It is only during the last few years that scholars like M. Granet in
France and Herr Schindler in Germany have attempted to pierce the
cloud of the Confucian tradition and to reconstitute the ideas and institutions of the more primitive stages of Chinese civilisation.

As M. Granet has said, the official history of China is a result of the
projection into the past of the controversies and ideals of a later period.
The China of the age of Confucius was very far from being the Confucian China that the classical authors depict. It was a simpler society
which still preserved the traces of a more barbarous culture, and at the
same time it was more original and richer in creative forces. Nevertheless, even in feudal times, Chinese civilisation had already begun to
acquire the spirit of formalism and etiquette that has been so characteristic of it ever since.

Its religion may be compared to that of the Romans, alike in its
merits and its defects—in its strong moral emphasis on the qualities of

Pietas and Gravitas, and in its legal punctiliousness in the performance of official rites and ceremonies and the importance that it attached to omens and augury. Every act of public and private life was regulated by an elaborate ceremonial code. Manners were inseparable from morals, and the observance of diplomatic and political precedents had the importance of an act of religious ritual. Thus there grew up a class of specialists in ceremonial and tradition, and each of the little states of which feudal China was composed had its own school of ritual lawyers, as one may term them, without whose advice no important political action could be undertaken. Now the importance of Confucius consisted in the new spirit that he brought to this ceremonial tradition. His school was, like the rest, a school of ritual specialists, but instead of being concerned solely with problems of formal correctness, he based his teaching on general principles of moral and philosophical import. For him the secret of the true performance of the rites lay in the complete conformity and adhesion of the individual mind to the conventional acts that were laid down by the ritual tradition. This is the great Confucian virtue of Sincerity, through which the individual participates in the universal order which governs not only the life of society, but the whole course of nature. Thus the essence of Confucianism consists not in its ethical ideals by themselves, but in their application to the old ritual tradition of the pre-existing culture of ancient China. Hence the paradox of Chinese civilisation, which never fails to perplex the Western observer. On the one hand its principles are so rational that they would not be out of place in the mouth of an eighteenth-century French philosopher (as indeed the latter was the first to realise) but at the same time they find their practical application and exemplification in the carrying out of a multitude of rites and traditions which have their origin in a much more primitive stage of culture. Yet it is this paradox which explains the extraordinary permanence and continuity of Chinese civilisation. There has been no break in the Chinese development such as occurred in the West with the adoption of Christianity. We can imagine a parallel state of things, if Europe instead of accepting the Gospel had remained faithful to the official religion of the Roman Empire as rationalised and re-edited by a Cicero or a Varro. Indeed, during the Augustan restoration, when the ceremonies of a primitive agrarian cult were sedulously practised on principles of social expediency by men of high philosophic culture, we do witness an approach to the state of things that obtained in the classical Chinese culture. Nevertheless, the spirit of the Augustan revival was never either quite so naif or quite so positivist as that of orthodox Confucianism. Roman religion, even in its most artificial phases, preserved a sense of the supernatural and the divine that was almost entirely lacking in the official religion of China. It is true that the emotional strength and conviction of Confucianism were far greater. It produced its saints, its ascetics and even its martyrs. But these did not sacrifice themselves to any supernatural ideal, but to the concrete ends of the social order. In no other civilisation do we find so absolute a subordination of the individual to the social organism, though the latter finds its ideal embodiment for the Chinaman in the Family rather than in the state. It has been well said that the national religion of China is an emotional cultus with its centre of gravity shifted from God to the idealised parent, so that in place of God being a "Father-substitute" as the psycho-analysts have taught, it is the Father who becomes a "God-substitute." It is true that the religious instincts, for which Confucianism leaves no room, do find an inevitable outlet even in China. The extraordinary popularity of Taoism and Buddhism, especially during the Middle Ages, bears witness to the appeal of mysticism and supernaturalism to the Chinese mind, and for a time it seemed as though Buddhism might replace Confucianism as the official religion of the Empire. But the learned class, as custodians of the national tradition, firmly resisted such attempts. "Where was the sense," asked Han Yu, in a celebrated memorial to the emperor, "in worshipping Buddha, a mere foreign barbarian, who could not speak a word of Chinese and who was ignorant of the first principles of Confucian teaching?"

Ultimately the common sense and self-confidence of such men won the day, and the influence of Buddhism steadily declined until in the eighteenth century, under the great Manchu emperors K'ang Hsi and Ch'ien Lung, the Confucian order seemed to stand firmer than ever before. There can be little doubt that it would be still intact to-day had it not been for the forcible impact of Western civilisation during the nineteenth century. The old regime inevitably suffered a loss of prestige from its complete failure to withstand the material forces of the European peoples who had hitherto been despised as mere barbarians. Moreover, however passionately the Chinese people might resent the aggressions of the foreigner, they could not entirely avoid being affected by the new knowledge and the new ideas which followed in the wake of the European economic and military expansion. Thus it came about that the very men who were the leaders in the campaign for national revival were those who were most under the influence of Western culture, and when they were ultimately successful, the fall of the Manchu Dynasty was accompanied by the introduction of Western institutions and the destruction of the old Confucian order.

To-day the sacred rites round which the life of China had revolved from immemorial antiquity have ceased. The Son of Heaven no longer offers the great sacrifices at the winter solstice, and a bandstand has been set up in the sacred field where the imperial ploughman had opened the first furrow and inaugurated the agricultural year. Even the Confucian teachings no longer receive the old unquestioning allegiance, and a new class of students and politicians of Western education and modern ideas have taken the place of the almost sacred caste of Confucian literati who were the uncrowned rulers of China for more than 2,000 years.

It would seem as though the impalpable walls of custom and tradition which have made China a world apart have been suddenly broken down, and that the Chinese people is about to enter the modern world on an equal footing with the Western nations.

But for all this the deep-rooted, instinctive opposition of the Chinese spirit to the foreign civilisation of the West has not ceased, it has only changed its mode of expression. For the Nationalist movement, which began as a protest against Manchu misgovernment under the influence of Western democratic ideals, has become transformed into a crusade against Western Imperialism.

It is, however, no longer a blind instinctive reaction like the Boxer movement of 1900; it appeals to general principles and employs the phraseology of Western liberalism and socialism. This appears very clearly in the official statement of the Nationalist programme, which has been translated into English by Mr. Wong Ching-Wai; in his *China and the Nations.* According to the author, the aim of the Chinese revolution is the destruction of foreign Imperialism, which he defines as the process of economic penetration by the forces of Western Capitalism. This so-called "Imperialism" is a menace to the existence, of all the non-European peoples. "Its main effects have been to extinguish or enslave three and a half of the five great races of mankind, and to change the colour of three and a half of the five continents." "The Red People in America, the Negroes in Africa and the Brown Race in Australia, as well as the Yellow Race in Central and Western Asia *(sic),* all are dominated by the European." "All Peoples who desire emancipation from servitude and deliverance from death must fight against Imperialism. There is no choice."

It is clear that these ideas bear a considerable resemblance to the doctrines of Moscow; indeed, there can be no doubt that the change in the attitude of the Nationalist party during recent years is due in large measure to the effect produced in the Far East by the Russian Revolution. The abandonment by the Soviet Government in 1924 of the extra-territorial rights formerly possessed by Russia naturally evoked the enthusiastic approval of the Nationalists. "Compare this agreement," says Mr. Wong, "with all our other treaties contracted since the Opium War. We shall then perceive the true natures of Imperialism and of Revolution: the one determined on an uncompromising policy of encroachment in China, the other on the inauguration of a policy towards her based on truth and equality."

It is true that this *entente* with Russia does not necessarily involve the conversion of the Nationalist party to Communism; indeed, many leading Nationalists have expressly denied the possibility of such a development. On the other hand, a steady increase of Communist propaganda has accompanied the recent advance of the Nationalist armies, and it would be premature to conclude that there is no possibility of its taking root in China. For the conditions in China and Russia are not so dissimilar as they appear at first sight. The Russian revolution itself can be viewed from two different points of view. It may be regarded as the realisation of a social programme of Western origin which is the logical development in the economic sphere of the democratic movement of modern Europe. On the other hand, it can be plausibly argued that the success of the Revolution was due not to its Socialist doctrines, but to the complete break that it involved with the rest of Western Europe. It was the national revolt of a semi-Asiatic people against an alien civilisation which had been forced upon an unwilling country by a German dynasty and its servants, the drill sergeants, the bureaucrats and the engineers from the West. Lenin was Russia's answer to Peter the Great. Each of these aspects of the Revolution is reflected in the policy of the Soviet. On the one hand, Moscow appeals to the proletariat of the Western countries to combine in a class war against the forces of capitalism, on the other, it has attempted to arouse all the peoples of Asia—Turks, Afghans, Indians, Chinese, and Japanese—in a national crusade against the Imperialism of the West.

Now this Soviet policy makes special appeal to China in her present situation. The collapse of the Manchu regime and the social order that went with it has left China temporarily without settled traditions and beliefs. The full acceptance of the ideals of Western liberalism and representative government seems to imply the recognition of the superiority of European culture, and yet the antipathy to the foreign trader and the foreign missionary remains one of the most deep-seated instincts of the Chinese soul. But in Soviet Russia the Chinese Nationalist finds an ally which is at once modern and anti-Western, which is equally hostile to the economic supremacy of the Western trader and to the religious propaganda of the Christian missionary. Moreover, the Soviet system, with its combination of democracy and despotism, of secrecy and popular appeal, of violence and discipline, stands far closer to the oriental traditions of government than the individualism and liberalism of the Western bourgeois parliamentary state. And we must recognise that the main factors which render Communist propaganda unpalatable to the other Asiatic peoples are practically non-existent in China. There is no hereditary aristocracy, no warrior nobility, no regime of caste. Above all, there is no strong religious feeling to stand in the way as in India or the lands of Islam. An age-long tradition has made the Chinaman a positivist who recognises social utility and practical expediency as the only ultimate laws, and the very characteristics that make Chinese civilisation appear artificial and slightly inhuman to the Western mind are in reality the evidence of a higher degree of socialisation.

It is obvious that the victory of Communism in China would be an event of incalculable importance for the whole future of civilisation. It would mean the coming into existence of a vast anti-Western bloc extending from the Baltic to the Yellow Sea and gradually tending to draw into its orbit all the other peoples of Asia. The European world hegemony has already been gravely shaken by the events of the last twelve years. What would the situation be if more than 400 million people were suddenly thrown into the scale on the other side of the globe? The vast resources and population of a modernised China may well be the governing factor in any cosmopolitan order of the future, and if these resources were organised in a spirit of hostility to Europe it would be the greatest possible menace to the continued existence of the current form of modern occidental civilisation. These dangers are certainly not entirely chimerical. Nevertheless, there is reason to doubt whether the changes that we are witnessing in China are really so profound as they appear at the moment. Foreign influences have not been at work for centuries, undermining the bases of the native culture, as they have been in Russia. The main current of Chinese life goes on unchanged. Even the present movement of social unrest can be only partially explained by the influence of foreign ideas; it also has its roots deep in Chinese history.

· The modern Chinese revolutionary is the heir not of Lenin and Karl Marx, but of the tradition of the native secret societies and heretical sects, such as the White Lotus Society, the Sect of the Eight Diagrams, and many more, whose periodical outbreaks form a long and sinister chapter in Chinese history. In the last century, the Tai Ping movement, which owed its origin to a convert of the Christian missionaries, spread its propaganda of "the Great Peace" throughout Southern China. Like the modern Nationalist movement, it began as a protest against the misgovernment of the Manchu Dynasty, and it also spread triumphantly over Southern China as far as Hankow and Nanking. It ended some ten years later in a carnival of slaughter and destruction, which is said to have cost the country a hundred million lives,[1] and the life of China

---

1. I quote Mr. Wong's estimate. The real figure was probably no higher than ten million.

went on its way as before. The modern Nationalist movement, even if it does not end in a similar cataclysm, may prove to be an equally transient episode in the history of China. The work of twenty centuries cannot be undone by a few years of political agitation. Although the rites have ceased, the spirit of Confucianism still lives on, and moulds the mind of society. The family with its ideals of filial piety and its ancestral cult, still remains the foundation stone of Chinese life, and, so long as it is intact, it poses a barrier alike to Russian communism and Western individualism. When the present storm has died away, there can be little doubt that the Confucian spirit, though not necessarily in its traditional form, will resume its former dominion. We must remember that hitherto Northern China, at the mercy of the militarist parties, has not made its voice heard, but it is the valley of the Yellow River and not the Yangtze Kiang or the river of Canton that is the true heart of China, the old Middle Kingdom, the original home of the Chinese people and the Confucian culture. And though the slow-going Northerner is inferior to the Southerner in mental alertness and quickness of tongue, he has usually had the last word in the fate of China. If the Nationalist movement succeeds in eliminating the Tuchuns and the Militarist factions and reconstitutes the unity of China, it will thereby make it possible for the North to collaborate with the rest of the country in the work of national restoration. It is impossible to forecast the outcome of the present situation, but, whatever the ultimate result may be, there can be no doubt that we shall never understand the future of China unless we understand its past.

1927

IX

Rationalism and Intellectualism

The Religious Elements in the
Rationalist Tradition

I

Rationalism is usually regarded as the natural enemy of religion; in fact, rationalists have tended to conceive the history of human thought in a frankly dualist spirit as a long warfare between the powers of light and the powers of darkness, in which the cause of rationalism is the cause of civilisation, science and progress, while religion is the dark and sinister power that holds humanity back from the path of enlightenment.

And this is far from being a peculiarly modern point of view. It received a classical expression nearly two thousand years ago in that great epic of rationalism which anticipated in such a remarkable manner the leading ideas of modern scientific rationalism. To Lucretius as to the modern rationalist religion was the enemy and the one power that was capable of freeing mankind from the terrors of superstition and the fear of the unknown was the scientific knowledge of nature.

"When human life," he writes, "lay shamefully prostrate, crushed down to the ground by the weight of religion, which showed its head from the skies lowering over mortals with hideous aspect, a man of Greece first dared to raise his eyes and stand against it. Neither the fame of the gods nor thunderbolts nor the threatening roar of heaven could daunt him; they only fired his spirit with the desire to be the first

A Paper read to the Conway Discussion Group of the Rationalist Press Association.

to burst the closed bars of the gates of nature. And so the living force of his mind was victorious and he passed beyond the flaming ramparts of the world and traversed in spirit the boundless universe, whence he returned a victor to tell us what can and what cannot be, and how to every power is set a fixed limit which it may not transgress. And so religion, in turn, is cast down and trodden under foot and its defeat raises us to heaven."

The rationalist spirit has never found a higher or more profound expression than in the work of Lucretius. Even the ablest and most brilliant of modern rationalist writers seem superficial and weak in comparison with him. And yet he has never been as popular with rationalists as one might have expected: They have as a rule chosen Voltaire rather than Lucretius as their patron and model: Voltaire who had the face to praise the worthy Cardinal de Polignac as the avenger of Heaven and the conqueror of Lucretius. And there is good reason for this, since Lucretius by his very genius transcends the limits of rationalism and reveals an inner contradiction in his own position. No one who reads his poem with an open mind can avoid the feeling that Lucretius for all his denunciations of religion was himself a religious man. Voltaire called himself a Deist, and remained an entirely irreligious nature— *naturaliter irreligiosa anima*—but Lucretius denounces religion in a religious spirit like a Hebrew prophet denouncing the false creeds of the heathen. "There is no piety in being often seen with veiled head adoring a stone and visiting every shrine, or falling prostrate on the ground and raising the hands to the images of the gods, nor in sprinkling the altar with much blood of beasts and piling vow on vow but rather in looking on all things with a mind at peace." Who, in fact, was the religious man—Lucretius announcing the spiritual deliverance of mankind from the chains of error and superstition, or the official representative of established Roman religion winking at his fellow-augur before the altar? There is no doubt that it was Lucretius who was on the side of the angels, though he would have consigned the latter to the dignified retirement of the inter-mundane spaces.

The fact is that rationalism itself is or may be a kind of religion, and in the ancient world, at any rate, it was the rationalists and not the priests who were the real theologians. No doubt there is a rationalism that is irreligious in the absolute sense: I mean the attitude of negative scepticism that has no positive content and confines itself to criticising and questioning any doctrine or theory which transcends the limits of everyday experience. This common-sense empirical rationalism is always with us, and is found among peasants and savages no less than among educated people. It is the rationalism of the philistine who despises theorists and of the canny country bumpkin who refuses to believe anything that he has not seen. But it is no more to be identified with the great creative tradition of rationalism than superstition is to be identified with religion. This other rationalism is one of the chief formative elements in Western culture and distinguishes it from the civilisations of the oriental world. It may be defined as a belief in the supremacy of reason; the conviction that the human mind is capable of understanding the world and consequently that reality is itself intelligible and in a manner rational. This positive rationalism had its origin in ancient Greece and was, in fact, the peculiar creation of the Greek genius, for all the later developments of rationalism are tributaries of the Hellenic achievement, and without it there would have been no rationalism and no natural science in the West worth speaking of. The whole development of Greek thought from the Ionians to the Alexandrians was dominated by this rationalist ideal. It was responsible not only for the rationalisation of nature by science and mathematics, but also for the rationalisation of human conduct by scientific ethics, and for the rationalisation of religion by philosophy. But inasmuch as Greek rationalism tended to replace traditional religion, it became itself a religion, and a religion of a very high order. Greek rationalism finds its ultimate expression in Logos worship—in the deification of intelligence as the supreme cosmic principle.

This tendency is to be found in Greek thought from its beginnings. We see it in the Pythagoreans, in Xenophanes and Parmenides, in Heraclitus and Empedocles. All of them were not only philosophers and scientists, but religious reformers and prophets of the Logos. Their criticism of the anthropomorphism and superstition of the popular religion was not merely destructive. They substituted a philosophical theism for the traditional cults of Greek paganism. Thus Xenophanes spoke of the "one God neither in form nor thought like unto mortals." And Empedocles writes: "it is not possible to set God before our eyes or to lay hold of him with our hands. . . . But he is only a sacred and unutterable mind flashing through the whole world with rapid thoughts." "Wisdom," says Heraclitus, " is one only. It is willing and unwilling to be called by the name of Zeus."

All this takes us a long way from rationalism in the modern acceptation of the word. That only emerges for the first time in the fifth century with the coming of the Sophists. Thenceforward it is possible to segregate the two tendencies in Greek thought and to distinguish the rationalism of the Atomists from the pure intellectualism which attains classical expression in the work of Plato. Nevertheless, Greek rationalism in this limited sense is secondary and dependent on the intellectualist tradition, as we see from the influence of the Pythagorean and Eleatic traditions on the rise of Atomism. Moreover, the two currents still remain very closely related to one another, and the progress of Greek science in its golden age owes as much to the intellectualists as it does to the rationalists or more. Greek mathematics and astronomy are based on the traditions of Plato and the Pythagoreans, while Aristotle was not only the great logician and metaphysician, but also a great naturalist and the founder of scientific biology.

Even in the post-Aristotelian period when the main tendencies in Greek thought seem to become crystallised in the sharp opposition of the rival schools, the line of division is not so clear as a modern rationalist would expect. At first sight the school of Epicurus seems to embody the rationalist ideal in its purest form, while the Stoics seem to represent a mystical intellectualism which is religious rather than scientific. Yet the Stoics professed a pantheistic materialism not unlike that of certain modern rationalists, and maintained the principle of universal causation and an absolute determinism in which there is no room for free will or for the intervention of supernatural powers, while Epicurus was in many respects a scientific reactionary who rejected orthodox mathematics and astronomy, and maintained the principle of indeterminacy in so much as he endowed the atoms with a certain spontaneity of action which provided a physical basis for the theory of the freedom of the human will. This reactionary tendency in Greek rationalism is still more evident in the Sceptics, for ancient scepticism turned its weapons impartially against the rationalist and the intellectualist, and attacked scientists no less vigorously than the metaphysicians. Religion, on the other hand, they were prepared to accept, so long as it was regarded as a way of life and not as a doctrine. "We follow life without holding opinions in order not to give up action" was their motto, and by "life" they understood the whole complex of human activities and social conventions, including those of traditional religion. Thus classical scepticism finds its modern representatives in thinkers like Dean Mansel and Lord Balfour, rather than among the agnostics, who would have got short shrift as dogmatisers by Aenesidemus and Sextus Empiricus.

But where ancient rationalism differs most strikingly from that of modern times is in its moral attitude. Modern rationalism is closely associated with a faith in social progress and with moral optimism. But the ancient rationalist ideal was essentially a static one, which did not seek to change the world, but rather to obtain moral perfection and spiritual peace for the individual. It is true that the Epicureans, at least, accepted the idea of progress in the strict rational sense, and regarded human civilisation as the result of an age-long evolutionary process. But so far from making this theory the basis of their moral creed, they preferred to concentrate their attention on the reverse side of the process—on the movement of atomic disaggregation that dooms the universe to destruction.

To quote Mallock's paraphrase of Lucretius:

> No single thing abides; but all things flow;
> Fragment to fragment clings—the things thus grow
> Until we know and name them. By degrees
> They melt and are no more the things we know.
> Globed from the atoms falling slow and swift
> I see the suns, I see the systems lift,
> Their forms; and even the systems and the suns
> Shall go back slowly to the eternal drift.
> Thou too O earth—thine empires lands and seas—
> Least with thy stars, of all the galaxies,
> Globed from the drift like these, like these thou too
> Shalt go. Thou art going hour by hour like these.

Thus Lucretius regards the study of physical science not in the modern fashion as an instrument for the conquest of nature, but as a means of moral purification and a preparation for a good death. "If men understood the cause of their disease they would abandon everything else and study to learn the nature of things, for what is at stake is the state not of one hour but of all eternity." The Epicurean life was far from being the gross materialistic hedonism which its enemies supposed it to be: its essential notes, as Seneca remarks, were *sadness* and *sanctity*. It was essentially ascetic and aimed at freeing the soul from the fear of death and from what Lucretius calls "the evil desire of life—*mala vitai cupido.*" In fact, the ideal of the ancient rationalist has more in common with that of the mediaeval monk than with that of the modern secularist. Perhaps the closest parallel to it is to be found in the asceticism of the non-theistic Indian sects, such as the Buddhists and the Sankhya. For just as these arose as a reaction or subtraction from the pure idealism of Vedantist monism, so Epicureanism and Hellenic rationalism in general are a subtraction from the antecedent unity of Greek intellectualism.

II

And so the decline and fall of ancient rationalism in the limited sense did not mean the end of the Greek intellectual tradition. Greek intellectualism survived and was incorporated into the Christian tradition as a fundamental element in the new theological culture. From the point of view alike of the modern Protestant and the ancient Oriental this culture is itself a rationalistic one, and scholars like Ritschl and Harnack have viewed the history of dogma as a progressive rationalisation and Hellenisation of the Christian faith. "The formula of the Logos as it was almost universally understood," writes Harnack, "legitimised speculation within the creed of the Church. When Christ was designated the incarnate Logos, and when this was set up as his supreme characterisation, men were directed to think of the divine in Christ as the reason of God realised in the structure of the world and the history of mankind. This implied a definite philosophical view of God, of creation, and of the world; and the baptismal confession (the creed), became a compendium of scientific dogmatics, *i.e.,* of a system of doctrine entwined with the metaphysics of Plato and the Stoics."[1] Of course, what Harnack calls Rationalism is really Intellectualism, and Intellectualism in its most transcendental and mystical form. Nevertheless, as we have seen, Intellectualism and Rationalism are closely related to one another as two aspects of one tradition, and the incorporation of the former in Christian culture provided a basis for the subsequent development of free rational activity.

And this is what actually occurred in the historical development of Western culture. The revival of philosophy as an autonomous rational discipline and the beginnings of physical science as the systematic rationalisation of nature had their origins in the integral intellectualism of mediaeval scholasticism. The world is a rational whole created and ruled by the Divine Reason and the human reason which is a participation of the Divine is of its very nature capable of comprehending reality. Hence the scholastic ideal aimed at nothing short of a science that is conterminous with reality. As Harnack, who was no friend of the scholastics wrote, "Scholasticism is simply nothing else but scientific thought, and it is merely perpetuating an unwarranted prejudice when it is thought that this part of the general history of science should be designated by a special name. . . . The science of the Middle Ages gives practical proof of eagerness in thinking and exhibits an energy in subjecting all that is real and valuable to thought to which we can perhaps find no parallel in any other age."

This ideal of universal science is not of course rationalist, since it does not make the human reason the measure of all things, but, on the contrary, regards intelligence as a universal power of which the human reason is but a limited and partial reflection; a spark of the divine light burning fitfully and uncertainly in the obscurity of the world of sense. Nevertheless, this scholastic intellectualism lies at the basis of modern scientific rationalism in the same way as the Hellenic intellectualism was the foundation of ancient rationalism. For, as Professor Whitehead has pointed out, it was the mediaeval belief in the ultimate rationality of the world that prepared the European mind for the belief in the possibility

---

1. *History of Dogma,* Vol. III., p. 23 (English translation).

of science, while the clear distinction introduced by the Thomists between the province of natural reason and that of faith made it possible for the former to assert its independent rights in its own sphere.

So long as the Thomist synthesis was accepted, there was, of course, no room for rationalism in the strict sense of the word, but the later Middle Ages witnessed a progressive revolt against that synthesis which culminated in the Protestant Reformation. It was, however, by no means a revolt of Reason against Faith; it was rather a revolt of Religion against Intellectualism. First the Nominalists and then the Protestants denied the transcendence of reason, and set up against the Thomist Intellectualism a voluntarist non-intellectual act of faith as the sole authority in religious matters. Thus religion was de-intellectualised and reason was left to its own devices, at the very time when the Renaissance was restoring man's confidence in his own powers, and was giving him a new sense of the possibilities of human knowledge and culture. Nevertheless, this did not lead directly to the birth of modern rationalism, as one might have anticipated. On the contrary, the Renaissance turned back to the classical tradition of Hellenic intellectualism and found its inspiration not in Scepticism or Epicureanism, but in the pure Intellectualism of Plato and in the intellectualised Natural Religion of Cicero and the Stoics. This is to be seen above all in the founders of modern science, like Copernicus and Kepler, who were arch-intellectualists and derived their scientific ideals from the tradition of Plato and Pythagoras. The Renaissance rationalists, as represented by the so-called Libertines, were, on the other hand, as hostile to natural science as the sceptics of the ancient world, and it is interesting to note that the Catholic apologist, Mersenne, the friend of Galileo and Descartes, in his work on *The Truth of the Sciences against the Sceptics,* undertook the defence of the cause of Religion and Science against the common enemies of both.

The origins of modern rationalism as a historic movement are to be found not on the extreme left among the sceptics and atheists of the type of Vanini, but rather in the middle party of the moderates like Bodin and Montaigne, Lord Herbert and the Socinians, Locke and Shaftesbury, who followed the intellectualist tradition of Natural Religion. This tradition had its roots, as we have seen, both in Christian theology and in ancient philosophy, and, as the late A. W. Benn pointed out, it received a great access of popularity in post-Renaissance times from the humanist cult of Cicero, through whom it became the common property of every educated man. When the new movement began its struggle for the emancipation of the European mind from religious authority, and the reconstitution of culture on a purely rational basis, it found this tradition ready to its hand, and throughout the eighteenth century the cause of rationalism was regarded as practically identical with that of Deism and Natural Religion. But what had been a genuine religion with the Socinians and a mystical intellectualism with Spinoza, became in the hands of the rationalists little more than a weapon of anti-religious propaganda. The Deism of Voltaire is not a religion; it is little more than a guarantee of social respectability; it has become entirely divested of all spiritual significance. It is in Voltaire that modern rationalism first attained complete self-consciousness and existed in a pure state unalloyed with any foreign element. In his clarity and good sense, his hatred of stupidity and superstition, he is the perfect rationalist without a shred of mysticism or intellectualism in his composition. But at the same time he is a witness to the inherent weakness of the rationalist position, since his life and his writings show how difficult it is to maintain one's footing on the basis of pure rationalism without slipping into the morass of a vulgar Philistinism. We can understand how in the heat of conflict he might see nothing in Christianity but a mass of grotesque and repulsive absurdities, that he should describe the Bible as a monument of the most outrageous folly, and the Psalms as Barrack Room Ballads.[2] But this insensitiveness is not confined to religious matters. We all know what he thought of Shakespeare, "a low savage whose works were an enormous dunghill of abominable balderdash."[3] And the philosophers, with the exception of Locke, get short shrift from him. Descartes is a charlatan, Plato a madman, while as for St. Thomas,[4] to read his works is like taking a course at Bedlam. What is more surprising, however, is that the scientists themselves

2. *Essai sur les mœurs,* chap. 121, and *Letter* of June 4, 1761.
3. *Essai sur les mœurs,* chap. 121, and *Letter* of December 4th, 1765.
4. *Essai sur les mœurs,* chap. 121, and *Letters* of July 9th and 30th, 1766.

do not fare much better. The real scientist is the man who can make a watch or construct a mill, or, in fact, do anything useful. But he has no taste for abstract theorising. In a letter to D'Alembert he pours scorn on the infinitesimal calculus, and congratulates Euclid on avoiding such charlatanry.[5] No doubt his famous theory of the origin of fossils was of the nature of a *jeu d'esprit,* but the fact remains that his common-sense rationalism made him as much an obscurantist as the most reactionary theologian of the Sorbonne.

And in the same way his rationalism narrowed his social sympathies and his political ideas. He preached enlightenment, but it was to a privileged audience: "the little flock," as he says, "of rich polite educated people who are the flower of humanity, and for whom human pleasures are made." As for the rest, they must be left in their ignorance, "for when the populace begins to reason, all is lost." Christianity was made for the lower classes, and it would be a mistake to enlighten them. "We have never claimed to enlighten shoemakers and servant girls," he writes to D'Argental, "they are the portion of the apostles."

If rationalism had been left to Voltaire and his friends, it would never have transformed European society. It would have led no further than to the enlightened despotism of Frederick II and the great Catharine or to the enlightened aristocracy of the Whig oligarchs. The dynamic force in the new movement came not from the critical rationalism of Voltaire and his friends, but from the romantic humanitarianism of Rousseau. This moody neurotic dreamer was one of the few men who have moved the world profoundly. He provided the new social gospel which was to take the place of orthodox Christianity as the moral basis of Western society and the spiritual inspiration of Western culture. This was the source alike of the faith in Humanity and Progress, and of the revolutionary protest against social inequality and injustice which were together the driving forces in the transformation of the modern world. No doubt this creed differed little in formal content from the beliefs of the rationalists. It was equally hostile to religious authority and tradition, and it shared with the Deists their doctrine of Natural Religion. But while the Natural Religion of the Deists was the rationalisation

5. December 20th, 1766.

of an intellectualist tradition, that of Rousseau was neither rationalist nor intellectualist; it was a religious faith based on a non-rational intuitive experience which was half mystical and half emotional. It allied itself with the reforming ideas of the rationalist philosophers to form that great movement of humanitarian Liberalism which was the dominant power in nineteenth-century culture. Thanks to this alliance, the rationalists were able to carry through the practical reforms in which they were most interested, but on the other hand they were incapable of overcoming the logical inconsistencies that were inherent in the liberal tradition. They were rationalists in their criticism of traditional religion and social authority, but their own ideology continued to be based on a non-rational dogmatism. It was, no doubt, comparatively easy to shed the purely theological element which Liberalism inherited from Rousseau, but the resultant social idealism was not made more rational by being deprived of its theological foundation. The new faith in humanity was just as much a faith as the creed of Rousseau's Savoyard priest: indeed, it often assumed apocalyptic forms which were far less consistent with rationalism than was the old intellectualist theology.

The consequence of this anomalous situation is to be seen in the conflicting currents of modern European thought. One wing of the rationalist movement went on towards scientific materialism, while the other turned back towards philosophic intellectualism. The attempt of Kant to provide a rational foundation for the creed of Liberalism was perhaps the greatest achievement of eighteenth-century thought. But he succeeded only by transcending rationalism and returning to a genuine intellectualism. No doubt it was not the absolute intellectualism of Hellenic thought, since it no longer affirmed the power of intelligence to transcend the phenomenal world. Nevertheless, since it is reason that provides the intelligible forms or schemata under which we know reality, reason remains the foundation of the only reality that is accessible to us, and the formative principle of the only world we know. And the successors of Kant carried this idealist intellectualism still further by eliminating the Kantian postulate of an unknowable reality behind the world of experience and asserting the identity of subjective and objective reality in the higher unity of absolute spirit. On such an assumption it is not difficult for theology to come into its kingdom once more, and it is no accident that the age of idealism was also an age of religious revival. Hence it is that rationalists have generally regarded idealism with distrust and have refused to accept the Kantian justification of their own social and ethical ideals. They preferred to look for guidance towards the new scientific movement which seemed to offer a firmer foundation for the rationalist ideal than was to be found in any metaphysical system. The vast achievements of scientific discovery filled men's minds with new hopes and inspired them with the belief that science was destined to take the place of religion as an infallible teacher. This unbounded faith in science is typical of the nineteenth-century rationalists—of Comte and Littré and Bertholet in France, of Herbert Spencer and W. K. Clifford in England, and of Buchner and Haeckel in Germany. It finds a most striking expression in Renan's early work on *The Future of Science*. "We proclaim the right of reason to reform society by rational science and the theoretic knowledge of that which is. It is no exaggeration to say that science contains the future of humanity and that it alone can say the last word on human destiny and teach mankind how to reach its goal. . . . Science is only valuable in so far as it can take the place of religion."

And, in the strength of this conviction, he confronts the orthodox with a fervour equal to their own. "It is you," he writes, "who are the sceptics and we who are the believers. We believe in the work of modern times, in its sanctity, in its future, and you blaspheme it. We believe in humanity and its divine destiny, and you laugh at it; we believe in the dignity of man, in the goodness of nature, the rectitude of his heart, in his right to the attainment of perfection, and you shake your heads at these consoling truths and prefer to dwell on the dark side of things."[6]

But this naïve idealism was not altogether rational and it inevitably ended in disillusionment. In the preface which Renan wrote when he published the work of his youth forty years afterwards he speaks in a very different manner. "It seems possible," he writes, "that the collapse of supernatural belief will be followed by the collapse of moral convictions and that the moment when humanity sees the reality of things will

---

6. *L'Avenir de la Science*, p. 65.

mark a real moral decline. Under the influence of illusions the good gorilla succeeded in making an astonishing moral effort. Remove the illusions and a part of the factitious energy that they aroused will disappear. If you take away the working man's beer you must not expect to get the same amount of work out of him."[7]

This "good gorilla" of 1887 is rather a startling conclusion to the humanitarian optimism of 1848. Renan remained a good rationalist, but he lost his faith in humanity and a good deal of his faith in science, as he had lost his earlier faith in religion. Indeed, he came to recognise that the two faiths were much more closely connected than he had originally supposed. "We are living," he said, "on the perfume of an empty vase."

The fact is that the nineteenth-century attitude to science was still influenced by the intellectualism that it had formally abandoned. Men's minds were haunted by the intellectualist ideal of a pure deductive science that was absolutely true and certain, when they professed to be dealing with a practical inductive positive science that had nothing to do with the nature of reality, but was limited to the observation and control of matter.

But while it is easy to conceive of a religion of science if we adopt the old Greek intellectualist ideal of science as the pathway to reality, it is obvious that a science which is purely instrumental and concerned with *means* can never take the place of religion which is essentially concerned with ends. Such a science is more akin to technology than to religion or philosophy. It gives us the power of manipulating nature to our own ends, but not the power of understanding nature theoretically. In fact, as Bertrand Russell has said, "The hope of understanding the world is itself one of those day dreams that science tends to dissipate." I do not say that this view is really justified. It seems to me the *reductio ad absurdum* of rationalism, but it seems to be the inevitable conclusion of a rationalism that has finally severed its connection with the intellectualist tradition. And it brings us back to a new dogmatism which is more fatal to the rationalist ideal than the old theological orthodoxy. As the late A. W. Benn pointed out, science is a dangerous ally for ra-

7. *L'Avenir de la Science*, p. xviii.

tionalism, since it tends to substitute the authority of the specialist for the appeal to reason, and this danger is greatly accentuated if science is regarded not as a form of rational knowledge, but as an instrument of power. It will inevitably become the servant of the ruling power in society, whether that power is a revolutionary dictatorship as in Communist Russia or a conservative bureaucracy as in the Hegelian ideal of the Prussian state. The only escape for the rationalist is to take refuge in scepticism, and scepticism is of its nature ill-adapted for carrying on a successful warfare with any system of dogmatic belief. We see this in the French rationalists of the later nineteenth century, such as Renan and Taine and Anatole France. They were the legitimate heirs of the tradition of eighteenth-century rationalism, but they no longer possessed the sublime self-confidence of the Encyclopædists. Their scepticism led them to pessimism or to dilettantism. They became weary of controversy and sceptical of rationalism itself. And, consequently, they prepared the way for a return to authority and faith, whether by way of Bergsonian vitalism, or communist dogmatism, or religious orthodoxy.

Thus it seems to me doubtful whether rationalism will be able to survive the disappearance of the liberal synthesis with its creed of humanitarian optimism, and it may be that we shall witness the same reaction that took place in the ancient world under the Roman Empire. It is impossible for rationalism to survive in a culture that is anti-intellectualist.

Both in the ancient and the modern worlds rationalism has flourished only in ages and societies in which intellectualism was strong enough to colour men's minds and to set the standard of thought without being strong enough to preclude criticism. The chief function of rationalism is critical. It stands for freedom and enlightenment, but these are not absolutes. The absolute element in culture is provided by some positive faith, whether that faith is religious in the full sense, or intellectualist, or takes the form of a social idealism.

Rationalism is the complement of intellectualism, and cannot exist without it. It often appears to be the enemy of intellectualism, but at the same time it is dependent upon it, and its most valuable work is done in co-operation with it by preventing intellectualism from losing itself in the clouds of speculation and bringing it back to solid earth by its application to facts and by the rationalisation of nature and social life.

Our civilisation owes its distinctive character in modern times to its rationalism, but it has never been rationalist only, and it is more than doubtful if any civilisation ever can be. The religious element is even more permanent and essential, and if it disappears the vitality of society disappears with it.

Consequently, a man like Voltaire is not the representative type of our culture; he is an exaggeration, almost a caricature, of one side of it, just as Luther is an exaggeration of the other. The classical type of Western culture is, I think, rather to be found in the seventeenth century in men like Descartes and Leibniz in whom rationalism and religion meet without destroying one another on the foundation of a common intellectualism.

III

X

Islamic Mysticism

During recent years a great deal of attention has been devoted to the study of Mohammedan mysticism by European scholars. Nor is it difficult to understand the reason of this attraction, since of all types of mysticism that of Islam is the richest perhaps in the quantity and certainly in the quality of its literature. In the West, apart from a few outstanding exceptions, mysticism and literature have followed separate paths, and the man of letters often knows nothing of works which from the religious point of view are spiritual classics. In the East, however, this is not so. Mysticism and letters go hand in hand in all the Moslem countries—among the Persians, above all, but also among the Arabs and the Turks.[1] The greatest poets have devoted themselves to give literary expression to spiritual experience, and to fuse poetical and mystical ecstasy in a single flame. A short time ago only the great mystical poets of Persia—'Attar, Jalalu'ddin Rumi, Hafiz, and Jami— were well known in the West, and it was usual to regard Moslem mysticism as predominantly Persian, but the works of Professor Nicholson have now introduced us to the works of the great Arab mystics, such as Ibnu'l 'Arabi and Ibnu'l Farid, and it is at last possible for an Englishman to obtain some idea of the wealth and variety of Sufi literature.

It is true that it is difficult for the Western mind to appreciate Arabic poetry in the same way as Persian. The mystical poets of Persia belong to the literature of the world, and it is as easy for an Englishman as for an Oriental to understand the spiritual passion of Jalalu'ddin Rumi or the classical perfection of Jami's famous lines on the Divine Beauty:

1. Cf. especially E. J. W. Gibb's great *History of Ottoman Poetry.*

Beware! Say not, "He is All-Beautiful,
And we His lovers." Thou art but the glass,
And He the Face confronting it, which casts
Its image in the mirror. He alone
Is manifest, and thou in truth art hid.
Pure Love, like Beauty, coming but from Him,
Reveals itself in Thee. If steadfastly
Thou canst regard, thou wilt at length perceive
He is the mirror also—He alike
The Treasure and the Casket. "I" and "Thou"
Have here no place, and are but fantasies
Vain and unreal. Silence! for this tale
Is endless, and no eloquence hath power
To speak of Him. 'Tis but for us to love
And suffer silently, being as naught![2]

Arabic poetry, on the other hand, is alien from European standards both in form and content, and its combination of far-fetched symbolism with an acrid intensity of sensuous passion is disconcerting to the Western mind. Contrast, for example, with Jami's lines the following typical passage from Ibnu'l 'Arabi:

She is a bishopess, one of the daughters of Rome, unadorned; thou seest in her a radiant Goodness.
Wild is she, none can make her his friend; she has gotten in her solitary chamber a mausoleum for remembrance.
She has baffled everyone who is learned in our religion, every student of the Psalms of David, every Jewish doctor and every Christian priest. . . .
The day when they departed on the road, I prepared for war the armies of my patience host after host.
When my soul reached the throat, I besought that Beauty and that Grace to grant me relief,
And she yielded—may God preserve us from her evil and may the victorious King repel Iblis.[3]

It is not easy for us to realise either the literary attraction or the religious significance of such poetry; indeed, the detailed mystical in-

---

2. Trans. E. G. Browne.
3. *Tarjuman al-Ashwaq,* Ode II, p. 49 (trans. R. A. Nicholson).

terpretation with which it is accompanied only serves to increase our bewilderment. Nevertheless, we have in the work of St. John of the Cross an example nearer home of the same methods. He also uses the magic of strange words and obscure imagery to transport the mind to a suprarational sphere, and employs the language of human passion to express spiritual experiences. Indeed, in some of his verses the images and the turns of expression show an almost verbal similarity to those of Arabic poetry. Nevertheless, the magic of his poetry is perceptible even in an English version, whereas that of the Arabs is so closely bound up with their language that it cannot survive the test of translation into a European tongue.

There is nothing in the Arabic poetry translated by Professor Nicholson to compare with *En una noche oscura,* still less with those incomparable lines of the Spiritual Canticle:

> Hide thyself, O my Beloved!
> Turn thy face to the mountains.
> Do not speak, But regard the companions
> Of her who is travelling amidst strange islands.

Consequently, it is in their prose writings that the Arabic mystics are seen to most advantage. The genius of the language and the race lend themselves to the vivid portrayal of individual character and the eloquent expression of personal emotion, and there are many passages in the lives of the Sufi saints which are of unsurpassed beauty and religious significance.

Thus it is related of Rabi'a, the saintly freedwoman of Basra, that at night she would *go* up to the house-top and pray as follows: "O my Lord, the stars are shining and the eyes of men are closed, and the kings have shut their doors and every lover is alone with his beloved, and here am I alone with Thee."

Then she prayed all night, and when the dawn appeared she would say: "O God, the night has passed and the day has dawned; how I long to know if Thou hast accepted my prayers, or if Thou hast rejected them! Therefore console me, for it is Thine to console this state of mine. Thou hast given me life and cared for me, and Thine is the glory. If Thou wert to drive me from Thy door yet would

I not forsake it for the love that I bear in my heart towards Thee."[4]

Again she would say: "O my Lord, whatever share of this world Thou dost bestow on me, bestow it on Thine enemies, and whatever share of the next world Thou dost give me, give it to Thy friends; Thou art enough for me."[5]

Even more remarkable are the prayers of al-Hallaj, the great Martyr of Sufism, who suffered at Bagdad in A.D. 922, and whose life and teaching have been so admirably and exhaustively dealt with by M. Massignon.

His disciple Ibrahim ibn Fatik relates:

When Husayn ibn Mansur al-Hallaj was brought to be crucified, and saw the cross and the nails, he laughed so greatly that tears flowed from his eyes. Then he turned to the people, and, seeing Shibli among them, said to him: "O Abu Bakr, hast thou thy prayer carpet with thee?" Shibli answered: "Yes, O Shaykh!" Hallaj bade him spread it out, which he did. Then Hallaj stepped forward and prayed two rak'as on it, and I was near him. . . . And when he had finished he uttered a prayer of which I remember only these words: "O Lord, I beseech Thee to make me thankful for the grace that Thou hast bestowed upon me in concealing from the eyes of other men what Thou hast revealed to me of the splendours of Thy radiant countenance which is without a form, and in making it lawful for me to behold the mysteries of Thy inmost conscience which Thou hast made unlawful to other men. And these Thy servants who are gathered to slay me, in zeal for Thy religion and in desire to win Thy favour, pardon them and have mercy upon them; for verily if Thou hast revealed to them that which Thou hast revealed to me, they would not have done what they have done; and if Thou hast hidden from me that which Thou hast hidden from them, I should not have suffered this tribulation. Glory unto Thee in whatsoever Thou doest, and glory unto Thee in whatsoever Thou willest."[6]

What strikes us in these passages is not, however, their literary beauty so much as the extraordinary Christian spirit that they manifest. Nothing could be more unlike the harsh legalism and militant intolerance which we are accustomed to regard as characteristic of the religion

4. Margaret Smith: *Rabi'a the Mystic and Her Fellow Saints in Islam* (Cambridge, 1928), p. 27.

5. *Ibid.*, p. 30.

6. Louis Massignon: *La Passion d'al Hosayn ibn Mansour al Hallaj* (2 vols Paris, 1922), pp. 301–2; and R. A. Nicholson: *The Idea of Personality in Sufism* (Cambridge, 1923), p. 34.

of Islam. And this brings us to the fundamental problem of Sufism. Is it a genuinely Islamic movement? Or is it a foreign importation which has no real roots in the religion of the Prophet?

The majority of Western scholars have decided in favour of the latter alternative. Either with Renan they have regarded it as "the reaction of the Aryan [*sic.* Persian] genius against the frightful simplicity of the Semitic spirit," or they have looked to some other external source, whether Buddhist, Vedantist, Neoplatonist, or Gnostic, for the origin of the movement. Certainly it is impossible to deny the influence of some of these factors, at least in the later developments of Sufism. There is no disputing the neoplatonic inspiration of such writers as Ibnu'l 'Arabi, or the importance of the Persian contribution to Sufi literature. It is noteworthy that the majority of the more pantheistic mystics were of Persian origin, and that even Ibnu'l 'Arabi himself owed much to "Persian influences."[7] Nevertheless, the fact remains that Sufism originated as an historical movement not in Persia or Turkestan, but in the very centre of early Moslem orthodoxy in eighth-century Basra. Hence the ruling tendency among those who have made the closest study of Sufi origins—above all, M. Massignon—is to emphasise the Mohammedan character of Sufism and to seek its sources in the Koran and in orthodox Islamic tradition.

Now the religion of the Koran undoubtedly provides a certain foundation for mysticism. Its first principles are the same as those which the Epistle to the Hebrews lays down as the first conditions of Faith— namely, the belief that God is, and that He is a Rewarder of those that seek Him. Mohammed himself was a visionary with a profound sense of the reality of God, and of the transitory and dependent nature of created things. He lived in a continual meditation of the Four Last Things, and he taught his followers to do the same. But, apart from this, nothing could be less mystical than his religious teaching. It was a religion of fear rather than of love, and the goal of its striving was not the vision of God, but the sensible delights of the shady gardens of Paradise. And this was not simply due to lack of spirituality; it had a posi-

---

7. It is also noticeable that the great majority of Sufi saints and the founders of the dervish orders derive their origin from the most outlying regions of Islam—viz., Khorasan in the East and Morocco and Spain in the West.

tive theological basis. Man's reward was proportionate to his nature. God was so exalted above creation that any idea of human communion with the Divinity savoured of presumption. The duty of man was not the transformation of his interior life, but the objective establishment of the reign of God on earth by the sword and submission to the law of Islam.

Thus the religion of Mohammed has more in common with Mahdism than with mysticism. It is a militant puritanism of the same type as the modern Wahhabite movement. But it was never a purely external system. Its puritanism was not only that of the warrior, it was also that of the unworldly ascetic who spends his time in prayer and fasting and his goods in almsgiving. From the first there existed in Islam, side by side with the externalism and legalism of the canonists and theologians, a tradition of interior religion, an "Islam of the heart," which showed itself in the simple and unworldly piety of men, like Abu Dharr or Hodhayfah Ibn Hosayl, among the Companions of the Prophet. Such men, however, can hardly be called mystics, as they are by M. Massignon,[8] unless we use the word in a very extended sense.

It was only by slow degrees that this pietist movement developed a genuinely mystical character. During the period of fermentation and schism which followed the establishment of the Syrian Khalifate, the pietists, like the puritan Kharijites, though in a different sense, reacted against the growing worldliness of Islam and began to follow a definitely ascetic rule of life founded on prayer and retirement from the world. The great leader of the movement was Abu Sa'id Hasan (A.D. 643–728), who lived at Basra during the first century of the Hejira, and has always been regarded as the real founder of Sufism. Even he, however, was an ascetic rather than a mystic. His teaching, primarily concerned with penance and moral amendment, is marked by an intense preoccupation with the thought of death and the wrath to come. So great was his fear of Hell that when he heard of a man who was condemned to a thousand years in Hell before he could be saved, he wept and said, "Would that I were like that man." Nevertheless, his asceticism and his emphasis on the importance of prayer and detachment gave a

8. Massignon: *Essai sur les origines du lexique technique de la mystique musulmane* (Paris, 1922), pp. 135 ff.

great impulse to the development of religious life, and it was among his disciples at Basra during the two following generations that the first true mystics of Islam made their appearance. One of the greatest and certainly the most attractive of these early Sufis was the woman saint Rabi'a, to whom Miss Margaret Smith has recently devoted a monograph.[9] Her life is marked by the same asceticism and spirit of penance as that of Hasan, but in her the purely ascetic phase is definitely transcended, and later Sufi writers are fond of contrasting her spirit of pure love and self-abandonment with the less disinterested devotion of her predecessor Hasan.[10]

It is to her that the famous verses on the Two Loves are attributed, possibly with justice:

> I have loved Thee with two loves, a selfish love and a love that is worthy,
> As for the love which is selfish, I occupy myself therein with remembrance
>   of Thee to the exclusion of all others,
> As for that which is worthy of Thee, therein Thou raisest the veil that I may
>   see Thee.
> Yet there is no praise to me in this or in that.
> But the praise is to Thee whether in that or this.[11]

She is also the subject of an anecdote which has found its way into Christian literature.[12] She was seen one day running with a torch and a pitcher of water, and, when she was asked what she was doing, she replied: "I am going to set fire to Paradise and to extinguish the fire of Hell, so that both Veils may disappear from the Pilgrims, and their intention may be pure, and the servants of God may seek him without any object of hope or motive of fear."

The anecdote is no doubt legendary, but it harmonises well with her authentic utterances on the subject, one of which has been quoted above. This attitude is so unlike that of orthodox Islam that it is not surprising that she should have met with criticism from the traditional-

9. *Rabi'a the Mystic*, 1928.
10. No doubt these anecdotes are apocryphal, as Hasan died when she was still a child.
11. *Op. cit.*, pp. 102–3.
12. The story appears in Joinville's *Vie de St. Louis*, chap. 87, where it is told of an old woman of Damascus who met the envoy of St. Louis, Frère Yves le Breton. Thence it was taken by Jean Pierre Camus as the text of his treatise on pure love, *La Caritée ou le Portrait de la vraie Charité*, and also by Drexelius. Cf. Bremond: *L'Humanism Dévot*, pp. 183 ff.

ists and the doctors of the law. Indeed, the latter looked askance at the whole ascetic movement and even Hasan did not escape their criticisms. The introduction of the monastic life, the wearing of the woollen robe *(suf)* which became the badge of the movement, the practice of penances such as the wearing of a chain, and, above all, the doctrine of pure love, and of a reciprocal friendship between God and His creatures, were all looked upon as a departure from true Islamic principles and an approximation to Christian ideas. Ibn Sirin accuses the early ascetics of assuming the *suf* "in imitation of Jesus," instead of following the example of the Prophet who wore cotton, and Hamad ibn Salamah appealed to Farqad Sinji, the friend of Hasan, to "rid himself of Christianity."[13] The well-known hadith (traditional sayings) of Mohammed against monasticism—"there is no monasticism" [var. "celibacy"] "in Islam" and "the monastic life, for my community, is the Holy War"—were also probably fabricated by the traditionalists at this period as part of their anti-ascetic propaganda.[14]

These criticisms are not altogether unjustified. It would, in fact, be extremely surprising if the rise of the ascetic and mystical movement in Islam owed nothing to Christianity. Syriac Christianity had already begun to affect Arabia in the sixth century, and its influence is plainly perceptible in the rise of Islam itself. The conquest of Mesopotamia and Syria had brought the Arabs into still closer contact with a Christian population as well as with the various Gnostic and Manichaean sects which were still numerous in these regions. The latter had an obvious influence on the development of the Shi'ah and other heretical movements in Islam, and there are features in Sufism, such as the religious dance and the use of music and poetry to produce an orgy of collective emotion—the so-called *"sama"* or "spiritual concert"—which suggest analogies with the practices of the Messalians and similar sects.

But it was, above all, in the case of monasticism that Christian in-

13. Massignon: *Lexique,* pp. 131–2.
14. M. Massignon has shown that the passages dealing with monasticism in the Koran are to be interpreted in a favourable sense (*op. cit.,* pp. 123–131). The fabrication of traditional sayings of the Prophet in the interests of sects and parties and even on purely general grounds had attained vast proportions by the ninth century. There is even a *hadith* which justifies the forgery of *hadith* as follows: "If you come across a fine saying, don't hesitate to attribute it to me. I must have said it"!

fluence on the rise of Sufism is apparent. Spiritually minded Moslems could not but be interested in the life and ideals of the monks of the desert, and there are numerous references in Arabic literature to the impression created by their stories and sayings. Primitive Sufism was nothing less than an attempt to introduce the institution and ideals of Christian monasticism into the bosom of Islam. It is true that there was no attempt to tamper with Moslem dogma, and the earlier type of Sufi ascetic, such as Hasan of Basra, was thoroughly loyal to the religious law and traditions of Islam. Nevertheless, it is obvious that the substitution of a new ideal of interior piety for the militant puritanism of the early believers involved nothing less than a religious revolution of the most radical character. There was implicit in the movement a revolt against the whole legal and traditionalist conception of Islam. The latter felt no need for any intermediary, between God and man other than the written revelation of the Koran and the inspired teachings of the Prophet. It inculcated an attitude of submission to the power of Allah and a morality based on the exact performance of the ritual and religious law. Sufism, on the other hand, demanded the transformation of the inner man by which he should become the familiar friend of God and should attain to a union of divine love. And this acceptance of the Christian ideal of spiritual perfection brought with it a need for something corresponding to the Christian discipline of salvation. Islam possessed neither a sacramental system nor the belief in a personal mediator between God and man, but since the whole tendency of its creed was to emphasise the transcendence and power of God and the utter dependence and creature-liness of man, it was at first unconscious of any deficiency. The new tendencies that were at work in Islam from the ninth century and earlier led men to seek some solution which might bridge the unfathomable gulf between the Creator and the creature. Thus the Shi'ah found such a solution in the doctrine of the Imamate which made of Ali and his descendants the living representatives of God on earth, while the Ismaili went still further and introduced a whole system of Gnostic emanations to fill the gap. The Sufis avoided such manifest departures from Islamic tradition, but they attained the same goal by their doctrine of sainthood, which was their greatest contribution to Mohammedanism as a living religion.

"The *wali* (or saint)," writes Professor Nicholson, "bridges the chasm which the Koran and scholasticism have set between man and an absolutely transcendent God. He brings relief to the distressed, health to the sick, children to the childless, food to the famished, spiritual guidance to those who entrust their souls to his care, blessing to all who visit his tomb and invoke Allah in his name."[15]

And these features of the saint in popular cult are but the working out in practice of his position in Sufi theology as the bond between the One and the Many and the organ of the divine power in the cosmic order. This theory reached its full development in the doctrine of the Perfect Man elaborated by Ibnu'l 'Arabi and 'Abdu'l Karim al-Jili in the thirteenth and fourteenth centuries A.D.,[16] but its roots lie deep in the early history of Sufism. Mohasibi (781–857), one of the earliest systematic writers on Sufism, has a magnificent passage on God's choice of His saints from all eternity, that by means of them the creation may be brought to know and love Him. Finally, He sends them forth, saying: "O you, my witnesses! whosoever cometh to you sick, because he has not found Me, do ye heal him; a fugitive, because he flies from My service, bring him back to Me; forgetful of My succour and My graces, remind him of them. Verily I will be to you the best of Physicians, for I am merciful, and he who is merciful takes as his servants only those who are merciful."[17]

This doctrine of the saints, as the recipients of a divine mission for the service and salvation of mankind, became crystallised at an early date (the tenth century. A.D.?) in the theory of a spiritual hierarchy, consisting of a fixed number of saints headed by the Qutb or Pole and the four Awtad, who are the pivot of the world and upon whom depend the order and harmony of human affairs. "It is their office," writes Hujwiri (in the eleventh century A.D.), "to go round the whole world every night, and if there be any place on which their eyes have not fallen, next day some flaw will appear in that place; and they must then inform the Qutb, in order that he may direct his attention to the weak

---

15. Nicholson: *Idea*, p. 78.
16. Cf. especially "The Perfect Man," in Nicholson: *Studies in Islamic Mysticism* (Cambridge, 1921), pp. 77–161.
17. Massignon: *Lexique*, p. 219.

spot, and that by his blessing the imperfection may be remedied."[18]
These thaumaturgic supermen obviously have much more in common with the Hindu rishi or the "Pure Men" of Taoism than with the prophets and warriors who were the saints of primitive Islam. "Mohammed himself, as described in the Koran," writes Professor Nicholson, "is no more than a man subject to human weaknesses who receives at intervals the divine revelation, not from God, but from an angel. He has never seen God, he does not share God's secrets, he cannot foretell the future, he can work no miracle: he is only the servant and messenger of Allah."[19] The Wali, on the other hand, is a veritable divine man. He is not merely the preacher of the divine unity, he is one who has realised that unity in his own person, and through whom the divinity is manifested to men. Jalalu'ddin Rumi relates in the *Masnavi* how the Qutb met Bayazid of Bistam as he set forth to Mecca and absolved him from the necessity of the pilgrimage, saying:

> Of a Truth that is God which your soul sees in me,
> For God has chosen me to be His House.
> When you have seen me, you have seen God,
> And have circumambulated the real Ka'ba.
> To serve me is to worship and praise God;
> Think not that God is distinct from me.[20]

Sufism ultimately succeeded in reconciling these ideas with Moslem orthodoxy by means of a *tour de force* which, in defiance of history and of the evidence of the Koran, converted Mohammed himself from a simple messenger of Allah into the Spiritual Pole, the archetype of mystical sanctity, and of the whole lower creation—in other words, a Mohammedan Logos. In the ninth century, however, this development was still only in germ, and the new ideal of mystical sanctity was still unassimilated by Islamic theology. There were Sufis such as Ibn al-Hawwasi and al-Tirmidhi, who maintained the superiority of the saint over the Prophet, and who regarded Jesus, in accordance with certain passages of the Koran, as the type of sanctity and the Seal of the Saints as Mohammed is the Seal of the Prophets. This latent conflict between

---

18. Nicholson: *Studies*, p. 79.   19. Nicholson: *Idea*, p. 58.
20. *Ibid.*, p. 57.

the Religion of the Saint and the Religion of the Prophet came to a crisis in the case of al-Hallaj, whose life and death mark the turning-point of the whole Sufi movement. It is due to the epoch-making researches of M. Massignon that the true personality and religious significance of this remarkable figure in the history of Islam have at last been made clear after nearly a thousand years of misunderstanding. He has shown that al-Hallaj was not the pantheistic enthusiast of later Sufi tradition. His piety was founded on that of the earlier ascetics, and was far more traditional and Koranic than that of Ibnu'l 'Arabi or Jalalu'ddin Rumi. On the other hand, it was a consistent attempt to work out the Sufi ideal of the saintly vocation to its full practical conclusions, and thereby it came into a far sharper conflict with the orthodox piety of the theologians than did the esoteric theosophy of the later Sufis.

The early Sufis, with the exception of Rabi'a, had concentrated their attention on the negative aspect of the mystical way, which taken by itself must lead in M. Massignon's words to "the slow destruction of man, consumed away by the inaccessible sun of the divine unity." Al-Hallaj also emphasised this negative process, but he went beyond it and sought to realise the positive aspect of the mystical union. To him the mystery of creation was not, as to Mohammed, the divine Will—the sheer decree of divine Omnipotence; it was the divine Love, the Essence of the divine Essence in which man was called to participate. Hence the mystical union does not consist in that pure intuition of the divine unity which is the goal of later Sufism; it is a personal adhesion to the divine *fiat* which makes the soul of the mystic the organ of the Divine Spirit and causes it to participate in the life of God.[21]

This ideal of mystical conformity with the divine Will was personified in the person of Jesus, who even in the Koran appears as the typical representative of the outpouring of the Spirit, and of "those who have near access to God." Al-Hallaj, however, goes further and regards Jesus as the type of deified humanity—the second Adam[22] in whom the divine vocation of the human race is realised.

21. Massignon: *Passion,* pp. 514–521 A detailed summary of his conclusions will be found in Père Maréchal's essay "The Problem of Mystical Grace in Islam" in his *Studies in the Psychology of the Mystics,* translated by Algar Thorold, 1927.

22. Based on the passage in the Koran (III, 52): " The likeness (or analogy) of Jesus is as the likeness of Adam in the sight of God."

"Glory to God," he writes," whose Humanity has manifested to the Angels the secret of His radiant divinity" (*i.e.,* in Adam). "And who then has appeared to His creatures visibly in the charge of one who eats and drinks" (*i.e.,* Jesus).[23]

It was this new conception of the mystical vocation which led al-Hallaj to break away from the narrow circle of traditional Sufism and to embark on an apostolate which extended to every part of the Moslem world, from Mecca to India and the frontiers of China, and to every class of men; above all, to the Carmathian heretics who were regarded with fear and loathing by orthodox Islam.

And the same burning desire for the divine glory and the salvation of men leads al-Hallaj on to the supreme degree of heroic sanctity—the desire to die anathema for the sake of his brethren. We can trace in the story of his life a growing thirst for martyrdom which is, so far as I am aware, absolutely unparalleled in the life of any other Sufi saint.

The martyrdom of al-Hallaj is the culmination of the Christian tendencies which were already latent in the earlier Sufi movement. As M. Massignon has shown, al-Hallaj had founded his ideal of mystical sanctity on the Koranic tradition of Jesus, and this imitation of the Koranic Christ led him on to a literal conformity with the real Christ in His Passion and Death.

Many different causes contributed to bring about the death of al-Hallaj—the hostility of the theologians and canon lawyers, the scribes and Pharisees of Islam, the distrust of the government for his activity as a propagandist, and the disapproval of many of the Sufi leaders themselves; but behind them all there lay a conviction of the incompatibility of the Hallajian doctrine of mystical sanctification with Islamic orthodoxy—the conflict between the Religion of Law and the Religion of the Spirit. And, consequently, the condemnation of al-Hallaj was not an isolated episode. It was the decisive refusal of the dynamic and transforming power of sanctity. The rejection of al-Hallaj forced Sufism aside towards intellectualism and monism, and ultimately led to its absorption by the forces of an alien syncretism which were then beginning to invade the world of Islam.

23. Massignon: *Passion,* p. 602.

For the third century of the Hejira, which saw the full development of Moslem mysticism in such figures as Mohasibi, Bayazid of Bistam, Jonayd, and Hallaj, was an age of profound intellectual unrest and change. It was marked on the one hand by the introduction into Islamic culture of Greek neoplatonic philosophy and science, as interpreted by the Christian and "Sabæan" scholars of Mesopotamia, and on the other by the reappearance of the Gnostic tradition which had been preserved by the Manichæans and lesser sects, such as the Mandæans and the Bardesanians. Both these currents were united in the Ismailian or Carmathian movement, which organised an elaborate system of secret propaganda against the unity and even the social existence of Islam. The Ismailian doctrine is Gnostic in character and teaches the evolution of the world from the unknown and inaccessible Godhead through a series of seven emanations. The temporal order is likewise divided into a series of seven cycles, in each of which the Universal Intelligence manifests itself anew in human form. These seven manifestations are the Speakers or Prophets—Adam, Noah, Abraham, Moses, Jesus, Mohammed, and the Ismaili Messiah "The Master of the Hour." Corresponding to these are seven manifestations of the Universal Soul—the Helpers or Bases, whose function it is to manifest to the elect the esoteric meaning of the Speakers' teaching. Thus Aaron supplements Moses, Peter Jesus, and Ali Mohammed.

All these successive revelations, embodied in the world religions, are summed up in the Ismailian doctrine in which all veils are removed. But this doctrine is essentially esoteric, and is imparted only to those who have passed through the seven degrees of initiation which compose the Ismailian hierarchy. Only when the disciple has given himself up body and soul to the Imam and his representatives, the *da'is* or missionaries, is the *ta'lim,* the secret doctrine, revealed. The adept is then emancipated from all positive dogmas and religious obligations. He is taught the inner meaning which is hidden under the veils of dogma and rite in all the positive religions. All religions are false and all are true, but it is only "the Gnostic," the Ismailian initiate, who realises the truth of the divine unity—that God is One because God is All, and that every form of reality is but an aspect of the Divine Being. This esoteric theosophy, which is represented by the treatises of "the Brethren of Purity," dating from the eleventh century, was, however, unequally yoked with the sanguinary anarchism of the Carmathians and the political schemes of the founders of the Fatimid Caliphate. Consequently, it was regarded by the Islamic world in general with similar fear and repulsion to that evoked by anarchism or communism in modern times. By the thirteenth century the movement had collapsed as a social force and survived only in the form of scattered sects such as the Druses, who to-day still worship the mad Fatimid Caliph Hakim as the final incarnation of God and the consummation of revelation.[24]

The speculative and theosophical aspects of the movement, however, had a considerable influence on Islam and, above all, on Sufism. In fact, Sufism in its later developments may be regarded as a parallel movement to Ismailianism and the outcome of a similar process of syncretism. It also incorporated Neoplatonic, Gnostic, and cabalistic elements, and developed an esoteric theosophy very similar to that of the Ismailians. Like the latter, it made extensive use of the principle of the symbolical or esoteric interpretation of dogma and of the Koran. Thus Jalalu'ddin Rumi speaks of the seven successive meanings which every passage in the Koran contains, and adds:

Do not limit thyself, my son, to the external sense, like the demons who saw in Adam only the clay;

The external sense of the Koran is like the body of Adam, for its appearance alone is visible, but its soul is hidden.[25]

Indeed, some of the Sufis go even farther than the Ismailians by openly proclaiming the subversive doctrines which the latter kept as jealously guarded secrets. One of the quatrains attributed to Abu Sa'id Ibn Abi'l Khayr runs as follows:

So long as the mosques and colleges are not utterly destroyed, the work of the Qalenders (dervishes) will not be complete;
So long as faith and infidelity are not altogether similar, not a man will be a true Moslem.

24. The ass on which he rode was believed to typify the Speakers of the former religions which he had come to abrogate.
25. *Masnavi* (Whinfield), 169.

One of the great dervish orders, that of the Bektashis, which possessed exceptional importance in the Ottoman Empire owing to its influence on the corps of Janissaries, was really a secret society of Ismailian character, but such examples of direct contact and fusion between the Sufis and Ismailians. are rare. Esoteric Sufism is a parallel phenomenon to the esoteric Shi'a sects, but the two movements remain distinct and for the most part hostile to one another.

By far the most important representative of this movement of syncretism in orthodox Islam is Ibnu'l 'Arabi,[26] the great Spanish mystic, who is known as "The Great Shaykh," *par excellence,* since he was the first to organise it in a system of speculative thought dominated by a monism as absolute and as unflinching as that of the Vedanta. Being is one, whether it be pure and unmanifested or contingent and manifested. Pure Being is not God, since it cannot be known and is beyond existence; nor is Contingent Being God, since, though it is ultimately identical with Him, it has no independent subsistence, but is restricted to its particular mode of being. Creation is therefore necessary as the medium through which God realises Himself. The contradiction between the two forms of Being is resolved and transcended in man— not indeed in the rational man who only participates in the Universal Soul, but in the perfect or spiritual man who is the expression of the Universal Intelligence. He is to God as the pupil to the eye, by which God sees creation, and the mirror which displays God to himself. "Man is the substance of every attribute wherewith he endows God: when he contemplates God, he contemplates himself, and God contemplates Himself when He contemplates man."[27] He is the copy of God and the pattern of the world—a microcosm in which all attributes are united and by which creation is brought back from diversity to unity and from separation to union.

The perfect man is, of course, the type of Sufi saint, but primarily he is Mohammed, the archetype of the saints and the Divine Logos.

All the beauty of the world is borrowed from him and subsists through his beauty and his light. 'Tis his beauty that is beheld in every beauty; 'tis his light

26. Born 1165 at Murcia in Spain. Died 1240 at Damascus.
27. *Tarjuman al-Ashwaq,* p. v.

that is seen in every light, in the sun, the moon, and the stars. Those who love the Prophet ought to behold his perfection in all that is beautiful and meditate on him, revering him in their hearts and praising him with their tongues. I knew one of our Shaykhs who, whenever he saw or thought of anything beautiful, used to cry, "Blessings and peace on thee, O Apostle of God!"[28]

Thus Ibnu'l 'Arabi is trinitarian in a double sense: there is the triad that consists of The One, The Universal Intelligence, and The Universal Soul; and in the second place there is the triad—Pure Being, The Perfect Man, and The Phenomenal World, and in each triad the members are arranged in a descending hierarchy consisting of successive emanations.

The whole system resembles a Gnostic or Neoplatonic version of Christianity rather than an orthodox interpretation of Islam, and it is remarkable that it can ever have been regarded as tolerable in orthodox circles. Nevertheless, from the thirteenth century onwards Ibnu'l 'Arabi has been accepted as the great *doctor mysticus* of Islam, and has set his seal on the later development of Sufism. And this reception of his doctrine involves a vital change in the character of Moslem mysticism. It marks the triumph of an intellectualised theosophy over the experimental mysticism which the earlier Sufis had drawn from their life of prayer. It substituted an intellectual intuition of pure being for the transforming union of the will, and thus dispensed with the necessity for the moral discipline and renunciation which had been the foundation of the original movement. In the words of Professor Nicholson: "The living clash of personality, divine and human, resolves itself into a logical distinction between God and man as aspects of the One Essence, whose attributes receive their most perfect manifestation in the first-created Light of Mohammed, the Prophet of Allah."[29]

Consequently, M. Massignon is fully justified in regarding Ibnu'l 'Arabi as the evil genius of Sufism and as the chief agent in the divorce between Moslem mysticism and moral life and its stagnation in a speculative quietism. Nevertheless, we must not exaggerate his influence, since it is very possible that even without his intervention Islamic mys-

28. Quoted in Nicholson, *Idea,* p. 61.
29. Nicholson: *Idea,* p. 31.

ticism would have been forced by the internal logic of its development to a similar conclusion.

As early as the ninth century, in the case of Bayazid of Bistam, we see the emergence of the pantheistic and antinomian strain which ultimately came to predominate. Some of his utterances are as extravagant as anything that is to be found in the writings of the disciples of Ibnu'l 'Arabi. For example, "Allah is great, and I am greater still." "Praise be to Me, Praise be to Me, how great is My Glory!" Again, he said on one occasion to his disciple: "It is better for you to see me once than to see God a thousand times." He also claimed unlimited powers of intercession with God on behalf of the human race. "My standard" (of protection at the Last Day), he said, "is broader than the standard of Mohammed," since it extended even to the infidel and the souls in Hell. "On the Day of Judgement, I will draw nigh to the damned and I will say to Thee, 'Take me for their ransom; if not, I will teach them that Thy Paradise is nothing but a children's game'!"[30] No doubt these utterances are mystical paradoxes of the kind that we find in the poems of Angelus Silesius, and are not to be interpreted in the sense of the later monistic theosophy. Nevertheless, they had an unfortunate influence on Sufi piety.

In the year 1045 the great Sufi doctor, 'Abdu'l Karim al-Qushayri, addressed an epistle to all the Sufis of Islam, in which he complained that the whole movement was being compromised by the antinomian and unorthodox opinions which were then in the ascendant. Everywhere, he says, asceticism has been abandoned, and the Sufis, intoxicated by their sublime doctrines, regard themselves as emancipated from the most sacred duties of religion.[31]

The intervention of al-Qushayri, and still more that of al-Ghazali, the greatest of Moslem theologians, did much to stem this antinomian and pantheistic current and to establish a *via media* between the mystical extravagances of the dervishes and the narrow traditionalism of the canonists and the theologians. But this compromise was not perma-

---

30. Massignon: *Lexique*, pp. 247, 252–3.

31. Al-Qushayri's moderate and circumspect type of Sufism is also represented by his contemporary al-Hujwiri, the author of the oldest Persian manual on the subject, which has been translated by Professor Nicholson (1911). He adopts a distinctly unfavourable attitude to *sama'*, the use of ecstatic song and dance.

nently acceptable to either party, and it was the theosophical monism of Ibnu'l 'Arabi rather than the mystical theism of al-Ghazali which was ultimately victorious.

The fact is that when once the possibility of a living communion of the human soul with God and its progressive transformation by divine grace according to the teaching of al-Hallaj was excluded as savouring of dualism and *hulul* (incarnation or infusion), the solutions of the extremists became the only logical ones. The transcendence and omnipotence of Allah, carried to their logical conclusions, involved the denial of any ultimate reality to created being and to human experience. God was the Real (al-Haqq), all else was vanity and nothingness. God's Will and Power were the only source of movement in the world. The apparent activity of man as a free moral personality was but an illusion which veiled the operation of the one real agent—the Will of God. And this view finds its speculative and dogmatic justification in the orthodox Asharite doctrine, which denies not only moral freedom, but even the principle of causality in the interests of divine transcendence. There are no necessary principles of relationship or succession in the order of things or the order of consciousness, only a juxtaposition of unintelligible states of being called into existence and destroyed by the arbitrary *fiat* of divine omnipotence.

The natural outcome of this theory in the religious life is a blind fatalism which adheres to the strict fulfilment of the religious law and forbears to scrutinise the mystery of the divine purpose. Al-Ghazali writes:

He whom Allah wills to guide, he opens his breast to Islam; and he whom he wills to lead astray, he narrows his breast. He is the guider aright and the leader astray; he does what he wills, and decides what he wishes; there is no opposer of his decision and no repeller of his decree. He created the Garden (of Paradise) and created for it a people, then used them in obedience; and he created the Fire (of Hell) and created for it a people, then used them in rebellion. . . . Then he said, as has been handed down by the Prophet: "These are in the Garden and I care not; and these are in the Fire and I care not." So is Allah Most High, the King, the Reality; "He is not asked concerning what he does; but they are asked."[32]

32. D. B. Macdonald: *The Religious Attitude and Life in Islam,* pp. 300–1.

But the mystic cannot rest content with this external fatalism. The refusal of all moral and intelligible value to the phenomenal world only serves to throw him back upon the One Reality. If God alone Is, then all that is, is God, and the transitory being of creatures is but a veil thrown over the one true substance. Thus the Moslem theologian's insistence on divine transcendence and unity culminates in a monism no less complete than that of the neoplatonist philosopher. Indeed, the Sufi goes further, for he is not content to say that all the positive qualities of creatures are the reflections of the Divine Perfections; even the negative element in creation must be divine, as Jalalu'ddin declares in those marvellous lines of the Diwani Shamsi Tabriz:

> I am the theft of rogues, I am the pain of the sick,
> I am both cloud and rain, I have rained in the meadows.[33]

It is this intuition—*this realisation*—of the Divine Being as the One Reality which constitutes the essence of what the Sufi conceives to be mystical union, and all his spiritual life is orientated in this direction. In the words of Baba Kuhi, the eleventh-century mystic of Shiraz:

> In the market, in the cloister—only God I saw,
> In the valley and on the mountain—only God I saw.
>
> . . . . .
>
> In prayer and fasting, in praise and contemplation,
> In the religion of the Prophet—only God I saw.
> Neither soul nor body, accident nor substance,
> Qualities nor causes—only God I saw.
> Like a candle I was melting in His fire
> Amidst the flames outflashing—only God I saw.
> Myself with mine own eyes I saw most clearly,
> But when I looked with God's eyes—only God I saw.
> I passed away into nothingness, I vanished,
> And lo, I was the All-Living—only God I saw.[34]

Thus the mystical experience is not, as Hallaj and the Christian mystics taught, a real transformation or assimilation of the human soul to God. The Sufis themselves describe their doctrine as a Unitarian Gno-

---

33. Trans. Nicholson, *Selected Poems from the Diwani Shamsi Tabriz*, p. 332.
34. Trans. Nicholson in *Eastern Poetry and Prose*, p. 101.

sis, and it is impossible to define it more perfectly. It is simply the affirmation of a unity which has always been, and which will always be, a naked identity of pure being with itself. It leads not to the transfiguration, of the soul, but to its disintegration and annihilation. The same vision which unites the soul with God unites it with everything else and all distinctions vanish in an iridescent mist.

This pantheistic ecstasy is the characteristic note of later Sufism and is the inspiration of all the great mystical poets of Islam. It finds expression in Attar's curious allegory of the Quest of the Simurgh, a kind of mystical Hunting of the Snark; in the Masnavi of Jalalu'ddin, the Yusuf and Zuleika of Jami, and the odes of Ibnu'l 'Arabi and Ibnu'l Farid. We may quote as typical the following lines of Ni'matu'llah of Kirman:

> King and beggar are one, are one; foodless and food are one, are one.
> We are stricken with grief and drain the dregs; dregs and sorrow and cure are one.
> In all the world there is naught but One; talk not of "Two," for God is One.
> Mirrors a hundred thousand I see, but the face of that Giver of Life is One.
> We are plagued with the plague of one tall and fair, but we the plagued and the plague are one.
> Drop, wave, and sea, and the elements four without a doubt in our eyes are one.
> Ni'matu'llah is one in all the world; come seek him out, he is one, is one."[35]

And these lines of Jili:

> I am the existent and the non-existent, and the naughted and the everlasting.
> I am the avowed and the imagined and the snake and the charmer.
> I am the loosed and the bound, and the wine and the cupbearer.
> I am the treasure, I am poverty, I am my creatures and my Creator.[36]

It is true that the Christian mystic often uses language which is practically indistinguishable from that of the Gnostic—as, for instance, the famous stanzas of St. John of the Cross, beginning, "My Beloved is the mountains"[37] or the words of St. Catherine of Genoa, in which she declares that "my Me is God, nor do I recognise any other Me except my

35. Trans. E. G. Browne. 36. Nicholson: *Studies,* p. 90.
37. *The Spiritual Canticle,* stanzas XIV.–XV.

God Himself."[38] But then similarities of expression cover a profound divergence of moral attitude and theological doctrine. Christian mysticism is nothing but the experimental realisation and personal appropriation of the new relationship of mankind to God which is involved by the Incarnation. The sacramental economy is not transcended, but becomes the pathway to Reality and the organ of union. The Moslem, however, who is bound to reject the whole concept of Incarnation, has for a discipline of salvation only the strict traditional observance of the religious law. But the mystic necessarily transcends this external discipline, and is thereby left face to face with the Absolute. He is forced to find his own path, to build his own bridge between the world of sense and the world of spirit. Consequently, he is driven to create a pseudo-sacramentalism or pan-sacramentalism, in which every created form may serve as a means of access to God, since, as Shabistari says, "Beneath the veil of each atom is hidden the soul-ravishing beauty of the face of the Beloved."

Jami writes:

> Sometimes the wine, sometimes the cup, we call Thee.
> Sometimes the lure, sometimes the net, we call Thee.
> Except Thy name there is not a letter on the tablet of the universe.
> Say by what name shall we call Thee?

But it is, above all, in sexual love that the Sufi finds a symbol and sacrament of worship. Omar Ibnu'l Farid writes:

> Declare the absoluteness of beauty and be not moved to deem it finite by
>   thy longing for a tinselled gaud;
> For the charm of every fair youth or lovely woman is lent to them from
>   Her beauty.
> 'Twas She that crazed Qays the lover of Lubna; ay and every enamoured
>   man, like Layla's Majnun or 'Azzar's Kutbayyir.
> Every one of them passionately desired Her attribute (Absolute Beauty)
>   which She clothed in the form of a beauty which shone forth in a beauty
>   of form.

. . . . .

38. Cf. E. I. Watkin: *The Philosophy of Mysticism*, pp. 320 ff., which gives a catena of similar passages.

The loved women and their lovers—'tis no infirm judgement—were
manifestations in which we (my Beloved and I) displayed (our
attributes of) love and beauty.

Every lover, I am he, and She is every lover's beloved, and all (lovers and
loved) are but the names of a vesture,

Names of which I was the object in reality, and 'twas I that was made
apparent to myself by means of an invisible soul.

I was ever She, and She was ever I, with no difference; nay, my essence
loved my essence,

Though there was nothing in the world except myself beside me, and no
thought of besideness occurred to my mind.[39]

This erotic symbolism, together with that of wine and intoxication,
runs through Sufi literature and has done much to discredit it in Western eyes. No doubt in many cases the use of such imagery is as free
from sensuality as it is with the Catholic mystics. But the latter possess
a series of safeguards against moral antinomianism which are wholly
lacking in Islam. In the hands of a poet like Hafiz, for instance, mystical interpretation is a double-edged weapon which is deliberately used
to exalt earthly passion rather than to typify spiritual experience. Yet
even here it is not, as some have supposed, a mere literary device. It
is a sincere attempt to view earthly love *sub specie æternitatis*. "For all
eternity," he writes, "the perfume of love comes not to him who has not
swept with his cheek the dust from the tavern threshold." For Hafiz it
is only in love that the transcendent can be realised: "Heart and soul
are fixed upon the desire of the Beloved: this at least *is*, for, if not, heart
and soul are naught." Unfortunately, the same pan-sacramental theory
which inspires this worship of the Beautiful will also serve as a justification for what Père Lammens terms "Rasputin-ism." Many of the
Sufi saints were very queer saints indeed, as we may see from Professor
Nicholson's interesting account of the great Persian Shaykh Abu Sa'id
Ibn Abi'l Khayr[40] (A.D. 967–1049). In his youth he was famous for his
severe asceticism,[41] but in later life he laid aside his penances and spent

39. Nicholson: *Studies*, pp. 222–4.
40. Nicholson: *Studies*, chap. I.
41. On one occasion he recited the Koran standing on his head in order to imitate the
angels who were said to praise God in this attitude!

much of his time with his disciples in feasting and mystical revelry. It is probable that the famous quatrains which bear his name are not his own work, but at least they faithfully reflect his spirit:

> Thou bidst me love and midst Thy lovers pine
> Of Sense and Reason stripped this heart of mine;
> Devout and much revered was I, but now
> Toper and gadabout and libertine.[42]

His powers as a wonder-worker (which were largely employed in extracting money from wealthy admirers) were only surpassed by his boundless self-exaltation. When a critic asked him why his neck was too big for his collar, he replied: "I marvel how there is room for my neck in the seven heavens and earths after all that God has bestowed upon me! (You ask) why I have not performed the Pilgrimage (which is one of the five pillars of Islam incumbent on every believer). Is it so great a matter that thou shouldst tread under thy feet a thousand miles of ground in order to visit a stone house? The true man of God sits where he is, and the Bayt al-Ma'mur (the celestial Ka'ba) comes several times in a day and a night to visit him and performs the circumambulation above *his* head. 'Look and see!' All who were present looked and saw it."[43]

This antinomian attitude is not limited to matters of conduct, it is also applied to the sphere of religious belief. If every created form is a sacrament and a means of access to the Beloved, the same is likewise true of the forms of religious revelation. The general principle is laid down in one of the most beautiful of the quatrains attributed to Abu Sa'id:

> By whatsoever Path, blessed the Feet
> Which seek Thee; blessed He who strives to meet
> Thy Beauty; blessed they who on it gaze;
> And blessed every tongue which Thee doth greet![44]

And it is developed in detail by all the great later Sufi writers, such as Omar Ibnu'l Farid, Hafiz, Jalalu'ddin Rumi, and Ibnu'l A'rabi. The last writes:

---

42. Trans . E. G. Browne: *History of Persian Literature*, II, p. 265.
43. Nicholson: *Studies*, p. 62.
44. Trans. E. G. Browne, *op. cit.*, p. 266.

My heart has become capable of every form; it is a pasture for gazelles and a
convent for Christian monks,
And a temple for idols and the pilgrims Kaʻba and the tables of the Tora and
the book of the Koran.
I follow the religion of Love: whatever way Love's camels take, that is my
religion and my faith.[45]

Elsewhere in *The Bezels of Divine Wisdom* he develops the same idea
more systematically:

Those who adore God in the sun behold the sun, and those who adore Him in
living things see a living thing, and those who adore Him in lifeless things see
a lifeless thing, and those who adore Him as a Being unique and unparalleled
see that which has no like. Do not attach yourselves to any particular creed
exclusively so that you disbelieve in all the rest; otherwise, you will lose much
good, nay, you will fail to recognise the full truth of the matter. God, the om-
nipresent and omnipotent, is not limited by any one creed, for he says (in the
Koran), "Wheresoever ye turn, there is the face of Allah." Everyone praises what
he believes; his god is his own creature, and in praising it he praises himself.
Consequently he blames the beliefs of others which he would not do if he were
just, but his dislike is based on ignorance. If he knew Junayd's saying, "The
water takes its colour from the vessel containing it," he would not interfere with
other men's beliefs, but would perceive God in every form of belief.[46]

Here Sufism has reached its ultimate conclusion. The movement
which began as an extreme development of orthodox Islamic pietism
ended in a pantheistic universalism which transcended alike religious
dogma and moral law. In fact, Sufism in its extreme development may
be regarded as the most perfect and consistent type of an universalist
or undenominational religion which has ever been achieved. It seems
paradoxical to suggest that the dancing dervish is a truer undenomina-
tionalist than the Liberal Protestant, but it is justified by the fact that
his undenominationalism is the direct outcome of his religious experience, whereas in the other case it is an artificial construction. The dervish rejects dogma because of his overpowering realisation of the reality of God; the Liberal rejects it because he realises the importance of

45. *Tarjuman al-Ashwaq:* Ode XL, p. 67.
46. Nicholson: *The Mystics of Islam,* pp. 87–88; cf. *Studies,* pp. 159 and 263–5.

man and the inconveniences of sectarianism. It is part of a movement to humanise religion, and in the majority of cases to secularise it—to substitute social "uplift" for the service of God.

In Sufism, however, we see undenominationalism carried out consistently and unflinchingly as a religious movement and not as a secularising one, and, consequently, it leads to a purely religious conclusion, to spiritual ecstasy. But it is a sterile ecstasy which no longer fructifies the social life of the Islamic community, as it did in the days of Hasan of Basra, and Rabi'a and al-Hallaj, but which allows the vital sources of spiritual energy to waste away in a nihilistic quietism. It is remarkable that three writers who differ so widely in their general outlook, as Count Gobineau, Père Lammens, and M. Massignon, should all agree in their unfavourable verdict on the social and moral effects of the later Sufism. To Gobineau it is this quietism, this "passive disposition of spirit which surrounds with a nimbus of inert sentiment all conceptions of God, of man, and of the universe . . . that is the running sore of all Oriental countries." To M. Massignon it is the divorce between social life and mysticism and the degeneration of the latter into a kind of "supernatural opium smoking," which is, "far more profoundly than all the military and economic factors, the true cause of the present disintegration of the Moslem community," for the salvation of which the early ascetics and mystics had struggled and suffered.[47] It is no doubt due to a confused sense of these dangers that there has been so widespread a reaction against Sufism in modern Islam—a reaction which is represented both by the extreme Puritan traditionalism of the Wahabis, and by the ultra-modernist reform movement in post-war Turkey. The death of the last Grand Tchelebi, the lineal successor of Jalalu'ddin himself, who put an end to his own life after the dissolution of his order, is a tragic symbol of the failure of Sufism to face the harsh realities of existence. Yet the mystical tradition has entered so deeply into the mind of Islam that its disappearance would leave the religious life of the Moslem world disastrously impoverished. For with all its faults and weaknesses, the Sufi movement remains one of the great witnesses outside Christianity to the religious need of humanity. The Sufi is like the

47. Massignon: *Lexique*, p. 286.

merchant in the Gospel who found the pearl of great price; he found one truth—the Reality of God and the worthlessness and emptiness of all apart from Him—and for that truth he sacrificed every other. But that truth is so great that it suffices to outweigh a vast amount of speculative error. The Sufi held fast to this, and, consequently, in spite of his theoretic monism and pantheism, he preserves, unlike the Western philosophic monist, a genuine religious attitude. The Sufi may reason like a pantheist, but when he prays it is with the humility and adoration of a creature in the presence of his Creator; witness the prayer with which Jami concludes the preface to his *Lawa'ih:*[48]

My God, my God! Save us from preoccupation with trifles and show us the realities of things as they are. Withdraw from the eyes of our understanding the veil of heedlessness, and show us everything as it truly is. Display not to us Not-Being in the guise of Being, and place not a veil of Not-Being over the beauty of Being. Make these phenomenal forms a mirror of the effulgence of Thy Beauty, not a cause of veiling and remoteness, and cause these phantasmal pictures to become the means of our knowledge and vision, not a cause of ignorance and blindness. All our deprivation and banishment is from ourselves; leave us not with ourselves, but grant us deliverance from ourselves, and vouchsafe us knowledge of Thyself.

48. Quoted by E. G. Browne in his *History of Persian Literature under Tartar Dominion.*

XI

On Spiritual Intuition in
Christian Philosophy

The problem of spiritual intuition and its reconciliation with the natural conditions of human knowledge lies at the root of philosophic thought, and all the great metaphysical systems since the time of Plato have attempted to find a definitive solution. The subject is no less important for the theologian, since it enters so largely into the question of the nature of religious knowledge and the limits of religious experience. The orthodox Christian is, however, debarred from the two extreme philosophic solutions of pure idealism and radical empiricism, since the one leaves no place for faith and supernatural revelation, and the other cuts off the human mind entirely from all relation to spiritual reality. Yet even so there remains a vast range of possible solutions which have been advocated by Catholic thinkers from the empiricism of the mediaeval nominalists to the ontologism of Malebranche and Rosmini. Leaving aside the more eccentric and unrepresentative thinkers, we can distinguish two main currents in Catholic philosophy. On the one hand, there is the Platonic tradition that is represented by the Greek Fathers, and, above all, by St. Augustine and his mediaeval followers such as St. Bonaventure; on the other, the Aristotelian tradition which found classical expression in the philosophy of St. Thomas Aquinas. But it is important not to exaggerate the divergences between the two schools. Both of them seek to find a *via media* between the two extreme solutions. St. Bonaventure is not a pure Platonist, nor St. Thomas a pure Aristotelian. The former rejects the doctrine of innate ideas, while the latter finds the source of intelligibility in the divine ideas, and regards the human mind as receiving its light from the divine intelligence.[1] Hence, although Thomism insists on the derivation of our ideas from sensible experience, it is far from denying the existence of spiritual intuition. On this point I will quote the words of a French Dominican, Père Joret: "Let us not forget," he writes, "that the human intelligence, also, is intuitive by nature and predisposition. No doubt, as it is united substantially with matter, it cannot thenceforth know except by proceeding from sensible realities and by means of images. But, apart from this, our intelligence is intuitive. Its first act at the dawn of its life, at its awakening, is an intuition, the intuition of being, or, more concretely, of 'a thing which is,' and, at the same time, as though it already unconsciously carried them in itself, there suddenly appear with an ineluctable certainty the first principles" of identity, contradiction, causality, and the like. It is from our intuition of first principles that all our knowledge proceeds. St. Thomas says: "As the enquiry of reason starts from a simple intuition of the intelligence, so also it ends in the certainty of intelligence, when the conclusions that have been discovered are brought back to the principles from which they derive their certitude." Père Joret insists on the importance of this intuitive faculty as the natural foundation of religious experience. It is not itself mystical, but it is the essential natural preparation and prerequisite for mysticism. The failure to recognise this, which has been so common among theologians during the last two centuries, has, he says, been deplorable not only in its effects on the study of mysticism, but in its practical consequences for the spiritual life.[2]

It is easy to understand the reasons for this attitude of hesitation and distrust with regard to intuitive knowledge. If the intuition of pure being is interpreted in an excessively realist sense, we are led not merely to ontologism, but to pantheism—to the identification of that being which is common to everything which exists with the Transcendent and Absolute Being which is God. And this danger has led to the op-

---

1. St. Thomas himself insists on the fundamental agreement of the two theories. *Non multum autem refert dicere quod ipsa intelligibilia participantur a Deo, vel quod lumen faciens intelligibilia participetur.* Cf. Gilson, *Pourquoi S. Thomas à critiqué S. Augustin,* p. 119.

2. F. D. Joret, O.P., *La Contemplation Mystique d'après St. Thomas d'Aquin.* Bruges, 1923, pp. 83–90.

posite error of minimising the reality of the object of our intuition, and reducing it to a mere logical abstraction.

Here again it is necessary to follow the middle way. The being which is the object of our knowledge is neither wholly real nor purely logical and conceptual. The intuition of pure being is a very high and immaterialised form of knowledge, but it is not a direct intuition of spiritual reality. It stands midway, between the world of sensible experience and the world of spiritual reality. On the one hand it is the culminating point of our ordinary intellectual activity, and on the other it leads directly to the affirmation of the Absolute and the Transcendent.[3]

Hence it is always possible, as Père Maréchal shows,[4] that the intuition of pure being may become the occasion or starting-point of an intuition of a higher order. But it is difficult to decide, in concrete cases, whether the supreme intuition of the Neoplatonist or the Vedantist philosopher is simply the intuition of pure being interpreted in an ontologist sense, or whether it is a genuine intuition of spiritual reality. There is no *á priori* reason for excluding the latter alternative; indeed, in some cases it seems absolutely necessary to accept it. Nevertheless, this higher intuition is not necessarily always the same. It is possible to distinguish several different types of intuition, or to find several different explanations of it. In the first place there is the possibility of a very high form of metaphysical intuition by which the mind sees clearly the absolute transcendence of spirit in relation to sensible things and the element of nothingness or not-being which is inherent in the world of sensible experience.[5] This form of intuition seems adequate to explain the spiritual experience which is typical of the oriental religions, *e.g.,* the intuition of *advaita*—non-duality, which is characteristic of the

---

3. *Cette intuition (de l'être saisi par l'abstraction formel) est fugitive, et cependant l'on comprend en descendant de ce sommet—pour penser de nouveau l'être comme tout universel dans l'abstraction totale—que si l'intelligence n'avait pas foncièrement cette intuition, perpetuelle quoique enveloppée généralement de virtualités, la characteristique même de son activité disparaîtrait, et il lui serait impossible, en particulier, d'affirmer l'existence inconditionée d'un Etre qui dépasse l'expérience.*—P. J. Webert, O.P., *Essai de Métaphysique Thomiste,* p. 52. Cf. the whole of chaps. II and III.

4. Maréchal, *Op. cit.,* pp. 101, 133.

5. M. Maritain admits the possibility of this kind of intuition, but he regards it as an anomalous form of experience which is neither metaphysical nor mystical. Cf. "Expérience Mystique et Philosophic," in *Revue de Philosophie,* November, 1926, p. 606.

Vedanta. But there are other cases which suggest a higher form of experience, and one which is more strictly comparable to the higher experiences of the Christian mystic. In such cases the obvious explanation is that such experience is mystical in the full sense of the word, since we need not deny the existence of supernatural grace wherever the human mind turns towards God and does what lies in its power—*facienti quod in se est, Deus non denegat gratiam.*

But while we must admit the essentially supernatural character of all true mystical experience, it is still possible that this higher experience may have its psychological roots in a rudimentary natural capacity of the soul for the intuition of God. This is certainly not the common theological view, but there are, nevertheless, Catholic theologians, such as St. Bonaventure and, above all, the great mediaeval mystics of Germany and the Low Countries, who teach that the human soul possesses by its very nature a real but obscure knowledge of God. St. Bonaventure argues that Aristotle's theory of the sensible origin of all human knowledge only holds good of our knowledge of external reality, not of those realities which are essentially present to the soul itself; consequently, "the soul knows God and itself and the things that are in itself without the help of the exterior senses."[6] *Deus praesentissimus est ipsi animæ et eo ipso cognoscibilis.*

The mediaeval mystics base their whole theory of mysticism on this doctrine of the knowledge of God essentially present in the human soul. Underneath the surface of our ordinary consciousness, the sphere of the discursive reason, there is a deeper psychological level, "the ground of the soul," to which sensible images and the activity of the discursive reason cannot penetrate. This is the domain of the spiritual intuition, "the summit" of the mind and the spiritual will which is naturally directed towards God. Here the soul is in immediate contact with God, who is present to it as its cause and the principle of its activity. It is, in fact, a mirror which has only to be cleansed and turned towards its object to reflect the image of God. In the words of Ruysbroeck: "In the most noble part of the soul, the domain of our spiritual powers, we are constituted in the form of a living and eternal mirror

6. Bon. in II *Sent.*, d. 39, q. 2.

of God; we bear in it the imprint of His eternal image, and no other image can ever enter there." Unceasingly this mirror remains under the eyes of God, "and participates thus with the image that is graven there from God's eternity. It is in this image that God has known us in Himself before we were created, and that He knows us now in time, created as we are for Himself. This image is found essentially and personally in all men; each man possesses it whole and entire, and all men together possess no more of it than does each one. In this way we are all one, intimately united in our eternal image, which is the image of God and the source in us all of our life and of our coming into existence. Our created essence and our life are joined to it immediately as to their eternal cause. Yet our created being does not become God, any more than the image of God becomes a creature."[7]

The soul "in its created being incessantly receives the impress of its Eternal Archetype, like a flawless mirror, in which the image remains steadfast and in which the reflection is renewed without interruption by its ever new reception in new light. This essential union of our spirit with God does not exist in itself, but it dwells in God and it flows forth from God and it depends upon God and it returns to God as to its Eternal Origin. And in this wise, it has never been, nor ever shall be, separated from God; for this union is within us by our naked nature, and, were this nature to be separated from God, it would fall into pure nothingness. And this union is above time and space and is always and incessantly active according to the way of God. But our nature, forasmuch as it is indeed like unto God but in itself is creature, receives the impress of its Eternal Image passively. This is that nobleness which we possess by nature in the essential unity of our spirit, where it is united to God according to nature. *This neither makes us holy, nor blessed, for all men, whether good or evil, possess it within themselves; but it is certainly the first cause of all holiness and all blessedness.*"[8]

According to this view, every man naturally possesses an immediate contact with God in the deepest part of his soul; but he remains, as a rule, without the realisation and the enjoyment of it.

7. Ruysbroeck, *The Mirror of Eternal Salvation,* chap. VIII.
8. Ruysbroeck, *The Adornment of the Spiritual Marriage,* Bk. II, chap. LVII (trans. C. A. Wynschenk Dom).

His soul is turned outwards to the things of sense, and his will is directed to temporal goods. It is the work of grace to reconstitute this divine image, to bring a man back to his essential nature, to cleanse the mirror of his soul so that it once more receives the divine light. Nevertheless, even apart from grace, the divine image remains present in the depths of the soul, and whenever the mind withdraws itself from its surface activity and momentarily concentrates itself within itself, it is capable of an obscure consciousness of the presence of God and of its contact with divine reality.

This doctrine is undoubtedly orthodox, and involves neither illuminism nor ontologism, still less pantheism. Nevertheless, it runs counter to the tendency to asceticism which has been so powerful since the Reformation, and it is also difficult to reconcile with the strictly Aristotelian theory of knowledge and of the structure of the human mind as taught by St. Thomas. Recently, however, Père Picard has made a fresh survey of the problem, and has endeavoured to show that St. Thomas himself, in his commentary on the Sentences, admits the existence of this obscure intuition of God, and uses it as a proof of the soul's resemblance to the Trinity which was so often insisted on by St. Augustine.[9] He does not, however, base his view on the argument from authority so much as on general theological considerations, as the hypothesis which is most in harmony with the teaching and experience of Catholic mystics. Certainly, it seems, the existence of an obscure but profound and continuous intuition of God provides a far more satisfactory basis for an explanation of the facts of religious experience, as we see them in history, than a theory which leaves no place for any experience of spiritual reality, except a merely inferential rational knowledge on the one hand and on the other a revelation which is entirely derived from supernatural faith and has no natural psychological basis.

9. Cf. "La Saisie immédiate de Dieu dans les Etats Mystiques," by G. Picard, in *Revue d'Ascétique et de Mystique,* 1923, pp. 37–63, 156–181. The subject is also discussed by Père Hugueny, O.P., in his introduction to the new French translation of Tauler (Vol. I, 73–154). He concludes that Tauler's doctrine is based upon that of Albertus Magnus, and diverges on several points from that of St. Thomas.

XII

St. Augustine and His Age

I: THE DYING WORLD

The world itself now bears witness to its approaching end by the evidence of its failing powers. There is not so much rain in winter for fertilising the seeds, nor in summer is there so much warmth for ripening them. The springtime is no longer so mild, nor the autumn so rich in fruit. Less marble is quarried from the exhausted mountains, and the dwindling supplies of gold and silver show that the mines are worked out and the impoverished veins of metal diminish from day to day. The peasant is failing and disappearing from the fields, the sailor at sea, the soldier in the camp, uprightness in the forum, justice in the court, concord in friendships, skill in the arts, discipline in morals. Can anything that is old preserve the same powers that it had in the prime and vigour of its youth? It is inevitable that whatever is tending downwards to decay and approaches its end must decrease in strength, like the setting sun and the waning moon, and the dying tree and the failing stream. This is the sentence passed on the world; this is God's law: that all that has risen should fall and that all that has grown should wax old, and that strong things should become weak and great things should become small, and that when they have been weakened and diminished they should come to an end.

St. Cyprian, Ad Demetrianum, c iii.

St. Augustine has often been regarded as standing outside his own age—as the inaugurator of a new world and the first mediaeval man, while others, on the contrary, have seen in him rather the heir of the old classical culture and one of the last representatives of antiquity. There is an element of truth in both these views, but for all that he belongs neither to the mediaeval nor to the classical world. He is essentially a man of his own age—that strange age of the Christian Empire which has been so despised by the historians, but which nevertheless marks one of the vital moments in the history of the world. It witnessed the fall of Rome, the passing of that great order which had controlled the fortunes of the world for five centuries and more, and the laying of the foundations of a new world. And Augustine was no mere passive spectator of the crisis. He was, to a far greater degree than any emperor or general or barbarian war-lord, a maker of history and a builder of the bridge which was to lead from the old world to the new.

Unfortunately, although there is no lack of historical evidence, the real importance of this period is seldom appreciated. Ever since the Renaissance the teaching of ancient history has been treated as part of the study of the classics and consequently comes to an end with the age of the Antonines, while the teaching of modern history is equally bound up with the nationalist idea and begins with the rise of the existing European peoples. Consequently there is a gap of some five hundred years from the third to the seventh century in the knowledge of the ordinary educated person. It lasts from the collapse of the old Empire in the third century A.D. to the breakup of the reconstituted Eastern Empire in the seventh century under the stress of the Mohammedan invasions. This is the period of the Christian Empire, the Empire of Constantine and Justinian, the age of the Fathers and of the great Councils. It deserves to be studied as a whole and for its own sake, instead of piecemeal and from conflicting points of view. Hitherto the secular historians have confined themselves to one side of the evidence and the ecclesiastical historians to the other, without paying much attention to each other's results. We have to go back to the days of Tillemont to find an historian that was equally competent in both fields. The modern historians of the period have shown themselves notably unsympathetic to its religious achievements. The greatest of them—Gibbon and the late Professor Bury—were freethinkers with a strong bias against Christianity, while the remainder, from the days of Finlay and Burckhardt and Gregorovius to Seeck and Stein and Rostovtzeff in our time, all write from a secularist point of view. This is peculiarly unfortunate, not only because by far the larger part of the historical evidence has a religious character, but still more because the whole historical development becomes inexplicable when viewed from a purely secular standpoint. To neglect or despise the religious achievement of the age is, as fatal to any true understanding of it as a complete disregard of the economic factor would be in the case of nineteenth-century Europe. For the real interest and importance of that age are essentially religious. It marks the failure of the greatest experiment in secular civilisation that the world had ever seen, and the return of society to spiritual principles. It was at once an age of material loss and of spiritual recovery, when amidst the ruins of a bankrupt order men strove slowly and painfully to rebuild the house of life on eternal foundations.

This vital revolution owes nothing to the coming of the new peoples. It was already accomplished while the Roman Empire was intact and the Eternal City was still inviolate. Yet it was this change rather than the material collapse of the Roman state which marks the real break between the ancient classical civilisation and that of the Byzantine and mediaeval world.

Rome had won her world empire by her genius for military and political organisation, but her positive contribution to culture was comparatively small. She was rather an agent in the expansion of culture than its creator. Her part was that of the soldier and engineer who cleared the way and built the roads for the advance of civilisation. The cosmopolitan culture which became common to the whole Roman Empire was itself mainly the creation of the Hellenic genius. It had its origins in the life of the Greek city-state and had already acquired the character of a world civilisation in the great states of the Hellenistic world. Alexander the Great and his successors had made it their mission to spread this civilisation throughout the lands that they had conquered. All over the East, from the Mediterranean and the Black Sea to the Oxus and the Indus, countless cities sprang up which in their constitution, their social life and their buildings were modelled on the pattern of the Greek city. And each of these cities became a centre of diffusion for Western culture. The peasants no doubt continued to live their own life and served their new masters as they had served so many conquerors in the past, but the upper and middle classes were by degrees drawn into the privileged society and were either completely Hellenised or at least acquired a superficial veneer of Greek manners and culture. A single type of urban civilisation gradually came to prevail throughout the Hellenistic world.

Rome in her turn took on this inheritance from the great Hellenistic monarchies and carried on their work. But she did so in a strictly practical and utilitarian spirit. At first, indeed, her attitude was entirely selfish, and she organised the world only to exploit it. Roman capitalists, money-lenders, slave-dealers and tax-gatherers descended on the East like a swarm of locusts and sucked the life out of the dependent communities. Every Roman, from the aristocratic capitalist like Brutus or Lucullus down to the meanest agent of the great financial corporations, had his share in the plunder.[1] The age of the Republic culminated in an orgy of economic exploitation which ruined the prosperity of the subject peoples and brought Rome herself to the verge of destruction.

The crisis was averted by the foundation of the Empire. Julius Caesar and Augustus put an end to the misrule of the capitalist oligarchy and the tyranny of military adventurers and returned to the Hellenistic ideal of an enlightened monarchy. The provinces recovered their prosperity, and alike in the Hellenistic East and the Latin West there was a fresh expansion of urban civilisation. For two centuries the ancient world enjoyed an age of continuous material progress.

Everywhere from Britain to Arabia and from Morocco to Armenia wealth and prosperity were spreading, new cities were being founded, and the more backward peoples were adopting a higher form of civilisation. And nowhere was this process more striking than in Africa, where even to-day the stately ruins of so many Roman cities still remain to impress the modern tourist with their evidence of vanished civilisation. Even a comparatively remote and unimportant town like Timgad, in North Africa, possesses public buildings and monuments finer than those of many a modern city of vastly superior wealth and population. It had its theatres and amphitheatres in which free spectacles were provided for the entertainment of the people. It had porticoes and basilicas where the citizens could attend to public business or idle away their leisure time. It had baths and gymnasia, libraries and lecture halls, and temples which were not, like our churches, destined solely for religious

---

1. It is characteristic that Brutus, who was regarded in later times as a model of republican virtue, quarrelled with Cicero because the latter was forced to reduce the interest on Brutus's loans to the impoverished cities of Cilicia from 48 per cent to a beggarly 12 per cent!

worship, but were the centre of civic ceremonial and public festivities. There has probably never been an age in which the opportunities for living an enjoyable and civilised existence were so widely diffused. For the ancient city was not, like the average modern town, a factory or a place of business; it existed for the enjoyment of its citizens, and it was the centre of an active communal life, lived in public and at the public expense.

This was most strikingly exemplified at Rome itself, where the Greek democratic principle of the right of the citizen to be fed and amused at the expense of the state had been carried to its extreme conclusions. These rights were the only remaining privilege of the Roman democracy, which had completely lost all share in the government of the Empire, but, so far from disappearing with the loss of political rights, they continued to expand down to the last period of the Empire. The corn dole had been limited by Augustus to some 200,000 citizens, but even so it involved a vast organisation, the traces of which are to be seen in the remains of the great public corn *depôts* at Ostia, and the setting aside for the use of the capital of the chief corn-growing areas of the Mediterranean world—Egypt and Sicily. Moreover, in the course of time the free distribution of other articles such as oil, wine and bacon was added to the corn dole. Gifts of money had been common even in republican times, and during the reign of Augustus no less than six distributions of between £2 and £3 10s. per head were made to between 200,000 and 320,000 persons.

No less important was the amusement of the people. The games of the circus and the amphitheatre involved enormous expenditure and occupied a considerable part of the year. Apart from the special festivals, which might last as long as a hundred days on end, the regular games took up sixty-six days a year in the time of Augustus, and had increased to a hundred and seventy-five days by the fourth century.

Finally, vast sums of public money were absorbed by the public buildings. To some extent this expenditure served ends of real value, above all in the case of the great aqueducts which ensured to Rome a better water supply than that of most modern capitals. For the most part, however, it was entirely unproductive. The Colosseum—which has stood for eighteen centuries as a symbol of the material power of imperial Rome—was created to serve the brutal amusements of the Roman populace. The imperial palaces and fora, with their temples and libraries and porticoes, provided a sumptuous background for the social life of the Court and the capital. But the most characteristic monuments of the imperial period are the thermae, which continued to increase in size and splendour down to the age of Diocletian and Constantine. They were not mere public baths in our sense of the word, but true palaces for the people, of vast size, containing baths and gymnasia, lecture-rooms and libraries, and adorned with the masterpieces of Greek and Hellenistic art. Public building on such a scale far surpassed anything that the modern world has yet seen. Imperial Rome became a city of gold[2] and marble, a worthy incarnation of the *Dea Roma* whom her subjects worshipped. And the same ideal was pursued by all the cities of the Empire according to their capacity. Each tried to surpass its neighbour in the splendour of its public buildings and the number of its games and festivals. Not only millionaires, like Herodes Atticus, but every citizen of moderate wealth, used his money unstintingly in the service of his native city, either by building baths, theatres and porticoes, or by providing public spectacles or endowments for educational and charitable purposes.

All this testifies to a high level of material culture and to an admirable development of public spirit on the part of the citizen class, but from the moral and spiritual point of view it was less satisfactory. All the vast development of material prosperity and external display had no spiritual purpose behind it. Its ultimate end was the satisfaction of corporate selfishness. The religious element in ancient culture, which had been the inspiration of civic patriotism in the fifth and sixth centuries B.C., had almost disappeared from the cosmopolitan civilisation of the imperial age. The temples and the gods remained, but they had lost their spiritual significance and had become little more than an ornamental appendage to public life and an occasion for civic ceremonial. For the educated, the only real religion was philosophy—a philosophy

---

2. She was literally a "golden city," for the growing scarcity of precious metal which characterised the later Empire is attributed by historians in part to the enormous quantities of gold which were used to gild the roofs and domes of the temples and public buildings of Rome.

which provided high moral ideals for the *élite*, but which was incapable of influencing the mass of society.

The true religion of society was not the philosophic paganism of men like Marcus Aurelius or St. Augustine's correspondent, Maximus of Madaura, but the cult of material pleasure and success. Christianity had more to fear from Trimalchio than from Julian, and the real Antichrist was not Apollo, but Belial, "the prince of this world." And this is fully recognised by the majority of Christian writers from the time of St. Paul down to the fifth century. St. Augustine himself, in a well-known chapter of *The City of God,* reveals the naked materialism which lay behind the opposition of pagan society to Christianity, and shows that it was as irreconcilable with the old Roman traditions as with Christian teaching. Its ideal was not civic virtue and patriotism, but to have a good time and bigger and better shows. "They do not trouble," he writes, "about the moral degradation of the Empire; all that they ask is that it should be prosperous and secure. 'What concerns us,' they say, 'is that everyone should be able to increase his wealth so that he can afford a lavish expenditure and can keep the weaker in subjection. Let the poor serve the rich for the sake of their bellies and so that they can live in idleness under their protection, and let the rich use the poor as dependants and to enhance their prestige. . . . Let the laws protect the rights of property and leave men's morals alone. Let there be plenty of public prostitutes for whosoever wants them, above all for those who cannot afford to keep mistresses of their own. Let there be gorgeous palaces and sumptuous banquets, where anybody can play and drink and gorge himself and be dissipated by day or night, as much as he pleases or is able. Let the noise of dancing be everywhere, and let the theatres resound with lewd merriment and with every kind of cruel and vicious pleasure. Let the man who dislikes these pleasures be regarded as a public enemy, and if he tries to interfere with them, let the mob be free to hound him to death. But as for the rulers who devote themselves to giving the people a good time, let them be treated as gods and worshipped accordingly. Only let them take care that neither war nor plague nor any other calamity interfere with this reign of prosperity.'"[3]

---

3. Condensed from *De Civitate Dei,* II, xx; cf. *Ep.* cxxxviii, 3, 14.

This indictment of the spirit of hedonism and materialism which dominated Roman society runs through all the writings of the Fathers and is supported by many non-Christian writers. Even allowing for the exaggerations of the moralist, there can be little doubt of its substantial truth. Nor was this spirit confined to great cities such as Rome and Antioch and Carthage; it was also characteristic of provincial society, as St. Jerome testifies in a characteristic sentence[4] about his own countrymen. It is a mistake to suppose that the age of the Empire was a religious one because it was marked by so many new religious movements. The mystery religions and the tendency towards mysticism and asceticism are a proof of the religious bankruptcy of society which drove the religious-minded to seek spiritual life outside the life of the city and of society in an esoteric ideal of individual salvation. Even Stoicism, the one sect of the time which inculcated a disinterested ideal of social duty, was fundamentally an unsocial and individualistic creed. The reigning culture had become almost completely secularised, and the religious and the social instincts were becoming opposed to one another.

The one exception to this tendency is to be found in the Jewish tradition, and that was the one religious tradition which had preserved its independence in face of the cosmopolitan Hellenistic culture. The attempt of the Seleucid kings to Hellenise Judaea had led to the great national rising of the Maccabean period, which was nothing less than a crusade against Hellenism, and though the Roman Empire succeeded in breaking down the material resistance of the nation, it could not overcome their spiritual opposition. The Jews remained a people apart, and refused to submit to the dominant culture or to share in the life of the city. The primitive Church inherited this tradition. The Christians claimed, no less than the Jews, to be a people apart—"a chosen race, a royal priesthood, a holy nation." But this claim no longer involved any political aspirations. Throughout the centuries of persecution the Christians remained faithful to the teachings of St. Peter and St. Paul and submitted to the imperial government as a power ordained of God. St. Clement's noble prayer on behalf of princes and rulers would not be out of place in the altered circumstances of a Christian society.

---

4. *"In mea enim patria, rusticitatis vernacula, deus venter est et dedie vivitur, sanctior est ille qui ditior est."—Ep.* vii, 5.

But this political loyalty to the Empire as a state only throws into stronger relief the irreconcilable hostility of Christianity to the imperial culture. The Church was to a great extent an alternative and a substitute for the communal life of the city-state. It appealed to all those elements which failed to find satisfaction in the material prosperity of the dominant culture—the unprivileged classes, the poor and the oppressed, the subject oriental populations, and above all those who were dissatisfied with the materialism and sensuality of pagan society and who felt the need for a living religion on which to base their lives.

Consequently, it was inevitable that Christianity should come into conflict with the pagan government and society. To the ordinary man the Christian was an antisocial atheist, "an enemy of the human race," who cut himself off from everything that made life worth living. To the authorities he was a centre of passive disaffection, a disloyal subject who would not take his share of the public service or pay homage to the emperor. The Christian, on his part, regarded the official worship of the emperor as a supreme act of blasphemy—the deification of material power and the setting up of the creature in place of the Creator. So long as the Empire confined itself to its secular function as the guardian of peace and order, the Church was ready to recognise it as the representative of God, but as soon as it claimed an exclusive allegiance and attempted to dominate the souls as well as the bodies of its subjects, the Church condemned it as the representative of Antichrist. Thus the denunciations of the Apocalypse are as integral a part of the Christian attitude to the Empire as St. Paul's doctrine of loyal submission. To St. John the official cultus of the emperor, as organised in the province of Asia, is the worship of the Beast, and Rome herself, the *Dea Roma* of the state religion, is the great harlot enthroned upon the waters, drunken with the blood of the saints and the blood of the martyrs of Jesus. It is, however, important to notice that Rome is not described as a conquering military power, but as the centre of a luxurious cosmopolitan culture, the great market in which all the merchants of the earth congregate. It is the triumphant materialism of Rome, not her military and political oppression, which is denounced in the Apocalypse.

Nothing can give a more vivid impression of the failure of material civilisation to satisfy the needs of the human soul than St. John's vision of the arraignment of the great heathen world power before the eternal justice by the souls of its innocent victims. Ancient civilisation had set itself in opposition to the religious spirit and had alienated the deepest forces in the mind of the age, and thereby its ultimate doom was sealed. There is a remarkable passage in one of the sermons of St. Gregory in which he looks back from the disorder and misery of the age in which he lived to the material prosperity of the world in which the martyrs had suffered. In his own days the world seemed dying. "Everywhere death, everywhere mourning, everywhere desolation." In the age of Trajan, on the contrary, "there was long life and health, material prosperity, growth of population and the tranquillity of daily peace, yet while the world was still flourishing in itself, in their hearts it had already withered."[5] *In cordibus aruerat*—that was the innermost secret of the fall of ancient civilisation. It had lost its roots in the human soul and was growing more and more empty and sterile. The vital centre of the society of the future was to be found, not in the city-state, but in the Christian *ecclesia*.

Are we, then, to conclude with Renan that the rise of Christianity was the real cause of the decline of the Empire—that "Christianity was a vampire which sucked the life-blood of ancient society and produced that state of general enervation against which patriotic emperors struggled in vain."[6] Certainly the victory of Christianity does mark a most profound and vital aspect of the decline of the old culture, but it does not follow that it was directly responsible for it. The cosmopolitan urban culture of the later Empire broke down through its own inherent weaknesses, and even before the victory of Christianity it had already failed to justify itself on sociological and economic grounds.

In spite of its apparent prosperity and its brilliant outward appearance, the vast development of city life under the Empire was out of all proportion to its real strength. It was an elaborate superstructure built on relatively weak and unstable foundations. For the urban civilisation of the imperial age was essentially the civilisation of a leisured class, a society of consumers, which rested on a foundation of slave labour and rural serfdom. The vast civic expenditure on public buildings and

5. St. Gregory, *Hom.* xxviii.
6. Renan: *Marc-Aurèle*, p. 589.

public games was unproductive and entailed an increasing drain on the economic resources of the Empire. And at the same time the process of urbanisation led to a similar exhaustion of human resources. For the citizen class was extremely sterile and had to be constantly recruited by new elements usually drawn from the class of freedmen. Moreover, neither the upper nor the lower classes of the city provided suitable military material, and the Empire came to rely more and more on the rural population, especially the natives of the recently conquered and less-civilised provinces, for its supply of troops.[7]

The Roman Empire and the process of urbanisation which accompanied it were, in fact, a vast system of exploitation which organised the resources of the provinces and concentrated them in the hands of a privileged class. The system worked well so long as the Empire was expanding, for there was no lack of new territory to urbanise and new masses of cheap slave labour with which to cultivate it. But the close of the period of external expansion and internal peace at the end of the second century put an end to this state of things and the Empire was left with diminishing resources to face the growing menace of external invasion and internal disruption. In spite of its apparent wealth and splendour, the urban society of the Empire had no reserve forces either of men or of money, and it was unable to face the crisis. The wealthy provincial bourgeoisie, which had been the backbone of the Empire in the second century, was financially ruined and lost its hold on the government. Power passed to the soldiery, who belonged by origin to the peasant class and had no sympathy with the civic tradition.[8]

Thus the third century witnessed a social and constitutional revolution of the most far-reaching kind. The great break in the history of the ancient world—the end of the old society and the inauguration of a new order—took place not in the age of St. Augustine, when the barbarians conquered the Western provinces and the unity of the Empire was destroyed, but more than a century earlier, in the age of military anarchy which followed the fall of the house of Severus. When the

---

7. Cf. Rostovtzeff: *Social and Economic History of the Roman Empire* (1926), pp. 332–3.

8. According to Rostovtzeff (*op. cit.*, ch. xi), the motive force of this revolution is to be found in the class conflict between the peasant soldiery and the urban bourgeoisie, which he compares to the class conflict of bourgeois and proletariat in our own times.

Illyrian soldier-emperors succeeded in stemming the tide of anarchy and beating back the enemies of Rome, the Empire which they re-established was no longer the same state. The old civic society was moribund, and neither the Senate, nor the Italian citizen body, nor the provincial city-state, was any longer strong enough to form a satisfactory basis of government and administration. Only the army and the imperial power itself had survived as living forces. But the emperor was not only the first magistrate of the Roman republic, he was also the representative of the great Hellenistic monarchies which had themselves inherited the absolutist traditions of the oriental state. In the East, and above all in Egypt, the organisation of society was entirely different from that of the Graeco-Roman world. Instead of a free citizen class, based on slave labour, practically the whole population consisted either of serfs or officials and priests. The institutions of the city-state, private property and slavery hardly existed. The whole economic life of Egypt was directly controlled by the state, and every class was bound to its special task. It was, in fact, a great system of state socialism, in which the state was the one landowner and organised the manufacture and distribution of goods by means of state monopolies and state factories and warehouses.

It was from this source that the new principles were derived on which Diocletian and his successors based their work of reorganisation. The imperial office itself acquired the characteristics of an oriental kingdom. The emperor ceased to be primarily the *princeps* of the Roman state and the commander-in-chief of the Roman armies and became a sacred monarch surrounded by the ceremonial and solemn ritual of an oriental Court. "The Sacred Palace" became the centre of government and the apex of a vast official hierarchy. The Empire was no longer a federation of city-states, each of which was a self-governing unit, but a centralised bureaucratic state which controlled the life of its members down to the minutest detail. Society was based on the principle of compulsory state service, and every class and occupation was subjected to state regulation and tended to become a fixed hereditary caste. The trades which were most essential to the public service, especially those connected with the food supply, were organised as hereditary guilds which were corporately responsible for the fulfilment of their obligations. The same principle was applied even more strictly to the land, on which the state depended in the last resort alike for its food supply and its revenue. Consequently the government did all in its power to prevent land going out of cultivation. The peasant, whether a slave or a freeman, was bound to his holding and was forbidden to abandon its cultivation or to migrate elsewhere. If a holding became derelict, and no owner could be found, the neighbouring land-holders were jointly responsible for its cultivation and taxes. In the same way, the members of the citizen class became corporately liable for the payment of taxes on the whole city territory, and were bound to their curia—their town council—just as the peasant was bound to his land, so that a citizen who attempted to escape his financial burdens by entering the army or migrating elsewhere was liable to be arrested and sent back to his *curia* like a runaway slave.

Under these conditions the old civic ideal of the leisured classes passed away and was replaced by that of the servile state. The urban aristocracy lost its economic prosperity and its social prestige, and its place was taken by the members of the official hierarchy and by the great landowners who stood outside the *curia* and who were strong enough to hold their own against the exactions of the tax-gatherers and the oppression of the bureaucracy. Society tended more and more to return to an agrarian foundation, and the city-state was no longer the vital centre of the whole social structure, as it had been during the eight classical centuries of Mediterranean culture.

But this social revolution involved no less fundamental changes in the relations of the Empire to religion. The old official cultus was essentially bound up with the institutions of the city-state, and now that these had lost their vitality the state was in danger of being left without any religious foundation. The new unitary state required a religion of a more universal character than the polytheistic cults of the city-state possessed, and, as a matter of fact, we observe throughout the third century a tendency towards a vague semi-philosophic monotheism in pagan society.[9] This tendency finds expression in the worship of the

---

9. Cf. especially the hymn of the army of Licinius to the *Summus Deus* which has been preserved by Lactantius: *De mort. persecut.* xlvi, 6.

sun, which was adopted by Aurelian and his successors as the tutelary deity of the Empire. No doubt it owed much to Syrian and Persian influences, but we see in the writings of Julian[10] how easily it adapted itself to the ideals of contemporary philosophic speculation and how well suited it was to serve as a principle of inspiration in the religious life of the age and as the official cult of the new orientalised monarchy.

Nevertheless, this solution was not destined to prevail. For Constantine, instead of contenting himself with the vague solar monotheism which had been the religion of his house, made an abrupt break with tradition and found a new religious basis for the Empire in an alliance with the outlawed and persecuted Christian Church. It was an act of extraordinary courage, and it is not altogether surprising that many historians, from the time of Gibbon to Ferdinand Lot in our day, should regard it as an act of madness which endangered the stability of the Empire by sacrificing the interests of the most loyal and influential part of the citizens in order to conciliate an unpatriotic minority. Yet it is possible that Constantine, even as a statesman, was more farsighted than his critics. The Church was the one living creative force in the social and spiritual life of the age. It brought to society just those elements of freedom, private initiative and cooperative action of which the Empire itself stood most in need.

The life had gone out of the civic organisation, and citizenship meant little more than the obligation to pay taxes. The citizenship of the future was to be found in the Church. It was a far wider citizenship than that of the old city-state, since it was open to all, even to the slave, and the poor enjoyed a specially privileged position. They were the *plebs Christi*, the people of Christ, and the wealth of the Church was in a very real sense "the patrimony of the poor." In the same way the functions of the city magistrate as the representative and protector of the people passed to the magistrate of the new society—the Christian bishop. While the former had become a mere puppet in the hands of the bureaucracy, the latter was the one independent power in the society of the later Empire. The choice of the bishop was the last right which the people preserved, and we know from countless instances

10. *Oratio* iv.

how eagerly they availed themselves of it. A man who had the gift of leadership and who was trusted by the people was liable to be elected, whether he wished it or not. In the case of St. Ambrose we see a high secular official, who was not even baptised, being chosen bishop of the most important see in North Italy by popular acclamation and ordained in spite of his personal wishes. Even more strange is the case of Synesius, a Neo-platonist and a man of letters, who was chosen bishop of Ptolemais in Lybia mainly on account of his patriotism and as a bold defender of the rights of his fellow-citizens.[11]

The Christian bishop was, in fact, the dominant figure in the life of the time. His position was something entirely new, for which no precedent can be found in the old religion of the city-state or in the priesthoods of the oriental mystery religions. Not only did he possess enormous religious prestige as the head of the Christian Church, but he was the leader of the people in social matters also. He occupied the position of a popular tribune, whose duty it was to defend the poor and the oppressed and to see that the strong did not abuse their power. He alone stood between the people and the oppression of the bureaucracy. He was not afraid to withstand an unjust law or to excommunicate an oppressive governor, and the life and correspondence of St. Ambrose or St. Basil or Synesius or St. Augustine himself show how frequently a bishop was called upon to intervene between the government and the people, and how fearlessly he performed his duty. On one occasion it is recorded that the praetorian prefect was so offended by St. Basil's freedom of speech that he declared that he had never in his life been spoken to in such, a manner. "No doubt," replied St. Basil, "you have never met a bishop."

In the same way, it was the bishop rather than the city magistrate. who inherited the civic tradition of popular oratory. While the Forum and the Agora were silent, the Churches resounded to the applause and exclamations of crowds who were still swayed by the voice of the orator. In St. John Chrysostom's homilies *On the Statues,* delivered to the

---

11. In the case of St. Augustine's successor we have an instance of a more regular and ecclesiastical type of election, and the report of the proceedings which has been preserved in St. Augustine's letters (ccxiii) shows how closely the procedure resembled that of a civic assembly.

people of Antioch when the fate of their city hung in the balance, we hear the last echo of the great Hellenic tradition of oratory which goes back to the golden age of Athenian democracy. And if the sermons of St. Augustine lack the classical grace of his great Syrian contemporary, they are no less interesting as examples of genuine popular oratory adapted to the simpler and less refined tastes of an ordinary provincial audience.

The Church was also taking the place of the state as the organiser of charity and of the support of the poor. Every church had its *matriculum,* or list of persons in receipt of regular relief, and enormous sums were spent in every kind of charitable work. All over the Empire, hospitals, orphanages and hostels for travellers were being built and endowed; so that the basilica was often the centre of a whole quarter which lived by and for the Church. Thus the Church stands out in this dark age as the one hope of humanity both spiritually and materially. It saved the individual from being entirely crushed under the pressure of the servile state, and it opened to him a new world of social and spiritual activity in which the free personality had room to develop itself.

Hence, when the final collapse of the imperial government in the West took place, the bishop remained the natural leader of the Roman population. He was the representative of the old secular culture as well as of the new spiritual society, and it was through him, above all, that the continuity of Western civilisation was preserved.

> *Comme aux jours de scandales*
> *Un vieil évêque en sa ville assiégée*
> *Par des Alains, des Goths ou des Vandales*
>
> . . . . .
>
> *Son esprit las porte un double fardeau*
> *Derrière lui sur le mur noir et froid*
> *La vieille louve allaite lesjumeaux*
>
> *Et devant lui Jésus meurt sur la croix.*[12]

In the fourth century, however, these diverse traditions were still far from being completely reconciled with one another. There were, in

12. R. Salomé: *Notre Pays,* p. 52.

fact, three distinct elements—and even three distinct societies—in the culture of the later Empire.

There was the new religious society of the Christian Church, with its tradition of independent spiritual authority; there was the city-state, with its Hellenistic traditions of intellectual and material culture; and there was the Empire itself, which more and more was coming to represent the oriental tradition of sacred monarchy and bureaucratic collectivism. The Church no longer held itself entirely aloof from secular society, but it had not yet succeeded in Christianising it. The civic culture remained pagan in spirit and, to a great extent, in outward form. But while the Church remained hostile to the paganism and immorality of civic life, as seen above all in the public shows and the games of the amphitheatre, she could not refuse to recognise the value of the classical tradition in its intellectual aspects. The Fathers were, almost without exception, men who had passed through the schools of rhetoric and whose minds were steeped in classical literature. St. Basil and St. Gregory Nazianzen had studied at the university of Athens, the centre of pagan culture; St. John Chrysostom was the most brilliant pupil of Libanius, the greatest heathen professor of his time; St. Augustine was himself a professional teacher of rhetoric; while St. Jerome is, of all his generation, the most typical representative of the rhetorical tradition in all its strength and weakness.

Consequently the patristic culture is a blend of Christian and classical elements. The writings of St. Ambrose are as full of reminiscences of the classics as those of a Renaissance scholar. The two Apollinarii, St. Gregory Nazianzen, Paulinus and Prudentius did their best to create a Christian literature based upon classical models. It is true that in the case of St. Augustine we see a gradual evolution from the Christian humanism of Cassiciacum to the anti-Pelagian severity of his later years. But it is easy to exaggerate the change, since he continued to realise the educational value of classical literature and to acknowledge his sympathy with the Platonic tradition. Nor must we attach too much importance to the famous vision in which St. Jerome was condemned as "a Ciceronian and not a Christian." After all, as he himself observed, when Rufinus taxed him with inconsistency, it was only a dream, and in spite of his visionary experience he ultimately returned to his Plato and Cicero.

This fusion of the old culture with the new religion was of incalculable importance for the future of Europe. Although the secular culture of the ancient city passed away with the city itself, the patristic culture lived on in the Church. The course of studies which St. Augustine had described in his treatise *On Christian Doctrine* became the programme of the monastic schools, and bore fruit in men like Bede and Alcuin. Thanks to the work of the Fathers and of their age, the mediaeval world never entirely lost touch with the tradition of ancient civilisation.

In the same way the relations between the Church and the imperial order were becoming more intimate in this period. Although the Church condemned the cruelty and the oppression of the weak which were so prevalent during the later Empire, she was wholly favourable to the principles of authority and hierarchy on which the imperial order was based. The ideal of a world state which should secure universal peace and the reign of law was thoroughly in harmony with Christian principles; indeed, the political unity of the world empire seemed to be the natural counterpart of the spiritual unity of the Catholic Church. Hence we find a new attitude to the Empire in the Christian literature of the fifth century—an appreciation of the positive services which Rome had rendered to the cause of humanity and a realisation of the common unity of Roman civilisation—*Romania,* to use Orosius's expression—as something greater and more permanent than even the political structure of the imperial state. At the beginning of the fifth century the Spaniard Prudentius already anticipates Dante's belief in the providential mission of the Roman Empire as a preparation for the world religion of Christianity. "In all parts of the world," he writes, "men live to-day as members of the same city and children of the same hearth. Justice, the forum, commerce, the arts and marriage unite the inhabitants of the most distant shores; from the mingling of so many different bloods, a single race is born. Such is the fruit of the victories and triumphs of the Roman Empire: thus has the road been prepared for the coming of Christ."[13]

---

13. Prudentius: *Contra Symmachum,* 582–91. Cf. *Peristephanon,* II, 419 *seq.* The same idea appears in the anonymous *De Vocatione Gentium,* II, xvi, and is developed at greater length by St. Leo, *Sermo* lxxxi. It had, however, already appeared in the East, though in a less specifically Roman form, in the writings of Eusebius (esp. *Theophany,* III, i–ii) and in the Apology of Melito of Sardis.

But this new far-seeing spirit of Christian patriotism was confined to a small aristocratic circle, to men of letters like Prudentius and Paulinus of Nola. The average man who felt the heavy hand of the tax-gatherer and the quartermaster could not take so wide a view. The pessimism and defeatism of Salvian is no doubt inspired by moral preoccupations, but he also expresses the criticism and discontent which were widespread in the society of the time. The Church, as the representative of the poor and the oppressed, could not be a wholehearted supporter of the existing order. In the West, at least, the adherents of the old religion still claimed to be the true representatives of the national Roman tradition, and attributed all the misfortunes of the Empire to its abandonment of the service of the gods. It was natural that patriotic Romans, like Symmachus, should feel that the destinies of Rome were inseparably bound up with the religion of Numa and Augustus. To them the new religion, like the new capital, was an oriental *parvenu,* fit only for slaves and foreigners. A true Roman, they felt, could not abandon the temples and altars which had become doubly sacred from their glorious past.

In fact, even at the end of the fourth century the situation of Christianity in the West was still not altogether secure. Many of the highest positions in the Empire were in the hands of pagans, and the prætorian prefect, Flavian Nicomachus, took advantage of the revolt of Arbogast and Eugenius in 392–394 to reinstitute pagan worship and to reconsecrate the city by a solemn lustral purification. Moreover, the events which followed the victory of Theodosius only served to justify the criticism of the pagans. The reign of the miserable Honorius witnessed a continuous series of disasters, and if, as Claudian hoped, the conservative party could have found an able leader in the person of Stilicho, it is possible that there might have been yet another pagan reaction.

But this was not to be. Stilicho fell, and his fall was followed by that of Rome itself. To pagan and Christian alike it seemed the end of all things—in St. Jerome's words, "the light of the world was put out and the head of the Empire was cut off." It is true that Alaric's raid on Rome was not in itself decisive; it was an episode in a long-drawn-out tragedy. Every year the tide of barbarism rose higher and fresh territories were overwhelmed. It is the tendency of modern historians to

minimise the importance of the invasions, but it is difficult to exaggerate the horror and suffering which they involved. It was not war as we
understand it, but brigandage on a vast scale exercised upon an unwar-
like and almost defenceless population. It meant the sack of cities, the
massacre and enslavement of the population and the devastation of the
open country. In Macedonia the Roman envoys to Attila in 448 found
the once populous city of Naissus empty save for the dead, and they
were forced to camp outside. In Africa, if a city refused to surrender,
the Vandals would drive their captives up to the walls and slaughter
them in masses so that the stench of their corpses should render the
defences untenable.

"The mind shudders," wrote St. Jerome, "when dwelling on the ruin
of our day. For twenty years and more Roman blood has been flowing
ceaselessly over the broad countries between Constantinople and the
Julian Alps, where the Goths, the Huns and the Vandals spread ruin
and death. . . . How many Roman nobles have been their prey! How
many matrons and maidens have fallen victims to their lust! Bishops
live in prison, priests and clerics fall by the sword, churches are plun-
dered, Christ's altars are turned into feeding-troughs, the remains of
the martyrs are thrown out of their coffins. On every side sorrow, on
every side lamentation, everywhere the image of death."[14]

And this was in 396, when the storm was only beginning. It was
to last, not for decades, but for generations, until the very memory of
peace was gone. It was no ordinary political catastrophe, but "a day of
the Lord" such as the Hebrew prophets describe, a judgment of the nations in which a whole civilisation and social order which had failed to
justify their existence were rooted up and thrown into the fire.

. . . . .

It was in this age of ruin and distress that St. Augustine lived and
worked. To the materialist, nothing could be more futile than the spectacle of Augustine busying himself with the reunion of the African
Church and the refutation of the Pelagians, while civilisation was falling to pieces about his ears. It would seem like the activity of an ant
which works on while its nest is being destroyed. But St. Augustine

14. *Ep.* lx; cf. *Ep.* cxxiii, written in 409 on the destruction of Gaul.

saw things otherwise. To him the ruin of civilisation and the destruction of the Empire were not very important things. He looked beyond the aimless and bloody chaos of history to the world of eternal realities from which the world of sense derives all the significance which it possesses. His thoughts were fixed, not on the fate of the city of Rome or the city of Hippo, nor on the struggle of Roman and barbarian, but on those other cities which have their foundations in heaven and in hell, and on the warfare between "the world-rulers of the dark æon" and the princes of light. And, in fact, though the age of St. Augustine ended in ruin and though the Church of Africa, in the service of which he spent his life, was destined to be blotted out as completely as if it had never been, he was justified in his faith. The spirit of Augustine continued to live and bear fruit long after Christian Africa had ceased to exist. It entered into the tradition of the Western Church and moulded the thought of Western Christendom so that our very civilisation bears the imprint of his genius. However far we have travelled since the fifth century and however much we have learnt from other teachers, the work of St. Augustine still remains an inalienable part of our spiritual heritage.

II. THE CITY OF GOD

But you are come to Mount Sion, and to the city of the living God, the heavenly Jerusalem, and to the company of many thousands of angels, and to the assembly of the first-born, who are written in the heavens, and to God the Judge of all, and to the spirits of the just made perfect. . . .

Hebrews xii, 22–3.

St. Augustine's work *The City of God* was inspired by the circumstances described in the last chapter. It was, like all his books, a *livre de circonstance,* written with a definitely controversial aim in response to a particular need. But during the fourteen years—from 412 to 426—during which he was engaged upon it, the work developed from a controversial pamphlet into a vast synthesis which embraces the history of the whole human race and its destinies in time and eternity. It is the one great work of Christian antiquity which professedly deals with the relation of the state and of human society in general to Christian principles; and consequently it has had an incalculable influence on the development of European thought. Alike to Orosius and to Charlemagne, to Gregory I and Gregory VII, to St. Thomas and Bossuet, it remained the classical expression of Christian political thought and of the Christian attitude to history. And in modern times it has not lost its importance. It is the only one among the writings of the Fathers which the secular historian never altogether neglects, and throughout the nineteenth century it was generally regarded as justifying the right of St. Augustine to be treated as the founder of the philosophy of history.

Of late years, however, there had been a tendency, especially in Germany, to challenge this claim and to criticise St. Augustine's method as fundamentally anti-historical, since it interprets history according to a rigid theological scheme and regards the whole process of human development as predetermined by timeless and changeless transcendental principles.[15] Certainly *The City of God* is not a philosophical theory of history in the sense of rational induction from historical facts. St. Augustine does not discover anything from history, but merely sees in history the working out of universal principles. But we may well question whether Hegel or any of the nineteenth-century philosophers of history did otherwise. They did not derive their theories from history, but read their philosophy into history.

What St. Augustine does give us is a synthesis of universal history in the light of Christian principles. His theory of history is strictly deduced from his theory of human nature, which, in turn, follows necessarily from his theology of creation and grace. In so far as it begins and ends in revealed dogma, it is not a rational theory, but it is rational in the strict logic of its procedure and it involves a definitely rational and philosophic theory of the nature of society and law and of the relation of social life to ethics.

Herein consists its originality, since it unites in a coherent system two distinct intellectual traditions which had hitherto proved irreconcilable. The Hellenic world possessed a theory of society and a po-

---

15. *E.g.*, H. Grundmann: *Studien über Joachim von Floris* (1927), pp. 74–5; cf. also H. Scholz: *Glaube und Unglaube in der Weltgeschichte* (1911).

litical philosophy, but it had never arrived at a philosophy of history. The Greek mind tended towards cosmological rather than historical speculation. In the Greek view of things, Time had little significance or value. It was the bare "number of movement," an unintelligible element which intruded itself into reality in consequence of the impermanence and instability of sensible things. Consequently, it could possess no ultimate or spiritual meaning. It is intelligible only in so far as it is regular—that is to say, tending to a recurrent identity. And this element of recurrence is due to the influence of the heavenly bodies, those eternal and divine existences whose movement imparts to this lower world all that it has of order and intelligibility.

Consequently, in so far as human history consists of unique and individual events it is unworthy of science and philosophy. Its value is to be found only in that aspect of it which is independent of time— in the ideal character of the hero, the ideal wisdom of the sage, and the ideal order of the good commonwealth. The only spiritual meaning that history possesses is to be found in the examples that it gives of moral virtue or political wisdom or their opposites. Like Greek art, Greek history created a series of classical types which were transmitted as a permanent possession to later antiquity. Certainly Greece had its philosophical historians, such as Thucydides and, above all, Polybius, but to them also the power which governs history is an external necessity—Nemesis or Tyche—which lessens rather than increases the intrinsic importance of human affairs.

The Christian, on the other hand, possessed no philosophy of society or politics, but he had a theory of history. The time element, in his view of the world, was all-important. The idea, so shocking to the Hellenic mind or to that of the modern rationalist, that God intervenes in history and that a small and uncultured Semitic people had been made the vehicle of an absolute divine purpose, was to him the very centre and basis of his faith. Instead of the theogonies and mythologies which were the characteristic forms of expression in Greek and oriental religion, Christianity from the first based its teaching on a *sacred history*.[16]

Moreover, this history was not merely a record of past events; it

16. Cf. for example, the speech of Stephen in *Acts* vii.

was conceived as the revelation of a divine plan which embraced all ages and peoples. As the Hebrew prophets had already taught that the changes of secular history, the rise and fall of kingdoms and nations, were designed to serve God's ultimate purpose in the salvation of Israel and the establishment of His Kingdom, so the New Testament teaches that the whole Jewish dispensation was itself a stage in the divine plan, and that the barrier between Jew and Gentile was now to be removed so that humanity might be united in an organic spiritual unity.[17] The coming of Christ is the turning-point of history. It marks "the fullness of times,"[18] the coming of age of humanity and the fulfilment of the cosmic purpose. Henceforward mankind had entered on a new phase. The old things had passed away and all things were become new.

Consequently the existing order of things had no finality for the Christian. The kingdoms of the world were judged and their ultimate doom was sealed. The building had been condemned and the mine which was to destroy it was laid, though the exact moment of the explosion was uncertain. The Christian had to keep his eyes fixed on the future like a servant who waits for the return of his master. He had to detach himself from the present order and prepare himself for the coming of the Kingdom.

Now from the modern point of view this may seem to destroy the meaning of history no less effectively than the Hellenic view of the insignificance of time. As Newman writes, "When once the Christ had come . . . nothing remained but to gather in His Saints. No higher Priest could come, no truer doctrine. The Light and Life of men had appeared and had suffered and had risen again; and nothing more was left to do. Earth had had its most solemn event, and seen its most august sight; and therefore it was the last time. And hence, though time intervene between Christ's first and second coming, it is not *recognised* (as I may say) in the Gospel Scheme, but is, as it were, an accident. . . . When He says that He will come soon, 'soon' is not a word of time but of natural order. This present state of things, 'the present distress,' as

---

17. *Eph.* ii.

18. St. Paul uses two expressions (*Gal.* iv, 4, and *Eph.* i, 10): πλήρωμα τοῦ χρόνου — the fullness of time in respect of man's age, and πλήρωμα τῶν καιρῶν — the completion of the cycle of seasons. Cf. Prat: *Theologie de S. Paul* (second edition), II, 151.

St. Paul calls it, is ever *close upon* the next world and resolves itself into it."[19]

But, on the other hand, although the kingdom for which the Christian hoped was a spiritual and eternal one, it was not a kind of abstract Nirvana, it was a real kingdom which was to be the crown and culmination of history and the realisation of the destiny of the human race. Indeed, it was often conceived in a temporal and earthly form; for the majority of the early Fathers interpreted the Apocalypse in a literal sense and believed that Christ would reign with His saints on earth for a thousand years before the final judgment.[20] So vivid and intense was this expectation that the new Jerusalem seemed already hovering over the earth in readiness for its descent, and Tertullian records how the soldiers of Severus's army had seen its walls on the horizon, shining in the light of dawn, for forty days, as they marched through Palestine. Such a state of mind might easily lead, as it did in the case of Tertullian, to the visionary fanaticism of Montanism. But even in its excesses it was less dangerous to orthodoxy than the spiritualistic theosophy of the Gnostics, which dissolved the whole historical basis of Christianity, and consequently it was defended by apologists, such as Justin Martyr and Irenaeus, as a bulwark of the concrete reality of the Christian hope.

Moreover, all Christians, whether they were millenniarists or not, believed that they already possessed a pledge and foretaste of the future kingdom in the Church. They were not, like the other religious bodies of the time, a group of individuals united by common beliefs and a common worship, they were a true people. All the wealth of historical associations and social emotion which was contained in the Old Testament had been separated from its national and racial limitations and transferred to the new international spiritual community. Thereby the Church acquired many of the characteristics of a political society; that is to say, Christians possessed a real social tradition of their own and a kind of patriotism which was distinct from that of the secular state in which they lived.

19. *Parochial Sermons*, VI, xvii.
20. Tixeront: *Histoire des Dogmes* I, 217 ff. On millenniarism at Rome in the third century cf. d'Alès: *La Théologie de S. Hippolyte*, v.

This social dualism is one of the most striking characteristics of early Christianity. Indeed, it is characteristic of Christianity in general; for the idea of the two societies and the twofold citizenship is found nowhere else in the same form. It entered deeply into St. Augustine's thought and supplied the fundamental theme of *The City of God*. In fact, St. Augustine's idea of the two cities is no new discovery, but a direct inheritance from tradition. In its early Christian form, however, this dualism was much simpler and more concrete than it afterwards became. The mediaeval problem of the co-existence of the two societies and the two authorities within the unity of the Christian people was yet to arise. Instead there was the abrupt contrast of two opposing orders—the Kingdom of God and the kingdom of this world—the present age and the age to come. The Empire was the society of the past, and the Church was the society of the future, and, though they met and mingled physically, there was no spiritual contact between them. It is true, as we have seen, that the Christian recognised the powers of this world as ordained by God and observed a strict but passive obedience to the Empire. But this loyalty to the state was purely external. It simply meant, as St. Augustine says, that the Church during her commixture with Babylon must recognise the external order of the earthly state which was to the advantage of both *utamur et nos sua pace.*[21]

Hence there could be no bond of spiritual fellowship or common citizenship between the members of the two societies. In his relations with the state and secular society the Christian felt himself to be an alien—*peregrinus;* his true citizenship was in the Kingdom of Heaven. Tertullian writes, "Your citizenship, your magistracies and the very name of your *curia* is the Church of Christ. . . . We are called away even from dwelling in this Babylon of the Apocalypse, how much more from sharing in its pomps? . . . For you are an alien in this world, and a citizen of the city of Jerusalem that is above."[22]

It is true that Tertullian was a rigorist, but in this respect, at any rate, his attitude does not differ essentially from that of St. Cyprian or of the earlier tradition in general. There was, however, a growing tendency in

---

21. *De Civitate Dei,* XIX, xxvi. "That the peace of God's enemies is useful to the piety of His friends as long as their earthly pilgrimage lasts." Cf. also *ibid.,* xvii.
22. *De Corona,* xiii.

the third century for Christians to enter into closer relations with the outer world and to assimilate Greek thought and culture. This culminated in Origen's synthesis of Christianity and Hellenism, which had a profound influence, not only on theology, but also on the social and political attitude of Christians. Porphyry remarks that "though Origen was a Christian in his manner of life, he was an Hellene in his religious thought and surreptitiously introduced Greek ideas into alien myths."

This is, of course, the exaggeration of a hostile critic; nevertheless, it is impossible to deny that Origen is completely Greek in his attitude to history and cosmology. He broke entirely, not only with the millenniarist tradition, but also with the concrete realism of Christian eschatology, and substituted in its place the cosmological speculations of later Greek philosophy. The Kingdom of God was conceived by him in a metaphysical sense as the realm of spiritual reality—the supersensuous and intelligible world. The historical facts of Christian revelation consequently tended to lose their unique value and became the symbols of higher immaterial realities—a kind of Christian *Mythos*. In place of the *sacred history* of humanity from the Fall to the Redemption we have a vast cosmic drama like that of the Gnostic systems, in which the heavenly spirits fall from their immaterial bliss into the bondage of matter, or into the form of demons. Salvation consists not in the redemption of the body, but in the liberation of the soul from the bondage of matter and its gradual return through the seven planetary heavens to its original home. Consequently, there is no longer any real unity in the human race, since it consists of a number of individual spirits which have become men, so to speak, accidentally in consequence of their own faults in a previous state of existence.

No doubt these ideas are not the centre of Origen's faith. They are counterbalanced by his orthodoxy of intention and his desire to adhere to Catholic tradition. Nevertheless, they inevitably produced a new attitude to the Church and a new view of its relation to humanity. The traditional conception of the Church as an objective society, the new Israel, and the forerunner of the Kingdom of God fell into the background as compared with a more intellectualist view of the Church as the teacher of an esoteric doctrine or *gnosis* which leads the human soul from time to eternity. Here again Origen is the representative of the

Græco-oriental ideals which found their full expression in the mystery religions.

The result of this change of emphasis was to reduce the opposition which had previously existed between the Church and secular society. Unlike the earlier Fathers, Origen was quite prepared to admit the possibility of a general conversion of the Empire, and in his work against Celsus he paints a glowing picture of the advantages that the Empire would enjoy if it was united in one great "City of God" under the Christian faith. But Origen's City of God, unlike Augustine's, has perhaps more affinity with the world state of the Stoics than with the divine Kingdom of Jewish and Christian prophecy. It found its fulfilment in the Christian Empire of Constantine and his successors, as we can see from the writings of Eusebius of Cæsarea, the greatest representative of the tradition of Origen in the following age.

Eusebius goes further than any of the other Fathers in his rejection of millenniarism and of the old realistic eschatology. For him prophecy finds an adequate fulfilment in the historical circumstances of his own age. The Messianic Kingdom of Isaiah is the Christian Empire, and Constantine himself is the new David, while the new Jerusalem which St. John saw descending from heaven like a bride adorned for her husband means to Eusebius nothing more than the building of the Church of the Holy Sepulchre at Constantine's orders.[23]

Such a standpoint leaves no room for the old Christian and Jewish social dualism. The emperor is not only the leader of the Christian people, his monarchy is the earthly counterpart and reflection of the rule of the Divine Word. As the Word reigns in heaven, so Constantine reigns on earth, purging it from idolatry and error and preparing men's minds to receive the truth. The kingdoms of this world have become the Kingdom of God and of His Christ, and nothing more remains to do this side of eternity.[24]

It is not enough to dismiss all this as mere flattery on the part of a

---

23. *Life of Constantine*, III, xxxiii. So too he applies the passage in *Dan.* vii, 17. ("And the saints of the Most High shall receive the Kingdom") to Dalmatius and Hannibalianus, who were made Caesars by Constantine (*Oration on the Tricennalia of Constantine*, iii).

24. Eusebius develops the parallel at great length in his *Oration on the Tricennalia of Constantine*, ii–x.

courtier prelate. The Eusebian ideal of monarchy has a great philosophical and historical tradition behind it. It goes back, on the one hand, to the Hellenistic theory of kingship, as represented by Dio Chrysostom, and, on the other, to the oriental tradition of sacred monarchy which is as old as civilisation itself. It is true that it is not specifically Christian and it is entirely irreconcilable with the strictly religious attitude of men like Athanasius, who were prepared to sacrifice the unity of the Empire to a theological principle. Nevertheless, it was ultimately destined to triumph, at least in the East, for it finds its fulfilment in the Byzantine Church-state indissolubly united under the rule of an Orthodox emperor.

In the West, however, Christian thought followed an entirely different course of development. At the time when Origen was creating a speculative theology and a philosophy of religion, the attention of the Western Church was concentrated on the concrete problems of its corporate life. From an intellectual point of view the controversies on discipline and Church order which occupied the Western mind seem barren and uninteresting in comparison with the great doctrinal issues which were being debated in the East. But historically they are the proof of a strong social tradition and of an autonomous and vigorous corporate life.

Nowhere was this tradition so strong as in Africa; indeed, so far as its literary and intellectual expression is concerned, Africa was actually the creator of the Western tradition. By far the larger part of Latin Christian literature is African in origin, and the rest of the Latin West produced no writers, save Ambrose and Jerome, who are worthy to be compared with the great African doctors. This, no doubt, was largely due to the fact that Africa possessed a more strongly marked national character than any other Western province. The old Libyo-Phœnicean population had been submerged by the tide of Roman culture, but it still subsisted, and during the later Empire it began to reassert its national individuality in the same way as did the subject nationalities of the Eastern provinces. And, as in Syria and Egypt, this revival of national feeling found an outlet through religious channels. It did not go so far as to create a new vernacular Christian literature, as was the case in Syria, for the old Punic tongue survived mainly among the peasants and the uneducated classes,[25] but though it expressed itself in a Latin medium, its content was far more original and characteristic than that of the Syriac or Coptic literatures.

This is already apparent in the work of Tertullian, perhaps the most original genius whom the Church of Africa ever produced. After the smooth commonplaces of Fronto or the florid preciosity of Apuleius the rhetoric of Tertullian is at once exhilarating and terrific.[26] It is as though one were to go out of a literary *salon* into a thunderstorm. His work is marked by a spirit of fierce and indomitable hostility to the whole tradition of pagan civilisation, both social and intellectual. He has no desire to minimise the opposition between the Church and the Empire, for all his hopes are fixed on the passing of the present order and the coming of the Kingdom of the Saints. Similarly, he has no sympathy with the conciliatory attitude of the Alexandrian School towards Greek philosophy. "What has Athens to do with Jerusalem?" he writes. "What concord is there between the Academy and the Church?" . . . "Our instruction comes from the Porch of Solomon who taught that the Lord should be sought in simplicity of heart. Away with all attempts to produce a mottled Christianity of Stoic, Platonic and dialectic composition. We want no curious disputation after possessing Christ Jesus. . . ."[27]

This uncompromising spirit remained characteristic of the African Church, so that Carthage became the antithesis of Alexandria in the development of Christian thought. It remained a stronghold of the old realistic eschatology and of millenniarist ideas, which were held not only by Tertullian, but by Arnobius and Lactantius and Commodian. The work of the latter, especially, shows how the apocalyptic ideas of the Christians might become charged with a feeling of hostility to the injustice of the social order and to the Roman Empire itself. In his strangely barbaric verses, which, nevertheless, sometimes possess a certain rugged grandeur, Commodian inveighs against the luxury and

---

25. Although the emperor Severus, according to his biographer, found it easier to express himself in Punic than in Latin.

26. It is true that Tertullian's style is no less artificial than that of Apuleius, by whom he was perhaps influenced, but the general effect that it produces is utterly different.

27. *De Praescriptione*, vii. (Homes's trans.).

oppression of the rich and exults over the approaching doom of the heathen world-power.

> *Tollatur imperium, quod fuit inique repletum,*
> *Quod per tributa mala diu macerabat omnes*
>
> . . . . .
>
> *Haec quidem gaudebat, sed tota terra gemebat;*
> *Vix tamen advenit illi retributio digna*
> *Luget in æternum qua se jactabat æterna.*[28]

And the same intransigent spirit shows itself in the cult of martyrdom, which attained an extraordinary high development in Africa, especially among the lower classes. Cultivated pagans saw in the martyrs the rivals and substitutes of the old gods and regarded their cult as typical of the barbarous anti-Roman or anti-Hellenic spirit of the new religion. Maximus, the old pagan scholar of Madaura, protested to St. Augustine that he could not bear to see Romans leaving their ancestral temples to worship at the tombs of low-born criminals with vile Punic names, such as Mygdo and Lucitas and Namphanio, "and others in an endless list with names abhorred both by gods and men." And he concludes: "It almost seems to me at this time as if a second battle of Actium had begun in which Egyptian monsters, doomed soon to perish, dare to raise their weapons against the gods of the Romans."[29]

In fact, the conversion of the Empire had not altered the fierce and uncompromising spirit of African Christianity. On the contrary, the peace of the Church was in Africa merely the occasion of fresh wars. The Donatist movement had its origin, like so many other schisms, in a local dispute on the question of the position of those who had lapsed or compromised their loyalty under the stress of persecution. But the intervention of the Roman state changed what might have been an unimportant local schism into a movement of almost national importance, and roused the native fanaticism of the African spirit. To the Donatists

---

28. *Carmen apologeticum*, 889–90 and 921–3. "May the Empire be destroyed which was filled with injustice and which long afflicted the world with heavy taxes. . . . Rome rejoiced while the whole earth groaned. Yet at last due retribution falls upon her. She who boasted herself eternal shall mourn eternally."

29. *Ep.* xvi.

the Catholic Church was "the Church of the traitors,"[30] which had sold its birthright and leagued itself "with the princes of this world for the slaughter of the saints." They themselves claimed to be the true representatives of the glorious tradition of the old African Church, for they also were persecuted by the world, they also were a martyr Church, the faithful remnant of the saints.

The African Church had been called by Christ to share in His passion, and the persecution of the Donatists was the first act of the final struggle of the forces of evil against the Kingdom of God. *"Sicut enim in Africa factum est,"* writes Tyconius, *"ita fieri oportet in toto mundo, revelari Antichristum sicut et nobis ex parte revelatum est." "Ex Africa manifestabitur omnis ecclesia."*[31]

But the Donatist movement was not only a spiritual protest against any compromise with the world; it also roused all the forces of social discontent and national fanaticism. The wild peasant bands of the Circumcellions, who roamed the country, with their war-cry of *"Deo laudes,"* were primarily religious fanatics who sought an opportunity of martyrdom. But they were also champions of the poor and the oppressed, who forced the landlords to enfranchise their slaves and free their debtors, and who, when they met a rich man driving in his chariot, would make him yield his place to his footman, as a literal fulfilment of the words of the Magnificat, *deposuit potentes de sede et exaltavit humiles.* In fact, we have in Donatism a typical example of the results of an exclusive insistence on the apocalyptic and anti-secular aspects of Christianity, a tendency which was destined to reappear at a later period in the excesses of the Taborites, the Anabaptists and some of the Puritan sects.

The existence of this movement, so powerful, so self-confident and so uncompromising, had a profound effect on Augustine's life and thought. The situation of the Church in Africa was essentially different from any-

30. *Traditores*—primarily those who had delivered *(tradere)* the sacred books to the authorities during the persecution of Diocletian, but the word also has the evil association of our "traitor."

31. From the *Commentary on the Apocalypse* of Beatus in Monceaux. *Hist. Litt. de l'Afrique Chretiénne,* V, p. 288, notes 2 and 3: "For as it has been done in Africa, so it must be done in the whole world and Antichrist must be revealed, as has been revealed to us in part." "Out of Africa all the Church shall be revealed."

thing which existed elsewhere. The Catholics were not, as in many of the Eastern provinces, the dominant element in society, nor were they, as in other parts of the West, the acknowledged representatives of the new faith against paganism. In numbers they were probably equal to the Donatists, but intellectually they were the weaker party, since with the exception of Optatus of Milevis the whole literary tradition of African Christianity had been in the hands of the Donatists; indeed, from the schism to the time of Optatus, a space of more than fifty years, not a single literary representative of the Catholic cause had appeared.

Hence, during the thirty years of his ecclesiastical life St. Augustine had to fight a continuous battle, not only against the paganism and unbelief of the open enemies of Christianity, but also against the fanaticism and sectarianism of his fellow-Christians. The extinction of the Donatist schism was the work to which before all others his later life was dedicated, and it inevitably affected his views of the nature of the Church and its relation to the secular power. The Catholics had been in alliance with the state, since the time of Constantine, and relied upon the help of the secular arm both for their own protection and for the suppression of the schismatics. Consequently, Augustine could no longer maintain the attitude of hostile independence towards the state which marked the African spirit, and which the Donatists still preserved. Nevertheless, he was himself a true African. Indeed, we may say that he was an African first and a Roman afterwards, since, in spite of his genuine loyalty towards the Empire, he shows none of the specifically Roman patriotism which marks Ambrose or Prudentius. Rome is to him always " the second Babylon,"[32] the supreme example of human pride and ambition, and he seems to take a bitter pleasure in recounting the crimes and misfortunes of her history.[33] On the other hand, he often shows his African patriotism, notably in his reply to the letter of Maximus of Madaura, to which I have already referred, where he defends the Punic language from the charge of barbarism.[34]

It is true that there is nothing provincial about Augustine's mind,

32. *De Civitate Dei*, XVIII, ii, xxii.
33. *E.g.*, the passage on Rome after Cannae in *De Civitate Dei*, III, xix.
34. "Surely, considering that you are an African and that we are both settled in Africa, you could not have so forgotten yourself when writing to Africans as to think that Punic

for he had assimilated classical culture and especially Greek thought to a greater extent than any other Western Father. But for all that he remained an African, the last and greatest representative of the tradition of Tertullian and Cyprian, and when he took up the task of defending Christianity against the attacks of the pagans he was carrying on not only their work, but also their spirit and their thought. If we compare *The City of God* with the works of the great Greek apologists, the *Contra Celsum* of Origen, the *Contra Gentes* of Athanasius and the *Praeparatio Evangelica* of Eusebius, we are at once struck by the contrast of his method. He does not base his treatment of the subject on philosophic and metaphysical arguments, as the Greek Fathers had done, but on the eschatological and social dualism, which, as we have seen, was characteristic of the earliest Christian teaching and to which the African tradition, as a whole, had proved so faithful.

Moreover, the particular form in which Augustine expresses this dualism, and which supplies the central unifying idea of the whole work, was itself derived from an African source, namely from Tyconius, the most original Donatist writer of the fourth-century.[35] Tyconius represents the African tradition in its purest and most uncontaminated form. He owes nothing to classical culture or to philosophic ideas; his inspiration is entirely Biblical and Hebraic. Indeed, his interpretation of the Bible resembles that of the Jewish Midrash far more than the ordinary type of patristic exegesis. It is a proof of the two-sidedness of Augustine's genius that he could appreciate the obscure and tortuous originality of Tyconius as well as the limpid classicism of Cicero. He was deeply influenced by Tyconius, not only in his interpretation of scripture,[36] but also in his theology and in his attitude to history;

---

names were a fit theme for censure. . . . And if the Punic language is rejected by you, you virtually deny what has been admitted by most learned men, that many things have been wisely preserved from oblivion in books written in the Punic tongue. Nay, you ought even to be ashamed of having been born in the country in which the cradle of this language is still warm." *Ep.* xvii (trans. J. G. Cunningham). Julian of Eclanum often sneers at St. Augustine as "a Punic Aristotle" and *"philosophaster Pœnorum."*

35. Strictly speaking, Tyconius was not a Donatist, but an "Afro Catholic," since he believed not that the Donatists were the only true Church, but that they formed part of the Catholic Church, although they were not in communion with it.

36. Cf. especially Augustine's incorporation of the "Rules" of Tyconius in his *De Doctrina Christiana.*

above all, in his central doctrine of the Two Cities. In his commentary on the Apocalypse, Tyconius had written, "Behold two cities, the City of God and the City of the Devil. . . . Of them, one desires to serve the world, and the other to serve Christ; one seeks to reign in this world, the other to fly from this world. One is afflicted, and the other rejoices; one smites, and the other is smitten; one slays, and the other is slain; the one in order to be the more justified thereby, the other to fill up the measure of its iniquities. And they both strive together, the one that it may receive damnation, the other that it may acquire salvation."[37]

This idea had entered deeply into Augustine's thought from the first. He was already meditating on it at Tagaste in 390; in 400 he makes use of it in his treatise *On Catechising the Unlearned*, and, finally, in *The City of God*, he makes it the subject of his greatest work. In his mind, however, the idea had acquired a more profound significance than that which Tyconius had given it. To the latter, the Two Cities were apocalyptic symbols derived from the imagery of the Bible and bound up with his realistic eschatological ideas. To Augustine, on the other hand, they had acquired a philosophic meaning and had been related to a rational theory of sociology. He taught that every human society finds its constituent principle in a common will—a will to life, a will to enjoyment, above all, a will to peace. He defines a people as a "multitude of rational creatures associated in a common agreement as to the things which it loves."[38] Hence, in order to see what a people is like we must consider the objects of its love. If the society is associated in a love of that which is good, it will be a good society; if the objects of its love are evil, it will be bad. And thus the moral law of individual and social life is the same, since both to the city and to the individual we can apply the same principle—*non faciunt bonos vel malos mores nisi boni vel mali amores.*

And thus the sociology of St. Augustine is based on the same psychological principle which pervades his whole thought—the principle of the all-importance of the will and the sovereignty of love. The power of love has the same importance in the spiritual world as the force of

37. Beatus, *Comm. in Apocalypsin,* ed. Florez, pp. 506–7.
38. *De Civitate Dei,* XIX, xxiv.

gravity possesses in the physical world.[39] As a man's love moves him, so must he go, and so must he become; *pondus meum amor meus, eo feror quocumque feror.*

And though the desires of men appear to be infinite they are in reality reducible to one. All men desire happiness, all seek after peace; and all their lusts and hates and hopes and fears are directed to that final end. The only essential difference consists in the nature of the peace and happiness that are desired, for, by the very fact of his spiritual autonomy, man has the power to choose his own good; either to find his peace in subordinating his will to the divine order, or to refer all things to the satisfaction of his own desires and to make himself the centre of his universe—"a darkened image of the divine Omnipotence." It is here and here only that the root of dualism is to be found: in the opposition between the "natural man" who lives for himself and desires only a material felicity and a temporal peace, and the spiritual man who lives for God and seeks a spiritual beatitude and a peace which is eternal. The two tendencies of will produce two kinds of men and two types of society, and so we finally come to the great generalisation on which St. Augustine's work is founded. "Two loves built two cities—the earthly, which is built up by the love of self to the contempt of God, and the heavenly which is built up by the love of God to the contempt of self."[40]

From this generalisation springs the whole Augustinian theory of history, since the two cities "have been running their course mingling one with the other through all the changes of times from the beginning of the human race, and shall so move on together until the end of the world, when they are destined, to be separated at the last judgment."[41]

In the latter part of *The City of God* (books xv to xviii) St. Augustine gives a brief synopsis of world history from this point of view. On the one hand he follows the course of the earthly city—the mystical Babylon—through the ages, and finds its completest manifestation in the two world empires of Assyria and Rome "to which all the other

---

39. Following the Aristotelian theory according to which every substance naturally tends to its "proper place"—τόπος οἰκεῖος; cf. Augustine, *Confessions,* XIII, i, x; *De Civitate Dei,* XI, xxviii.

40. *De Civitate Dei,* XIV. xxviii.

41. *De Catechizandis Rudibus,* XXI, xxxvii; cf. *ibid.,* XIX, xxxi, and *De Civitate Dei,* XIV, i, xxviii; XV, i, ii.

Kingdoms are but appendices." On the other hand, he traces the development of the heavenly city: from its beginnings with the patriarchs, through the history of Israel and the holy city of the first Jerusalem, down to its final earthly manifestation in the Catholic Church.

The rigid simplification of history which such a sketch demands necessarily emphasises the uncompromising severity of St. Augustine's thought. At first sight he seems, no less than Tertullian or Commodian, to condemn the state and all secular civilisation as founded on human pride and selfishness, and to find the only good society in the Church and the Kingdom of the Saints. And in a sense this conclusion does follow from the Augustinian doctrine of man. The human race has been vitiated at its source. It has become a waste product—a *massa damnata*. The process of redemption consists in grafting a new humanity on to the old stock, and in building a new world out of the debris of the old. Consequently, in the social life of unregenerate humanity St. Augustine sees a flood of infectious and hereditary evil against which the unassisted power of the individual will struggles in vain. "Woe to thee," he cries, "thou river of human custom! Who shall stop thy course? How long will it be before thou art dried up? How long wilt thou roll the sons of Eve into that great and fearful ocean which even they who are clinging to the wood (of the Cross) can scarcely cross?"[42]

This view of human nature and of the social burden of evil finds still further confirmation in the spectacle of universal history. St. Augustine, no less than St. Cyprian,[43] sees the kingdoms of the world founded in injustice and prospering by bloodshed and oppression. He did not share the patriotic optimism of writers like Eusebius and Prudentius, for he realised, more keenly perhaps than any other ancient writer, at what a cost of human suffering the benefits of the imperial unity had been purchased. "The imperial city," he writes, " endeavours to communicate her language to all the lands she has subdued to procure a fuller society and a greater abundance of interpreters on both sides. It is true, but how many lives has this cost! and, suppose that done, the worst is not past, for . . . the wider extension of her empire produced still greater wars. . . . Wherefore he that does but consider with com-

42. *Confessions,* I, xxv.
43. Cf. especially St. Cyprian's *Epistle to Donatus.*

passion all these extremes of sorrow and bloodshed must needs say that this is a mystery. But he that endures them without a sorrowful emotion or thought thereof is far more wretched to imagine he has the bliss of a god when he has lost the natural feelings of a man."[44]

In the same way the vaunted blessings of Roman law are only secured by an infinity of acts of injustice to individuals by the torture of innocent witnesses and the condemnation of the guiltless. The magistrate would think it wrong not to discharge the duties of his office, "but he never holds it a sin to torture innocent witnesses, and when he has made them their own accusers, to put them to death as guilty."[45] Consequently, the consideration of history leads Augustine to reject the political idealism of the philosophers and to dispute Cicero's thesis that the state rests essentially on justice. If this were the case, he argues, Rome itself would be no state; in fact, since true justice is not to be found in any earthly kingdom, the only true state will be the City of God.[46] Accordingly, in order to avoid this extreme conclusion, he eliminates all moral elements from his definition of the state, and describes it, in the passage to which I have already referred, as based on a common will, whether the object of that will be good or bad.

The drastic realism of this definition has proved shocking to several modern writers on Augustine. Indeed, so distinguished a student of political thought as Dr. A. J. Carlyle is unwilling to admit that St. Augustine really meant what he said,[47] and he cites the famous passage in book iv, chapter 4, "Set justice aside and what are kingdoms but great robberies,"[48] to show that the quality of justice is essential to any real state. The actual tendency of the passage, however, appears to be quite the contrary. St. Augustine is arguing that there is no difference between the conqueror and the robber except the scale of their operations, for, he continues, "What is banditry but a little kingdom?" and he approves the reply of the pirate to Alexander the Great, "Because I do it with a

44. *De Civitate Dei*, XIX, vii (trans. J. Healey).
45. *De Civitate Dei*, XIX, vi.
46. *De Civitate Dei*, II, xxi.
47. "If he did," he writes, "I cannot but feel that it was a deplorable error for a great Christian teacher." *Social and Political Ideas of Some Great Mediaeval Thinkers*, ed. F. J. C. Hearnshaw, p. 51.
48. *Remota justitia quid regna nisi magna latrocinia?*

little ship, I am called a robber, and you, because you do it with a great fleet, are called an emperor."

In reality there is nothing inconsistent or morally discreditable about St. Augustine's views. They follow necessarily from his doctrine of original sin; indeed, they are implicit in the whole Christian social tradition and they frequently find expression in later Christian literature. The famous passage in the letter of Pope Gregory VII to Hermann of Metz, which has been regarded by many modern writers as showing his belief in the diabolic origin of the state, is simply an assertion of the same point of view; while Newman, who in this, as in so many other respects, is a faithful follower of the patristic tradition, affirms the same principle in the most uncompromising terms. "Earthly kingdoms," he says, "are founded, not in justice, but in injustice. They are created by the sword, by robbery, cruelty, perjury, craft and fraud. There never was a kingdom, except Christ's, which was not conceived and born, nurtured and educated, in sin. There never was a state, but was committed to acts and maxims, which it is its crime to maintain and its ruin to abandon. What monarchy is there but began in invasion or usurpation? What revolution has been effected without self-will, violence, or hypocrisy? What popular government but is blown about by every wind, as if it had no conscience and no responsibilities? What dominion of the few but is selfish and unscrupulous? Where is military strength without the passion for war? Where is trade without the love of filthy lucre, which is the root of all evil?"[49]

But from this condemnation of the actual reign of injustice in human society it does not follow that either Newman or Augustine intended to suggest that the state belonged to a non-moral sphere and that men in their social relations might follow a different law to that which governed their moral life as individuals. On the contrary, St. Augustine frequently insists that it is Christianity which makes good citizens, and that the one remedy for the ills of society is to be found in the same power which heals the moral weakness of the individual soul. "Here also is security for the welfare and renown of a commonwealth;

---

49. From "Sanctity the Token of the Christian Empire" in *Sermons on Subjects of the Day*, p. 273 (first edition).

for no state is perfectly established and preserved otherwise than on the foundations and by the bond of faith and of firm concord, when the highest and truest good, namely God, is loved by all, and men love each other in Him without dissimulation because they love one another for His sake."[50]

Moreover, though St. Augustine emphasises so strongly the moral dualism which is inherent in the Christian theory of life, he differs from the earlier representatives of the African school in his intense realisation of a universal reasonable order which binds all nature together and which governs alike the stars in their courses and the rise and fall of kingdoms. This belief is one of the fundamental elements in Augustine's thought. It dominated his mind in the first days of his conversion, when he composed the treatise *De Ordine,* and it was preserved unimpaired to the last. It finds typical expression in the following passage in *The City of God:* "The true God-from Whom is all being, beauty, form and number, weight and measure; He from Whom all nature, mean and excellent, all seeds of forms, all forms of seeds, all motions both of forms and seeds, derive and have being; . . . He (I say) having left neither heaven nor earth, nor angel nor man, no, nor the most base and contemptible creature, neither the bird's feather, nor the herb's flower, nor the tree's leaf, without the true harmony of their parts, and peaceful concord of composition; it is in no way credible that He would leave the kingdoms of men and their bondages and freedoms loose and uncomprised in the laws of His eternal providence."[51]

Here Augustine is nearer to Origen than Tertullian; in fact, this fundamental concept of the Universal Law—*lex æterna*—is derived from purely Hellenic sources. It is the characteristically Greek idea of cosmic order which pervades the whole Hellenic tradition from Heraclitus and Pythagoras to the later Stoics and neo-Platonists, and which had reached Augustine by way of Cicero and Plotinus.[52] This Hellenic influence is to be seen above all in Augustine's profound sense of the aesthetic beauty of order and in his doctrine that even the evil and suf-

---

50. *Ep.* cxxxvii, 5, 18 (trans. Cunningham); cf. *Ep.* cxxxviii, 15 and 17.
51. *De Civitate Dei,* V, xi (trans. J. Healey).
52. Cf. P. A. Schubert, *Augustins Lex Æterna Lehre nach Inhalt und Quellen* (1924).

fering of the world find their aesthetic justification in the universal harmony of creation, an idea which had already found classic expression in
the great lines of Cleanthes's Hymn to Zeus:

"Thou knowest how to make even that which is uneven and to order what is
disordered, and unlovely things are lovely to Thee. For so Thou bringest together all things in one, the good with the bad, that there results from all one
reasonable order abiding for ever."

Thus St. Augustine was able to view history from a much wider
standpoint than that of Tertullian or the Donatists. He can admit that
the Earthly City also has its place in the universal order, and that the
social virtues of the worldly, which from a religious point of view are
often nothing but "splendid vices," yet possess a real value in their own
order, and bear their appropriate fruits in social life. And in the same
way he believes that the disorder and confusion of history are only apparent, and that God orders all events by His Providence in a universal
harmony which the created mind cannot grasp.

This philosophic universalism is not confined to Augustine's conception of the order of nature; it also affects his eschatology and his doctrine of the Church. Above all, it determined his treatment of the central
theme of his great work—*The City of God*—and entirely alienated him
from the realistic literalism of the old apocalyptic tradition. To Augustine, the City of God is not the concrete millennial kingdom of the older
apologists, nor is it the visible hierarchical Church. It is a transcendent
and timeless reality, a society of which "the King is Truth, the law is
Love and the duration is Eternity."[53] It is older than the world, since its
first and truest citizens are the angels. It is as wide as humanity, since
"in all successive ages Christ is the same Son of God, co-eternal with
the Father, and the unchangeable Wisdom by Whom universal nature
was called into existence and by participation in Whom every rational
soul is made blessed." Consequently, "from the beginning of the human
race whosoever believed in Him and in any way knew Him, and lived
in a pious and just manner according to His precepts, was undoubtedly
saved by Him in whatsoever time and place he may have lived."[54]

53. *Ep.* cxxxviii, 3, 17.
54. *Ep.* cii, 2, 11 and, 12.

Thus the City of God is co-extensive with the spiritual creation in so far as it has not been vitiated by sin. It is, in fact, nothing less than the spiritual unity of the whole universe, as planned by the Divine Providence, and the ultimate goal of creation.

These conceptions are quite irreconcilable with the old millenniarist belief which was still so strong in the West, and which Augustine himself had formerly accepted. They led him to adopt Tyconius's interpretation of the crucial passage in the Apocalypse, according to which the earthly reign of Christ is nothing else but the life of the Church militant: an explanation which henceforth gained general acceptance in the West. Moreover, he went further than Tyconius himself and the great majority of earlier writers by abandoning all attempts to give the data of prophecy an exact chronological interpretation with regard to the future, and by discouraging the prevalent assumption of the imminence of the end of the world.[55]

Thus St. Augustine influenced Christian eschatology in the West no less decisively than Origen had done in the East almost two centuries earlier, and to some extent their influences tended in the same direction. To Augustine, as to Origen, the ideal of the Kingdom of God acquired a metaphysical form, and became identified with the ultimate timeless reality of spiritual being. The Augustinian City of God bears a certain resemblance to the neo Platonic concept of the Intelligible World—$\varkappa\acute{o}\sigma\mu o\varsigma$ $\nu o\eta\tau\grave{o}\varsigma$: indeed, the Christian Platonists of later times, who were equally devoted to Augustine and Plotinus, deliberately make a conflation of the two ideas. Thus John Norris of Bemerton writes of his "Ideal World": "Thou art that Glorious Jerusalem, whose foundations are upon the Holy Hills, the everlasting Mountains, even the Eternal Essences and Immutable Ideas of Things Here are $\tau\grave{\alpha}$ $\acute{o}\nu\tau\alpha$— the Things that are and that truly and chiefly are *quæ vere summeque sunt,* as St. Austin speaks, and that because they necessarily and immutably are, and cannot either not be or be otherwise. Here live, flourish and shine those bright and unperishing Realities whereof the Things of

---

55. *Ep.* cxcix. In another passage he even goes so far as to entertain the hypothesis of the world being still in existence 500,000 years hence (*De Civitate Dei*, XII, xii); elsewhere, however, he speaks of the world having reached old age (*e.g., Sermo* xxxi, 8; *Ep.* cxxxvii, 16).

this World are but the Image, the Reflection, the Shadow, the Echo."[56]

This Platonic idealism did indeed leave a deep imprint on St. Augustine's thought. Nevertheless, he never went so far in this direction as Origen had done, for his Platonism did not destroy his sense of the reality and importance of the historical process. To Origen, on the contrary, the temporal process had no finality. There was an infinite succession of worlds through which the immortal soul pursued its endless course. Since "the soul is immortal and eternal, it is possible that, in the many and endless periods of duration in the immeasurable and different worlds, it may descend from the highest good to the lowest evil, or be restored from the lowest evil to the highest good."[57] This is not precisely the classical Hellenic doctrine, since, as I have pointed out elsewhere,[58] Origen expressly rejects the theory of the Return of All Things as irreconcilable with a belief in free will. It has a much closer resemblance to the Hindu doctrine of *samsara*—the endless chain of existences, which are the fruit of the soul's own acts. But, although this theory allows for the freedom of the will, it is destructive of the organic unity of humanity and of the significance of its social destinies to an even greater extent than the purely Hellenic doctrine. Consequently, St. Augustine rejected it no less firmly than the theory of cyclic recurrence. He admits that the idea of a perpetual return is a natural consequence of the belief in the eternity of the world, but if we once accept the doctrine of Creation, as Origen himself did, there is no further need for the theory of "the circumrotation of souls," or for the belief that nothing new or final can take place in time. Humanity has had an absolute beginning and travels to an absolute goal. There can be no return. That which is begun in time is consummated in eternity.[59] Hence time is not a perpetually revolving image of eternity; it is an irreversible process moving in a definite direction.

This recognition of the uniqueness and irreversibility of the temporal process—this "explosion of the perpetual cycles"—is one of the

---

56. J. Norris, *An Essay Towards the Theory of the Ideal or Intelligible World*, I, 430–6 (1701).

57. Origen: *De Principiis*, III, i, 21 (trans. I. Crombie).

58. *Progress and Religion*, p. 156.

59. *De Civitate Dei*, XII, xi–xx; XXI, xvii.

most remarkable achievements of St. Augustine's thought. It is true that the change of attitude was implicit in Christianity itself, since the whole Christian revelation rests on temporal events which nevertheless possess an absolute significance and an eternal value. As St. Augustine says, Christ is the straight way by which the mind escapes from the circular maze of pagan thought.[60] But although this change had been realised by faith and religious experience, it still awaited philosophic analysis and definition. This it received from St. Augustine, who was not only founder of the Christian philosophy of history, but was actually the first man in the world to discover the meaning of time.

His subtle and profound mind found a peculiar attraction in the contemplation of the mystery of time which is so essentially bound up with the mystery of created being.[61] He was intensely sensitive to the pathos of mutability—*omnis quippe iste ordo pulcherrima rerum valde bonarum modis suis peractis transiturus est; et mane quippe in eis factum est et vespera*[62]—but he felt that the very possibility of this act of contemplation showed that the mind in some sense transcended the process which it contemplated. Consequently, he could not rest satisfied with the naïve objectivism of Greek science which identified time with the movement of the heavenly bodies.[63] If the movement of bodies is the only measure of time, how can we speak of past and future? A movement which has passed has ceased to exist, and a movement which is to come has not begun exist. There remains only the present of the passing moment; a moving point in nothingness. Therefore, he concludes, the measure of time is not to be found in things, but in the soul—time is spiritual extension—*distentio animæ*.

Thus the past is the soul's remembrance, the future is its expectation, and the present is its attention. The future, which does not exist, cannot be long; what we mean by a long future is a long expectation of the future, and a long past means a long memory of the past. "It is,

---

60. *"Viam rectam sequentes, quae nobis est Cristus, eo duce et salvatore a vano et inepto impiorum circumitu iter fidei mentemque avertamus." De Civitate Dei*, XII, xx.

61. Cf. *De Civitate Dei*, XII, xv, xi, vi.

62. *Confessions*, XIII, xxxv. "For all this most fair order of things truly good will pass away when its measures are accomplished, and they have their morning and their evening."

63. *Confessions*, XI, xxiii.

then, in thee, my soul, that I measure time. . . . The impression which things make upon thee as they pass and which remains when they have passed away is what I measure. I measure this which is present, and not the things which have passed away that it might be. Therefore this is time *(tempora)* or else I must say that I do not measure time at all."[64]

Finally, he compares the time-process with the recitation of a poem which a man knows by heart. Before it is begun the recitation exists only in anticipation; when it is finished it is all in the memory; but while it is in progress it exists, like time, in three dimensions—"the life of this my action is extended into the memory, on account of what I have said, and into expectation, on account of what I am about to say; yet my attention remains present and it is through this that what was future is transposed and becomes past." And what is true of the poem holds good equally of each line and syllable of it, and of the wider action of which it forms part, and also of the life of man which is composed of a series of such actions, and of the whole world of man which is the sum of individual lives.[65]

Now this new theory of time which St. Augustine originated also renders possible a new conception of history. If man is not the slave and creature of time, but its master and creator, then history also becomes a creative process. It does not repeat itself meaninglessly; it grows into organic unity with the growth of human experience. The past does not die; it becomes incorporated in humanity. And hence progress is possible, since the life of society and of humanity itself possesses continuity and the capacity for spiritual growth no less than the life of the individual.

How far St. Augustine realised all this may indeed be questioned. Many modern writers do, in fact, deny that he conceived of the possibility of progress or that he had any real historical sense. They argue, as I said before, that *The City of God* conceives humanity as divided between two static eternal orders whose eternal lot is predestined from the beginning. But this criticism is, I think, due to a misconception of the Augustinian attitude to history. It is true that Augustine did not

---

64. *Ibid.,* XI, xxvii.
65. *Confessions,* XI, xxviii.

consider the problem of secular progress, but then secular history, in his view, was essentially unprogressive. It was the spectacle of humanity perpetually engaged in chasing its own tail. The true history of the human race is to be found in the process of enlightenment and salvation by which human nature is liberated and restored to spiritual freedom. Nor did Augustine view this process in an abstract and unhistorical way. For he constantly insists on the organic unity of the history of humanity, which passes through a regular succession of ages, like the life of an individual man;[66] and he shows how "the epochs of the world are linked together in a wonderful way" by the gradual development of the divine plan.[67] For God, who is "the unchangeable Governor as He is the unchangeable Creator of mutable things, orders all events in His providence until the beauty of the completed course of time, of which the component parts are the dispensations adapted to each successive age, shall be finished, like the grand melody of some ineffably wise master of song."[68]

It is true, as we have already seen, that in *The City of God* St. Augustine always emphasises the eternal and transcendent character of the Heavenly City in contrast to the mutability and evil of earthly life. It is impossible to identify the City of God with the Church as some writers have done, since in the Heavenly City there is no room for evil or imperfection, no admixture of sinners with the saints. But, on the other hand, it is an even more serious error to separate the two concepts completely and to conclude that St. Augustine assigned no absolute and transcendent value to the hierarchical Church. Certainly the Church is not the eternal City of God, but it is its organ and representative in the world. It is the point at which the transcendent spiritual order inserts itself into the sensible world, the one bridge by which the creature can pass from Time to Eternity. St. Augustine's point of view is, in fact, precisely the same as that which Newman so often expresses, though their terminology is somewhat different. Like Augustine, Newman emphasises the spiritual and eternal character of the City of God and regards the visible Church as its earthly manifestation. " The un-

---

66. *e.g., De Vera Religione,* XXVII, 1.   67. *Ep.* cxxxvii, 15.
68. *Ep.* cxxxviii, 5 (trans. Cunningham).

seen world through God's secret power and mercy encroaches upon this; and the Church that is seen is just that portion of it by which it encroaches, it is like the islands in the sea, which are in truth but the tops of the everlasting hills, high and vast and deeply rooted, which a deluge covers."[69]

And neither in the case of St. Augustine nor in that of Newman does this emphasising of the transcendence and spirituality of the City of God lead to any depreciation of the hierarchical Church. The latter describes the Christian Church as an Imperial power—"not a mere creed or philosophy but a *counter kingdom*." "It occupied ground; it claimed to rule over those whom hitherto this world's governments ruled over without rival; and it is only in proportion as things that are are brought into this kingdom and made subservient to it; it is only as kings and princes, nobles and rulers, men of business and men of letters, the craftsman and the trader and the labourer humble themselves to Christ's Church and (in the language of the prophet Isaiah) 'bow down to her with their faces toward the earth and lick up the dust of her feet,' that the world becomes living and spiritual, and a fit object of love and a resting-place for Christians."[70]

The late Dr. Figgis, in his admirable lectures: *The Political Aspects of St. Augustine's "City of God"* has referred to this sermon of Newman as showing how far later Western *tradition* carried "the political way of thinking about the Church, which had been inaugurated by St. Augustine." But here again Newman's teaching really represents, not the views of his own time nor even those of the Middle Ages, but a deliberate revival of the patristic Augustinian doctrines. We have seen how primitive Christianity, and the early Western tradition in particular, showed an intense social realism in their eschatology and in their conception of the Church and the Kingdom of God. St. Augustine definitely abandoned the millenniarist tradition and adopted a thoroughly spiritual eschatology. But he preserved the traditional social realism in his attitude to the Church: indeed, he reinforced it by his identification of the Church with the millennial kingdom of the Apocalypse. *Ecclesia*

---

69. "The Communion of Saints" in *Parochial Sermons* (first edition), IV, p. 201.
70. *Sermons Bearing on Subjects of the Day* (first edition), pp. 257 and 120.

et nunc est regnum Christi regnumque cœlorum.[71] Consequently, it is in the Church that the prophecies of the kingdom find their fulfilment, and even those which seem to refer to the last Judgment may really be applied "to that advent of the Saviour by which He is coming through all the present time in His Church, that is to say, in His members, gradually and little by little, for it is all His Body."[72]

"*O beata ecclesia,*" he writes, "*quodam tempore audisti, quodam tempore vidisti. . . . Omnia enim quæ modo complentur antea prophetata sunt. Erige oculos ergo, et diffunde per mundum: vide jam hereditatem usque ad terminos orbis terræ. Vide jam impleri quod dictum est: Adorabunt eum omnes reges teræ, omnes gentes servient illi.*"[73]

The grain of mustard-seed has grown until it is greater than all the herbs, and the great ones of this world have taken refuge under its branches. The yoke of Christ is on the neck of kings, and we have seen the head of the greatest empire that the world has known laying aside his crown and kneeling before the tomb of the Fisherman.[74]

Hence Augustine bases his claim to make use of the secular power against the Donatists, not on the rights of the state to intervene in religious matters, but on the right of the Church to make use of the powers of this world which God has subdued to Christ according to His prophecy: "All the kings of the earth shall adore Him and all nations shall serve Him."—"*et ideo hac Ecclesiæ potestate utimur, quam ei Domininus et promisit et dedit.*"[75]

To some—notably to Reuter and Harnack—this exaltation of the visible Church has seemed fundamentally inconsistent with the Augustinian doctrine of grace. It is indeed difficult to understand Augustine's

---

71. *De Civitate Dei*, XX, x.

72. *De Civitate Dei*, XX, v.

73. *Enarrationes in Psalmos*, LXVII, vii. "O blessed Church, once thou hast heard, now thou hast seen. For what the Church has heard in promises, she now sees manifested. For all things that were formerly prophesied, are now fulfilled. Lift up thine eyes and look abroad over the world. Behold now thine inheritance even to the ends of the earth. See now fulfilled what was spoken: 'All the kings of the earth shall worship Him, all nations shall do Him service.'"

74. *Sermo* xliv, 2; *Ep.* cxxxii, 3. We may observe that the same facts on which Eusebius rests his glorification of the Emperor are used by Augustine to exalt the Church.

75. *Ep.* cv, 5, 6; cf. *Ep.*, xxxv, 3. "And, therefore, we are making use of this power which the Lord both promised and gave to the Church."

theology if we approach it from the standpoint of the principles of the Reformation. But if we ignore modern developments, and study Augustine's doctrine of grace and the Church from a purely Augustinian standpoint, its unity and consistency are manifest.

St. Augustine never separates the moral from the social life. The dynamic force of both the individual and the society is found in the will, and the object of their will determines the moral character of their life. And as the corruption of the will by original sin in Adam becomes a social evil by an hereditary transmission through the flesh which unites fallen humanity in the common slavery of concupiscence, so too the restoration of the will by grace in Christ is a social good which is transmitted sacramentally by the action of the Spirit and unites regenerate humanity in a free spiritual society under the law of charity. The grace of Christ is only found in "the society of Christ." " Whence," says he, "should the City of God originally begin or progressively develop or ultimately attain its end, unless the life of the saints is a social one?"[76] Thus the Church is actually the new humanity in process of formation, and its earthly history is that of the building of the City of God which has its completion in eternity, *"Adhuc ædificatur templum Dei."*[77] *"Vos tanquam lapides vivi coædificamini in templum Dei."*[78] Hence, in spite of all the imperfections of the earthly Church, it is nevertheless the most perfect society that this world can know. Indeed, it is the only true society, because it is the only society which has its source in a spiritual will. The kingdoms of the earth seek after the goods of the earth; the Church, and the Church alone, seeks spiritual goods and a peace which is eternal.

Such a doctrine may seem to leave little room for the claims of the state. In fact, it is difficult to deny that the state does occupy a very subordinate position in St. Augustine's view. At its worst it is a hostile power, the incarnation of injustice and self-will. At its best, it is a perfectly legitimate and necessary society, but one which is limited to temporary and partial ends, and it is bound to subordinate itself to the greater and more universal spiritual society in which even its own members find their real citizenship. In fact, the state bears much the

76. *De Civitate Dei*, XIX, v.
78. *Ibid.*, clvi, 12, 13.

77. *Sermo* clxiii, 3.

same relation to the Church that a Friendly Society or a guild bears to the state: it fulfils a useful function and has a right to the loyalty of its members, but it can never claim to be the equal of the larger society or to act as a substitute for it.

It is on the ground of these conceptions that St. Augustine has so often been regarded as the originator of the mediaeval theocratic ideal, and even (by Reuter) as "the founder of Roman Catholicism."[79] And indeed it is to him more than any other individual that we owe the characteristically Western ideal of the Church as a dynamic social power in contrast to the static and metaphysical conceptions which dominated Byzantine Christianity. But it does not necessarily follow that the influence of St. Augustine tended to weaken the moral authority of the state or to deprive ordinary social life of spiritual significance. If we consider the matter, not from the narrow standpoint of the juristic relations of Church and state, but as St. Augustine himself did, from the point of view of the relative importance of the spiritual and material element in life, we shall see that his doctrine really made for moral freedom and responsibility. Under the Roman Empire, as in the sacred monarchies of the oriental type, the state was exalted as a superhuman power against which the individual personality had no rights and the individual will had no power. In the East, even Christianity proved powerless to change this tradition, and alike in the Byzantine Empire and in Russia the Church consecrated anew the old oriental ideal of an omnipotent sacred state and a passive people. In the West, however, St. Augustine broke decisively with this tradition by depriving the state of its aura of divinity and seeking the principle of social order in the human will. In this way the Augustinian theory, for all its otherworldliness, first made possible the ideal of a social order resting upon the free personality and a common effort towards moral ends. And thus the Western ideals of freedom and progress and social justice owe more than we realise to the profound thought of the great African who was himself indifferent to secular progress and to the transitory fortunes of the earthly state, "for he looked for a city that has foundations whose builder and maker is God."

79. Cf. C. H. Turner in the *Cambridge Mediaeval History*, I, 173: " St. Augustine's theory of the *Civitas Dei* was, in germ, that of the mediaeval papacy, without the name of Rome."

XIII

Christianity and Sex

I

Western civilisation at the present day is passing through a crisis which is essentially different from anything that has been previously experienced. Other societies in the past have changed their social institutions or their religious beliefs under the influence of external forces or the slow development of internal growth. But none, like our own, has ever consciously faced the prospect of a fundamental alteration of the beliefs and institutions on which the whole fabric of social life rests. Underneath the self-conscious activity of the ruling classes the daily life of the majority of men went on unchanged. The statesmen of the past would no more have thought of altering the fundamental social and moral relations than of interfering with the course of the seasons. But, on the contrary, the change which is actually taking place in the modern world leaves no aspect of social life or moral life unaffected. Civilisation is being uprooted from its foundations in nature and tradition and is being reconstituted in a new organisation which is as artificial and mechanical as a modern factory.

In Western Europe, however, the traditions of the older culture, although greatly weakened, are still strong enough to prevent the full development of this process. It is in the outlying territories of our civilisation, in Russia on the one hand, and in North America on the other, that its success has been greatest and that its results can be most easily studied. In Russia the change is being carried through consciously and deliberately by the power of the government in the face of the passive resistance of a society which still rests largely on the foundations of a primitive peasant culture. In America, on the other hand, it is the unfettered development of the new economic forces which has produced the change, and public opinion and social authority still attempt to preserve as far as possible the moral and social traditions of the older culture. But in spite of this important difference, there is a curious similarity between the two societies. In both cases there is the same cult of the machine and the same tendency to subordinate every other side of human life to economic activity. In both the individual is subjected to a ruthless pressure which produces a standardised type of mass civilisation. And finally we see in both societies the breaking down of the family as a fixed social unit and the rise of a new type of morality, based upon the complete emancipation of sexual relations from the old social restrictions. Although America has not gone so far as Russia, where marriage is now a purely voluntary arrangement terminable on the demand of either party, it has rendered divorce exceedingly easy, and there are those, like Judge Lindsay, who believe that the institution of trial or "companionate" marriage is also necessary in order to introduce some regularity into the sexual relations of the rising generation.[1]

Of all the symptoms of change that I have mentioned, this breakdown of the traditional morality is undoubtedly the most important, for it involves a profound biological change in the life of society. A society can undergo a considerable transformation of its economic conditions and yet preserve its vital continuity, but if a fundamental social unit like the family loses its coherence and takes on a new form this continuity is destroyed and a new social organism comes into existence. This is not always recognised by the advocates of the new morality. Mr. Havelock Ellis has even gone so far as to maintain that the new

---

1. There is, moreover, a very noticeable tendency among the American protagonists of the new morality to follow the example of Russia. Mr. Calverton, for example, condemns companionate marriage as "a patch on the face of a volcano," and celebrates the Russian achievement in a strain of lyrical enthusiasm. "Love and sex-life," he writes, "have been freed of the superstitions and silences which clouded, confused and bound them; marriage has been liberated from the religious and ceremonial rites in which it had once been bound; divorce has been converted into an intelligent device, disenslaved from duplicity and deceit and accessible to all. As a result, morality has been emancipated from the stereotyped stupidities of an enforced convention and an inelastic code. . . . This new moral life which Soviet Russia has endeavoured to achieve is new only in social realisation for the radical. Far-flung Utopias had conjured it up in spheres remote from reality and sequestered from struggle. Dreamers had viewed it amid the effusions of fancy and talked of it as a hope winged upon angelic transformations."—*The Bankruptcy of Marriage*, p. 235.

tendencies may "purify and fortify, rather than weaken, the institution of the family." He writes: "The greater facility of divorce aids the formation of the most satisfactory unions. A greater freedom between the sexes before marriage, even if it has sometimes led to licence, is not only itself beneficial, but the proper method of preparing for a more intimate union. And the exercise of contraceptive control is the indispensable method of selecting the best possibilities of offspring and of excluding from the world those who ought never to be born. As a matter of fact, marriage, so far from dying out, tends in various countries of the West to increase in frequency."[2]

It is, of course, obvious that the frequency of marriage has nothing to do with the question. Under the Russian system, which is commended by Mr. Ellis, there is no reason why every adult should not have an annual marriage, but that does not mean that the institution of the family is flourishing. The fact is that, under the new conditions, marriage means something essentially different from what it has done in the past. In fact, as Mr. Justice Hill has decided in a recent lawsuit, the Russian form of marriage is not marriage at all, but a temporary arrangement.[3] According to European law and tradition, there can be no marriage without the intention of a permanent union, for it is obvious that only a marriage of this kind can render the family possible as a permanent social unit.

The European society of the past, like every other strong and healthy society, has always rested on this foundation. It is, however, incompatible with the complete mechanisation of social life which is the characteristic feature of the new type of civilisation.[4] For if the primary social unit is a natural biological group which is defended by the strongest

---

2. *The Family,* by Havelock Ellis, in *Whither Mankind, A Panorama of Modern Civilisation,* edited by C. Beard, 1928, pp. 208–228.

3. Cf. *The Times,* December 18th, 1929.

4. Mme. Kollontai, the Soviet Ambassador to Norway, states this opposition very clearly. "The old form of the family is passing away; the communist society has no use for it. The bourgeois world celebrated the isolation, the cutting off of the married pair from the collective weal; in the scattered and disjointed bourgeois society full of struggle and destruction, the family was the sole anchor of hope in the storms of life, the peaceful haven in the ocean of hostilities and competitions between persons. The family represented an individual class in the social unit. There can and must be no such thing in the communist society. For communist society as a whole represents such a fortress of the collective life,

moral and religious sanctions, society can never become sheer mechanism, nor can the economic organisation of the state absorb the whole life of the citizen. If, on the other hand, marriage is transformed into a temporary arrangement for the satisfaction of the sexual impulse and for mutual companionship, which is not intended to create a permanent social unit, it is clear that the family loses its social and economic importance and that the state will take its place as the guardian and educator of the children. Society will no longer consist of a number of organisms, each of which possess a limited autonomy, but will be one vast unit which controls the whole life of the individual citizen from the cradle to the grave.

Hence it is easy to understand the reasons for the hostility of the Communist, and even of the milder type of Socialist, represented by Mr. Bernard Shaw, to the traditional code of sexual morality and to the old form of marriage, since the destruction of these is an indispensable condition for the realisation of their social ideals. But this does not altogether explain the strength of the modern attack on marriage and morals. The ordinary follower of the new ethics is not necessarily an admirer of the ideals of social mechanisation and mass civilisation. He or she is often just the reverse—an individualist and a rebel who is in revolt against every kind of social discipline and external compulsion. He seeks not mechanism but freedom, and his hostility to marriage springs from a romantic idealisation of sex and a desire to free his emotional life from all social constraints. The intellectual propaganda against the traditional morality which is so evident in England to-day is, in fact, the tail-end of the great Liberal assault on authority and social tradition which had its origins in the eighteenth century. In Catholic countries the moral aspects of the Liberal revolt were evident from the beginning. The Encyclopædists attacked the moral code of Christianity even more fiercely than its theological doctrines, and all the stock arguments of the

precluding any possibility of the existence of an isolated class of family bodies, existing by itself, with its ties of birth, its love of family honour, its absolute segregation."

Mr. Calverton, who quotes this passage with approval, notes that some of the older Bolsheviks such as Lunacharsky regarded her views as "too rash and precocious." The recent modifications in the Soviet marriage laws, which remove the distinction between registered and unregistered unions, have, however, quite justified her views.—Calverton: *Bankruptcy of Marriage,* pp. 276–277, 281.

modern English sex reformers are to be found stated in their most incisive and paradoxical form in the writings of Diderot, La Mettrie and their friends. In Protestant lands, however, and above all in England and America, the revolt against tradition did not extend to moral principles. Indeed, the leaders of "advanced thought" and particularly the feminists were usually persons of exceptionally strict traditional morality, while the Victorian agnostics professed an unbounded admiration for the ethical ideals of the religion which they combated on intellectual grounds.

Today all this is changed. The attack on tradition has shifted to the sphere of morals, and men no longer believe that it is possible to throw over the religious doctrines of Christianity and yet preserve the moral and social traditions of European civilisation intact. Consequently, our civilisation is now faced with a definite issue. We have to choose between two contradictory ideals—on, the one hand, that of the traditional Christian morality, which finds its most complete expression in Catholicism—on the other, the ideal of a purely hedonist morality, which involves unrestricted freedom in sexual relations and the reorganisation of marriage and the family on the model of the new Russian legislation.

Faced with these alternatives, the ordinary Englishman is in a difficult position. He is instinctively favourable to the traditional morality on which English law and social organisation are based, and at the same time he is uneasily conscious of his lack of any clear system of ethical principles with which to justify his attitude. The defence of orthodox morality is consequently left more and more to those who still adhere to dogmatic Christianity, above all to the representatives of the Catholic Church. The advocates of the new morality, on their side, are only too ready to acknowledge the Catholic Church as the representative and champion of traditional ethics, for since their propaganda is based on the irrational character of orthodox morality, they are anxious to emphasise its theological origins. They maintain that the Christian view of marriage and of sexual morality in general has no basis in natural ethics. It is an irrational system of taboo created by mediaeval superstition and oriental asceticism. According to Mr. Bertrand Russell, "those who first inculcated such a view must have suffered from a diseased condition of body or mind or both." . . . "A view of this sort, which goes against all the biological facts, can only be regarded as a morbid aberration.

The fact that it is embedded in Christian ethics has made Christianity, throughout its whole history, a force tending towards mental disorders and unwholesome views of life."[5]

So too Dr. Briffault: "The moral standards applied to sex relations are the residual product of that exaltation of ritual purity which pronounced a curse upon sex, stigmatised women as the instrument of Satan and poured scorn upon motherhood. It is in the doctrines of Ambrose and of Origen, of Augustine and Jerome that European sexual morality has its roots." "To the Christian authorities of the patristic age, and for long after, it was more than doubtful whether the state of matrimony were not a state of sin. Married men commonly regarded themselves as unworthy of partaking the sacraments, and deferred doing so, even as regards baptism, until their wife's death or their own approaching end had placed them in a state of grace. The very suggestion that marriage should be regarded as a sacrament would to the Christian Fathers have been gross blasphemy."[6]

If this strange travesty of patristic teaching were to be believed, it is clear that the true representatives of Christian ethical tradition would be found, not in the Catholic Church, but among the most fanatical of the Russian sectaries, much as the Khlysti and Skoptsi. In reality, however, the Church has always based its teaching on marriage and sexual morality, not on its ideals of asceticism, nor even on its theological dogmas, but on broad grounds of natural law and social function. Even St. Augustine, who certainly develops the ascetic and anti-natural side of Christian ethics to its extreme conclusions, is far from being the Manichæan sex-maniac that so many moderns imagine. His fundamental attitude to sex is extraordinarily rational and even scientific. "What food is to the conservation of the individual," he writes, "that sexual intercourse is to the conservation of the race." Hence, in so far as the sexual appetite is directed to its true end, it is as healthy and good as the desire for food. But, on the other hand, any attempt on the part of the individual to separate the pleasure which he derives from the satisfaction of his sexual appetite from its social purpose is essentially immoral. And since the purpose of sex is social, it requires an appropri-

5. *Marriage and Morals,* pp. 50, 43.
6. R. Briffault, *The Mothers,* Vol. III, pp. 506, 248.

ate social organ for its fulfilment. This organ is the family, the union of man and wife "which is the first natural bond of human society." Nevertheless, St. Augustine teaches that the institution of marriage does not rest solely on its fulfilment of its primary function—the procreation of children. If so, there would be no permanence in a childless marriage. It has a "second good," the power of friendship, which has its root in the essentially social character of human nature. The union of male and female is necessary not only for the procreation of children, but also for mutual help, "so that when the warmth of youth has passed away, there yet lives in full vigour the order of charity between husband and wife." In other words, marriage has a spiritual as well as a physical foundation, and it is the union of these two principles, both alike social and natural, which determines the character of the family and the origin of all sexual morality.[7]

Thus the resistance of Catholicism to the hedonism and individualism of the new morality rests not on an irrational system of taboo, but on a solid foundation of biological and sociological principle. It condemns contraception as an unnatural attempt to divorce the sexual activity from its biological function; it forbids irregular sexual intercourse, because it involves the separation of sex from its proper social organ; and it is opposed to divorce and remarriage, because they destroy the permanence of the marriage bond and thus break down the organisation of the family as the primary sociological unit.

And for the same reasons the Church maintains the original and inalienable rights of the family against the claims of the modern state to override them. Leo XIII writes: "No human law can abolish the natural and original right of marriage, ordained by God's authority from the beginning. . . . Hence we have the Family, the society of a man's house, a society limited in numbers, but no less a true society anterior to every kind of state and nation, invested with, rights and duties of its own totally independent of the civil community."[8]

Hence, as Leo XIII pointed out elsewhere, in his encyclical on marriage,[9] the alteration by the state of the fundamental laws that gov-

7. St. Augustine, *De boni conjugali,* caps, 1, 3 and 18.
8. Encyclical *Rerum Novarum,* 1891.
9. Encyclical *Arcanum Divinum,* 1880.

ern marriage and family life will ultimately lead to the ruin of society itself. No doubt the state will gain in power and prestige as the family declines, but state and society are not identical. In fact, the state is often most omnipotent and universal in its claims at the moment when society is dying, as we see in the last age of the Roman Empire. As the vital energy of society declined, the machinery of bureaucratic administration grew more vast and more complicated, until the wretched provincial was often glad to abandon his household and take refuge in the desert or, among the barbarians in order to escape from the intolerable pressure exercised by the ubiquitous agents of the bureaucracy.

At the present day we have reason to ask ourselves whether modern civilisation is not threatened with a similar danger owing to the absorption of the whole of human life in the artificial order of bureaucracy and industrialism. The introduction of the new moral code would remove the last obstacle to the complete mechanisation of society and lead to the final supresession of the independent family by the state. No amount of governmental organisation can supply the place of the natural reserves of vitality on which social health depends. If the Catholic theory of society is true, the supersession of the family means not progress, but the death of society, the end of our age and the passing of European civilisation.

II

We have seen that the traditional Catholic attitude to marriage and morals is essentially social and takes full account of the primary biological significance of sex and of the sociological significance of the family. The partisans of the new morality, on the other hand, are for the most part singularly indifferent to the biological and sociological aspects of the problem. They base their propaganda on a superficial philosophy of hedonism and on an appeal to the romantic ideals of passionate love and emotional freedom. Some writers, such as Mr. Calverton, seem to be entirely reckless of the social consequences of their theories. In fact, their new morality consists simply in the emancipation of sex from all social restrictions. Others, like Bertrand Russell, adopt a more moderate position. The virulence of Bertrand Russell's contempt for Christian ethics and the boldness with which he states paradoxical opinions are apt to blind one to the fact that he is relatively conservative in his attitude to the family and to the question of divorce. He admits unrestricted sexual intercourse only on condition that the birth of children is avoided by the use of contraceptives, and he recognises the importance of preserving a quasi-permanent union from the moment that a child is born. He does not, however, explain how such a state of permanence is to be attained under the new conditions; indeed, it seems little more than a pious aspiration.

There are, however, a few writers, such as Mr. Havelock Ellis and Dr. Briffault, who approach the problem in a more scientific way and who justify the modern revolt from traditional morality on anthropological and sociological grounds. They regard the Christian doctrine of marriage and the family as based upon a misreading of history. The monogamous family has not the fundamental importance that has been attributed to it by Christian tradition. It is a temporary phenomenon, which originated in particular circumstances and which is bound to pass away with the change of economic and political conditions.

Now it is quite true that the traditional view of the family was founded on a somewhat naive and one-sided conception of history. The knowledge of the past was confined to the history of classical civilisation and to that of the Jews, in both of which the patriarchal family reigned supreme. But when the European horizon was widened by the geographical discoveries of modern times, men suddenly realised the existence of societies whose social organisation was utterly different to anything that they had imagined. The discovery of totemism and exogamy, of matrilinear institutions, of polyandry, and of customs of organised sexual licence, gave rise to a whole host of new theories concerning the origins of marriage and the family. Under the influence of the prevalent evolutionary philosophy, scholars like Lewis Morgan elaborated the theory of the gradual evolution of the family from a condition of primitive sexual promiscuity through various forms of group-marriage and temporary pairing up to the higher forms of patriarchal and monogamous marriage as they exist in developed civilisations. This theory naturally commended itself to socialists. It received the official imprimatur of the leaders of German Socialism in the later nineteenth century, and has become as much a part of orthodox socialist thought as the Marxian interpretation of history. It was, however, never fully accepted by the scientific world, and is today generally abandoned, although it still finds a few supporters among anthropologists. In England it is still maintained by Mr. E. S. Hartland and by Dr. Briffault, whose vast work *The Mothers* (3 vols. 1927) is entirely devoted to the subject. According to Briffault, primitive society was purely matriarchal in organisation, and the primitive family group consisted only of a woman and her offspring. A prolonged sexual association, such as we find in all existing forms of marriage, except in Russia, is neither natural nor primitive, and has no place in matriarchal society. The original social unit was not the family, but the clan which was based on matrilinear kinship and was entirely communistic in its sexual and economic relations. The family, as we understand it, owes nothing to biological or sexual causes, but is an economic institution arising from the development of private property and the consequent domination of women by men. It is "but a euphemism for the individualistic male with his subordinate dependents."

But in spite of its logical coherence, and the undoubted existence of matrilinear institutions in primitive society, this theory has not been borne out by recent investigations. The whole tendency of modern anthropology has been to discredit the old views regarding primitive promiscuity and sexual communism, and to emphasise the importance and universality of marriage. Whether the social organisation is matrilinear or patrilinear, whether morality is strict or loose, it is the universal rule of every known society that a woman before she bears a child must be married to an individual male partner. The importance of this rule has been clearly shown by Dr. Malinowski. "The universal postulate of legitimacy," he writes, "has a great sociological significance which is not yet sufficiently acknowledged. It means that in all human societies moral tradition and law decree that the group consisting of a woman and her offspring is not a sociologically complete unit. The ruling of culture runs here again on entirely the same lines as natural endowment; it declares that the human family must consist of the male as well as the female."[10]

10. B. Malinowski, *Sex and Repression in Savage Society* (1927), p. 213.

It is impossible to go back behind the family and find a state of society in which the sexual relations are in a pre-social stage, for the regulation of sexual relations is an essential prerequisite of any kind of culture. The family is not a product of culture; it is, as Malinowski shows, "the starting point of all human organisation "and "the cradle of nascent culture." Neither the sexual nor the parental instinct is distinctively human. They exist equally among the animals, and they only acquire cultural significance when their purely biological function is transcended by the attainment of a permanent social relation. Marriage is the social consecration of the biological functions, by which the instinctive activities of sex and parenthood are socialised and a new synthesis of cultural and natural elements is created in the shape of the family. This synthesis differs from anything that exists in the animal world in that it no longer leaves man free to follow his own sexual instincts; he is forced to conform them to a certain social pattern. The complete freedom from restraint which was formerly supposed to be characteristic of savage life is a romantic myth. In all primitive societies sexual relations are regulated by a complex and meticulous system of restrictions, any breach of which is regarded not merely as an offence against tribal law, but as morally sinful. These rules mostly have their origin in the fear of incest which is the fundamental crime against the family, since it leads to the disorganisation of family sentiment and the destruction of family authority. It is unnecessary to insist upon the importance of the consequences of this fear of incest in both individual and social psychology, since it is the fundamental thesis of Freud and his school. Unfortunately, in his historical treatment of the subject, in *Totem and Tabu,* he inverts the true relation, and derives the sociological structure from a pre-existent psychological complex instead of *vice versa.* In reality, as Dr. Malinowski has shown, the fundamental repression which lies at the root of social life is not the suppressed memory of an instinctive crime—Freud's prehistoric Œdipus tragedy—but a deliberate constructive repression of anti-social impulses. "The beginning of culture implies the repression of instincts, and all the essentials of the Œdipus complex or any other complex are necessary by-products in the gradual formation of culture."[11]

11. Malinowski, *op. cit.,* p. 182.

The institution of the family inevitably creates a vital tension which is creative as well as painful. For human culture is not instinctive. It has to be conquered by a continuous moral effort, which involves the repression of natural instinct and the subordination and sacrifice of the individual impulse to the social purpose. It is the fundamental error of the modern hedonist to believe that man can abandon moral effort and throw off every repression and spiritual discipline and yet preserve all the achievements of culture. It is the lesson of history that the higher the achievement of a culture the greater is the moral effort and the stricter is the social discipline that it demands. The old type of matrilinear society, though it is by no means devoid of moral discipline, involves considerably less repression and is consistent with a much laxer standard of sexual behaviour than is usual in patriarchal societies. But at the same time it is not capable of any high cultural achievement or of adapting itself to changed circumstances. It remains bound to its elaborate and cumbrous mechanism of tribal custom.

The patriarchal family, on the other hand, makes much greater demands on human nature. It requires chastity and self-sacrifice on the part of the wife and obedience and discipline on the part of the children, while even the father himself has to assume a heavy burden of responsibility and submit his personal feelings to the interests of the family tradition. But for these very reasons the patriarchal family is a much more efficient organ of cultural life. It is no longer limited to its primary sexual and reproductive functions. It becomes the dynamic principle of society and the source of social continuity. Hence, too, it acquires a distinctively religious character, which was absent in matrilinear societies, and which is now expressed in the worship of the family hearth or the sacred fire and the ceremonies of the ancestral cult. The fundamental idea in marriage is no longer the satisfaction of the sexual appetite, but, as Plato says: "the need that every man feels of clinging to the eternal life of nature by leaving behind him children's children who may minister to the gods in his stead."[12]

This religious exaltation of the family profoundly affects men's attitude to marriage and the sexual aspects of life in general. It is not

12. *Laws*, 773 F.

limited, as is often supposed, to the idealisation of the possessive male as father and head of the household; it equally transforms the conception of womanhood. It was the patriarchal family which created those spiritual ideals of motherhood and virginity which have had so deep an influence on the moral development of culture. No doubt the deification of womanhood through the worship of the Mother Goddess had its origin in the ancient matrilinear societies. But the primitive Mother Goddess is a barbaric and formidable deity who embodies the ruthless fecundity of nature, and her rites are usually marked by licentiousness and cruelty. It was the patriarchal culture which transformed this sinister goddess into the gracious figures of Demeter and Persephone and Aphrodite, and which created those higher types of divine virginity which we see in Athene, the giver of good counsel, and Artemis, the guardian of youth.

The patriarchal society was in fact the creator of those moral ideas which have entered so deeply into the texture of civilisation that they have become a part of our thought. Not only the names of piety and chastity, honour and modesty, but the values for which they stand are derived from this source, so that even where the patriarchal family has passed away we are still dependent on the moral tradition that it created.[13] Consequently, we find that the existing world civilisations from Europe to China are all founded on the tradition of the patriarchal family. It is to this that they owed the social strength which enabled them to prevail over the old cultures of matrilinear type which, alike in Europe and in Western Asia, in China and in India, had preceded the coming of the great classical cultures. Moreover, the stability of the latter has proved to be closely dependent on the preservation of the patriarchal ideal. A civilisation like that of China, in which the patriarchal family remained the corner-stone of society and the foundation of religion and ethics, has preserved its cultural traditions for more than 2,000 years without losing its vitality. In the classical cultures of the

---

13. For this reason the Catholic Church has always associated its teaching on marriage with the patriarchal tradition, and even to-day she still concludes the marriage service with the ancient patriarchal benediction: "May the God of Abraham, the God of Isaac, and the God of Jacob, be with you and may he fulfil his blessing upon you that you may see your children's children even to the third and fourth generation."

Mediterranean world, however, this was not the case. Here the patriarchal family failed to adapt itself to the urban conditions of the Hellenistic civilisation, and consequently the whole culture lost its stability. Conditions of life both in the Greek city state and in the Roman Empire favoured the man without a family who could devote his whole energies to the duties and pleasures of public life. Late marriages and small families became the rule, and men satisfied their sexual instincts by homosexuality or by relations with slaves and prostitutes. This aversion to marriage and the deliberate restriction of the family by the practice of infanticide and abortion was undoubtedly the main cause of the decline of ancient Greece, as Polybius pointed out in the second century B.C.[14] And the same factors were equally powerful in the society of the Empire, where the citizen class even in the provinces was extraordinarily sterile and was recruited not by natural increase, but by the constant introduction of alien elements, above all from the servile class. Thus the ancient world lost its roots alike in the family and in the land and became prematurely withered.

The reconstitution of Western civilisation was due to the coming of Christianity and the re-establishment of the family on a new basis. Though the Christian ideal of the family owes much to the patriarchal tradition which finds such a complete expression in the Old Testament, it was in several respects a new creation that differed essentially from anything that had previously existed. While the patriarchal family in its original form was an aristocratic institution which was the privilege of a ruling race or a patrician class, the Christian family was common to every class, even to the slaves.[15] Still more important was the fact that the Church insisted for the first time on the mutual and bilateral character of sexual obligations. The husband belonged to the wife as exclusively

14. He writes that in his days the diminution of population in Greece was so great that the towns were becoming deserted and the fields unfilled. The reason of this is neither war nor-pestilence, but because men "owing to vanity, avarice or cowardice, no longer wish to marry or to bring up children." In Boeotia especially he notes a tendency for men to leave their property to clubs for public benefactions instead of leaving it to their heirs, "so that the Boeotians often have more free dinners than there are days in the month."—*Polyb. Books* XXXVI, 17, and XX, 6.

15. The same change, however, has taken place in China, where, owing to the influence of Confucianism, the whole population has gradually acquired the family institutions which were originally peculiar to the members of the feudal nobility.

as the wife to the husband. This rendered marriage a more personal and individual relation than it had been under the patriarchal system. The family was no longer a subsidiary member of a larger unity—the kindred or *gens*. It was an autonomous self-contained unit which owed nothing to any power outside itself.

It is precisely this character of exclusiveness and strict mutual obligation which is the chief ground of objection among the modern critics of Christian morality. But whatever may be thought of it, there can be no doubt that the resultant type of monogamous and indissoluble marriage has been the foundation of European society and has conditioned the whole development of our civilisation. No doubt it involves a very severe effort of repression and discipline, but its upholders would maintain that it has rendered possible an achievement which could never have been equalled under the laxer conditions of polygamous or matrilinear societies. There is no historical justification for Bertrand Russell's belief that the Christian attitude to marriage has had a brutalising effect on sexual relations and has degraded the position of woman below even the level of ancient civilisation: on the contrary, women have always had a wider share in social life and a greater influence on civilisation in Europe than was the case either in Hellenic or oriental society: And this is in part due to those very ideals of asceticism and chastity which Bertrand Russell regards as the source of all our troubles. For in a Catholic civilisation the patriarchal ideal is counterbalanced by the ideal of virginity. The family for all its importance does not control the whole existence of its members. The spiritual side of life belongs to a spiritual society in which all authority is reserved to a celibate class. Thus in one of the most important aspects of life the sexual relation is transcended, and husband and wife stand on an equal footing. I believe that this is the chief reason why the feminine element has achieved fuller expression in Catholic culture and why, even at the present day, the feminine revolt against the restrictions of family life is so much less marked in Catholic society than elsewhere.

In Protestant Europe, on the other hand, the Reformation, by abandoning the ideal of virginity and by the destruction of monasticism and of the independent authority of the Church, accentuated the masculine element in the family. The Puritan spirit, nourished on the traditions of the Old Testament, created a new patriarchalism and made the family the religious as well as the social basis of society. Civilisation lost its communal and public character and became private and domestic. And yet, by a curious freak of historical development, it was this Puritan and patriarchal society which gave birth to the new economic order which now threatens to destroy the family. Industrialism grew up, not in the continental centres of urban culture, but in the most remote districts of rural England, in the homes of nonconformist weavers and ironworkers. The new industrial society was entirely destitute of the communal spirit and of the civic traditions which had marked the ancient and the mediaeval city. It existed simply for the production of wealth and left every other side of life to private initiative. Although the old rural culture, based on the household as an independent economic unit, was passing away for ever, the strict ethos of the Puritan family continued to rule men's lives.

This explains the anomalies of the Victorian period both in England and America. It was essentially an age of transition. Society had already entered on a phase of intense urban industrialism, while still remaining faithful to the patriarchal ideals of the old Puritan tradition. Both Puritan morality and industrial mass economy were excessive and one-sided developments, and when the two were brought together in one society they inevitably produced an impossible situation.

The problem that faces us to-day is, therefore, not so much the result of an intellectual revolt against the traditional Christian morality; it is due to the inherent contradictions of an abnormal state of culture. The natural tendency, which is even more clearly visible in America than in England, is for the Puritan tradition to be abandoned and for society to give itself up passively to the machinery of modern cosmopolitan life. But this is no solution. It leads merely to the breaking down of the old structure of society and the loss of the traditional moral standards without creating anything which can take their place. As in the decline of the ancient world, the family is steadily losing its form and its social significance, and the state absorbs more and more of the life of its members. The home is no longer a centre of social activity; it has become, merely a sleeping place for a number of independent wage-earners. The functions which were formerly fulfilled by the head of the family are now being taken over by the state, which educates the children and takes the responsibility for their maintenance and health. Consequently, the father no longer holds a vital position in the family: as Mr. Bertrand Russell says, he is often a comparative stranger to his children, who know him only as "that man who comes for week-ends." Moreover, the reaction against the restrictions of family life which in the ancient world was confined to the males of the citizen class, is to-day common to every class and to both sexes. To the modern girl marriage and motherhood appear not as the conditions of a wider life, as they did to her grandmother, but as involving the sacrifice of her independence and the abandonment of her career.

The only remaining safeguards of family life in modern urban civilisation are its social prestige and the sanctions of moral and religious tradition. Marriage is still the only form of sexual union which is openly tolerated by society, and the ordinary man and woman are usually ready to sacrifice their personal convenience rather than risk social ostracism. But if we accept the principles of the new morality, this last safeguard will be destroyed and the forces of dissolution will be allowed to operate unchecked. It is true that Mr. Russell, at least, is willing to leave us the institution of marriage, on condition that it is strictly demoralised and no longer makes any demands on continence. But it is obvious that these conditions reduce marriage to a very subordinate position. It is no longer the exclusive or even the normal form of sexual relations: it is entirely limited to the rearing of children. For, as Mr. Russell is never tired of pointing out, the use of contraceptives has made sexual intercourse independent of parenthood, and the marriage of the future will be confined to those who seek parenthood for its own sake rather than as the natural fulfilment of sexual love. But under these circumstances who will trouble to marry? Marriage will lose all attractions for the young and the pleasure-loving and the poor and the ambitious. The energy of youth will be devoted to contraceptive love and only when men and women have become prosperous and middle-aged will they think seriously of settling down to rear a strictly limited family.

It is impossible to imagine a system more contrary to the first principles of social well-being. So far from helping modern society to surmount its present difficulties, it only precipitates the crisis. It must lead

inevitably to a social decadence far more rapid and more universal than
that which brought about the disintegration of ancient civilisation. The
advocates of birth-control can hardly fail to realise the consequences
of a progressive decline of the population in a society in which it is
already almost stationary, but for all that their propaganda is entirely
directed towards a further diminution in the birth rate. Many of them,
like Dr. Stopes, are no doubt so much concerned with the problem of
individual happiness that they do not stop to consider how the race
is to be carried on. Others, such as Mr. Russell, are obsessed by the
idea that over-population is the main cause of war and that a diminishing birth rate is the best guarantee of international peace. There is,
however, nothing in history to justify this belief. The largest and most
prolific populations, such as the Chinese and the Hindus, have always
been singularly unaggressive. The most warlike peoples are usually
those who are relatively backward in culture and few in numbers, like
the Huns and the Mongols, or the English in the fifteenth century, the
Swedes in the seventeenth century, and the Prussians in the eighteenth
century. If, however, questions of population should give rise to war
in the future, there can be no doubt that it is nations with wide possessions and a dwindling population who will be most likely to pro-
voke an attack. But it is much more likely that the process will be a
peaceful one. The peoples who allow the natural bases of society to be
destroyed by the artificial conditions of the new urban civilisation will
gradually disappear and their place will be taken by those populations
which live under simpler conditions and preserve the traditional forms
of the family. Thus in England and Scotland the native population will
be replaced by Irish immigrants, in France by Spaniards and Italians, in
Germany by Slavs, and in the United States by Mexicans and negroes
and by immigrants from Eastern Europe.

Such a change would transform Western civilisation far more fundamentally than any social or political revolution. It is however probable
that, long before it has been accomplished, the state will abandon its
present attitude of *laissez-faire* and will take active measures to prevent
the diminution of the population. If by that time the principles of the
new morality are generally accepted, these measures would necessarily
involve the complete regulation of parenthood and procreation by the

state. Motherhood would be regarded as one of the chief branches of the public service and would be organised and controlled by the government on strictly scientific and impersonal principles. But such a system would outrage not only Christian morality, but the very ideals of individual liberty and freedom in love which have been the inspiration of the reformers themselves. If sex has been liberated from the restrictions of marriage only to fall into the hands of a government department, the final stage in the dehumanisation of culture will have been reached. It will mean the end of humanity as we have known it, and it will prove, as some have already suggested, that mankind is not the crown of creation, but is only an intermediate stage in the evolution of an ape into a machine.

Fortunately there is little reason to suppose that such things will be. The true alternative to social suicide is not sexual communism, but the restoration of the family. Sooner or later the state will realise that it can neither take the place of the family nor do without it, and, consequently, it will begin to use all the resources of legislation and social organisation, to protect the family organism. Housing policy, education and taxation, instead of penalising family life, will be directed to its protection and encouragement. Above all, the individualistic tendencies of industrialism must be limited by some system of family insurance or family endowment.

No doubt it will be said that it is impossible to bolster up by artificial means an institution which is no longer adapted to modern conditions. But if human life is to exist at all under the artificial conditions of modern civilisation, it must be safeguarded by artificial means. All our legislation for public health and social welfare is a recognition of the fact that nature can no longer be left to take care of itself. A simple peasant community can preserve its family life without external assistance, but it can also dispense with schools and drains and old age pensions and all the elaborate mechanism of urban civilisation. We are slow to realise the implications of the new order. When the age of transition has passed, if our civilisation has survived the crisis, the family will no longer be left to sink or swim in the economic current, it will be re-established not as an economic unit, but in its higher function as the primary organ of social life and the guardian of cultural tradition. The more we realise that the prosperity of society depends not on economic production but on the quality of the population, the greater will be. the importance of the family which is the only true guardian of the race. At the present day the cause of eugenics is suffering, above all in America, from the championship of cranks and fanatics who are prepared to castrate anybody who fails to conform to the accepted standards of successful mediocrity. But if it is to be taken seriously, eugenics must be based, in the future, on sound sociological, as well as biological, principles. True eugenics is the science of *good breeding*. It must aim at the improvement of the race by the combination of good blood with a high ethical and cultural tradition. This aim can only be fulfilled through the family, which, as we have seen, was founded from the beginning on a union of cultural and biological functions. In the past this aspect of the family has been overshadowed by economic needs, but it has never been entirely forgotten, and it still possesses vast potentialities for the enrichment and purification of social life. The ideals of eugenics can be best realised, not by governmental supervision and the sterilisation of the unfit, but by the creation of a strong and enlightened family feeling. The aristocratic ideal must be separated from economic circumstances and given the widest possible extension so that even the poorest man and woman may be proud of their blood and may be the conscious heirs of a high cultural and ethical tradition.

III

But however important is the social aspect of sex, it is not the only basis of morality. Men will never regulate their sexual life entirely, by considerations of social utility or the common good. Sexual passion is too strong for that. The attempt of the eugenist and the sexual reformer to treat sex purely as a matter of personal and social hygiene fails to take account of the elemental forces of human nature. For not only is man incapable of rationalising sexual passion, he is ready to make it an object of worship. All modern literature is full of the exaltation of passion and the glorification of the lover who defies social conventions and sacrifices honour and happiness in order to attain his desire. This romantic attitude towards sex is no less contrary to Christian morality than the rationalism of the advocates of sexual reform, but it is far more coloured by Christian ideas. It is, indeed, definitely religious in that it regards sexual love as a means of moral purification and spiritual enlightenment. It shuts its eyes to the physical aspects of sex and sees love only as the mating of souls. Unfortunately, this denial of the physical character of sex tends to produce not spirituality but an unhealthy and perverted sexuality. It finds its pleasure in frustration rather than in fulfilment. The greater the obstacles to the fulfilment of passion and the more hopeless its prospects, the more romantic it is. This explains the tendency to exalt whatever is forbidden, which we see in the romantic idealisation of incest which is characteristic of Byron and Shelley and Poe and in the attitude of modern romantics towards sexual perversion.

At the present day the old romantic attitude is no longer possible. Psychology and psycho-analysis have stripped away all poetical illusions and have pointed with brutal directness to the crude realities which underlie the romantic sentiment. We are actually suffering from an equally exaggerated insistence on the physical aspect of sex and from a reaction to crude materialism. Nevertheless, romanticism still colours our thought more than we are aware. Nothing could be more incisive than Bertrand Russell's criticism of the romantic view of love, and yet for all his rationalism and psychological knowledge we cannot but feel that his own attitude to sex is fundamentally romantic. And the same is true of almost all the advocates of the new morality, whether they are scholars like Mr. Havelock Ellis and Dr. Briffault or popular writers like Dr. Marie Stopes. Their rationalism is mixed with romanticism in an inextricable tangle, so that it is impossible to feel any confidence in their scientific impartiality. And if this is true of the intellectual leaders, the case of the ordinary man and woman is still worse. Their romanticism leads them to idealise their emotions, while their rationalism makes them sceptical of all ultimate principles. Consequently, for them sexual life loses its depth and permanence and mystery and becomes a surface activity, a form of amusement from which they hope to derive an emotional thrill only.

The evils of this state of things have been most clearly realised by the one modern writer on sex who has steered clear alike of the Scylla of rationalism and the romantic Charybdis—the late Mr. D. H. Lawrence. No one could accuse him of undervaluing or belittling sex. To him it was the most important thing in the world and the only thing that was sacred. But for that very reason he was at one with the traditionalist in his hostility to the romanticism and rationalism of the modern attitude towards it. He saw the source of evil in the modern tendency to "cerebralise" sex. As soon as we attempt to exploit love mentally, to make it an intellectual problem and a matter of conscious emotion, we make a mess of it, it becomes "mind-perverted, will-perverted, ego-perverted love." Sex is good, it is the intrusion of the mind that pollutes it and makes it turn rotten. Consequently, it was his ideal to keep it apart from the mind, to preserve the chastity of pure sex from being messed about by reason and conscious emotion, to return to the spontaneous natural sexuality of the animal.

Now it is true that natural sexuality is good, and that it is the highest and, as it were, the most religious activity of which the animal is capable. But in man this natural purity of sex is no longer possible, it is inevitably contaminated by egotism and conscious emotion. It passes beyond its natural function and becomes an outlet for all the unsatisfied cravings of the psychic life. It ceases to be a natural physical appetite and becomes a quasi-spiritual passion which absorbs the whole man and drags his nature awry.

Because Catholicism has always recognised this truth and has taught that concupiscence—the disorder of the sexual instinct—is an evil, it is condemned by writers like Bertrand Russell as a preacher of death. But the Catholic view is no Manichæan fancy, it is a fact of common experience which is amply confirmed by the teaching of modern psychology. Indeed, the Freudian psychologist insists even more strongly than the theologian that the sexual impulse is the chief source of psychic suffering and disorder. But he differs from the Catholic in that he believes that it is possible to heal this disorder by the methods of rational analysis. This may be successful as a means of curing the neuroses which are the most obvious symptom of the disorder, but it does not remove the spiritual conflict which lies behind them. The rationalisation of the sexual life and the removal of repressions do not suffice to give men back their peace of mind and spiritual unity. The modern generation seems none the happier for its emancipation. Indeed, if we may judge by the descriptions of Mr. Aldous Huxley and other observers of contemporary life, sex has become a source of torment and disgust rather than of pleasure.

We may refuse to accept the Catholic solution of the moral problem, but we cannot deny the existence of the problem itself. The rationalist who attacks Catholicism for its asceticism and its low views of human nature is himself more profoundly pessimistic. If Pascal views the world as a hospital, Voltaire sees it as a mad-house. Human nature has lost its dignity without losing its corruption. The evil is still there, but it has become disgusting instead of tragic.

Whether we view the world from a religious or a naturalistic standpoint, we have to admit that man is an unsatisfactory creature. Judged as an animal, he lacks the perfection of an animal, because his spiritual powers impart something monstrous to his animality. And as a rational being, even the rationalist must admit that he is a failure, since for the greater part of his life he is at the mercy of impulse and passion. If he attempts to suppress the animal side of his nature by a sheer effort of conscious will, nature finds a hundred unexpected and unpleasant ways to take its revenge. If, on the other hand, he tries to come to terms with his instincts by the removal of all repression and the relaxation of moral restrictions, his sexual life becomes trivial and empty and loses its contact with the deeper forces of the personality. In either case, the attempt to rationalise sex and to shut our eyes to the deeper realities that lie beneath and above reason ends in failure. If man shuts himself up in the narrow limits of his rational consciousness, his whole life becomes arid and stunted. In some way or other he must open his being to the greater forces that surround it. If no other way is open to him, he must seek relief, like Mr. D. H. Lawrence, in a direct contact with the unmentalised life of nature, above all, in the physical ecstasy of sex by which he merges his little drop of rational consciousness in the life-flux of the material organism.

There remains the Catholic solution. The concrete reality of sex, which is too strong for the abstract laws of reason, can be met only by the equally objective reality of spirit. Although sex cannot be rationalised, it can be spiritualised, for man finds in religion a force which is capable of taking possession of the will no less completely than physical passion. Of course, the very idea of spiritual reality is to-day generally rejected. The rationalist regards it as a metaphysical delusion, while to Mr. Lawrence it is itself the offspring of rationalism, an abstraction of" the white mind." To the religious mind, however, spiritual reality is not an ideal or a metaphysical abstraction, it is a living Being—*Deus fortis vivus*. And even those who refuse all objective validity to this belief cannot deny its tremendous psychological potency, for experience shows that it is the one power in the world that is stronger than self-interest and sensuality, and that it is capable of transforming human nature and altering the course of history. The real danger of religion is not that it is too weak or too abstract to affect human conduct, but rather that it is so absolute and uncompromising that nature may become crushed and overwhelmed:

> oppressa gravi sub religione
> Quae caput a coeli regionibus ostendebat
> Horribili super aspectu mortalibus instans.

This is no imaginary danger. We have in Buddhism the example of a great world-religion which has founded itself on the radical denial of life and which regards birth and sexual desire as unmitigated evils. Nor is this attitude peculiar to Buddhism. It was equally characteristic of the Gnostic and Manichæan movements which were the most dangerous rivals of early Christianity, and it affected the Christian mind itself through the apocryphal Gospels and Acts, and many other subterranean channels.

Nevertheless, this tendency never captured the Church. She insisted from the first that "marriage is honourable in all and the marriage bed undefiled." Although Catholicism conquered the world by its ideals of virginity and martyrdom, it never denied the good of marriage or the good of life. If the asceticism of the monks of the desert appears to us purely negative and hostile to life, we must remember that it was only by a complete break with the old world—by going out into the wilderness and making a fresh start—that it was possible to realise the independence and autonomy of Christian ideals. Above all, sex had to be rescued from the degradation and vulgarisation that had overtaken it in the decadence of Graeco-Roman society, and this could only be accomplished by a drastic process of discipline and purgation. Catholicism stood for the existence of absolute spiritual values in a disillusioned and hopeless world, and consequently it had to assert these values by the sacrifice of every lesser good, not only the good of marriage, but the good of life itself. The essentially positive character of the Christian ideal could only be completely realised when the struggle with the pagan world was over, and consequently it is in the lives of saints such as Francis of Assisi and Philip Neri rather than St. Anthony or St. Symeon Stylites that we may find the fullest expression of Christian asceticism—an asceticism which is fundamentally humane and friendly to life. It involves an heroic sacrifice of the natural life of sex and of the family to the service of God and the Christian people, but it is in no sense a denial of the values that it has transcended.

Moreover, Catholicism is not content simply to accept marriage as a natural good: from the first it has regarded marriage as possessing a positive spiritual value and significance—as a means of supernatural grace. This sacramental view of marriage finds its basis in the celebrated passage of the Epistle to the Ephesians[16] which compares the union of man and woman in marriage to the union of Christ and the Church—a passage which is strangely ignored by Bertrand Russell when he declares that St. Paul never "suggests that there may be any positive good in marriage or that affection between man and wife may be a beautiful and desirable thing."[17] In fact, it is precisely in the mystery of love that St. Paul finds the meaning of marriage. It is not merely a physical union of bodies under the blind compulsion of instinctive desire, nor is it an abstract moral union of wills. It is the physical expression or incarnation of a spiritual union in which the sexual act has become the vehicle of a higher creative purpose. It is for this reason that marriage is regarded by the Church as a type and a sacramental participation of the central mystery of the Faith—the marriage of God and man in the Incarnation. As humanity is saved and deified by Christ, so the natural functions of sex and reproduction are spiritualised by the sacrament of marriage.

---

16. *Ephesians*, v. 23–33.
17. *Marriage and Morals*, p. 42.

At first sight this doctrine may seem infinitely removed from the realities of life and of little assistance to the practical moralist. But if we once renounce the vain attempt to rationalise sexual life, we must be prepared to find in sex a mysterious element which is akin to the ultimate mysteries of life. The religious significance of sex has always been felt by man. Primitive religion regarded it as the supreme cosmic mystery, the source of the life and fruitfulness of the earth; while the higher religions also made it the basis of their view of life whether in a pessimistic sense, as in Buddhism, or, as in China, in the metaphysical idea of a rhythmic order pervading the life of the universe. Christianity went a step farther by attributing a positive spiritual significance to sex, and thus gave to Western civilisation a higher ideal of love and marriage than any other culture has known. If these characteristically European ideals are to survive, it is essential to preserve a spiritual basis for sexual life. Romanticism attempted to accomplish this by making a religion of sex and exalting passion itself into the place of a spiritual ideal, but, in doing so, it lost its hold alike on spiritual principles and physical realities. The true way of spiritualising sex is not to idealise our emotions and to hide physical appetite under a cloud of sentiment, but rather to bring our sexual life into relation with a more universal reality. The romantic idealisation of passion and the rationalist attempt to reduce love to the satisfaction of physical desire alike fail to create that permanent basis of sexual life which can only be found in a spiritual order which transcends the appetites and the self-will of the individual. It is only when a man accepts marriage as something greater than himself, a sacred obligation to which he must conform himself, that he is able to realise all its spiritual and social possibilities.

Hence the restoration of the religious view of marriage which is the Catholic ideal is the most important of all the conditions for a solution of our present difficulties. Its importance cannot be measured by practical considerations, for it means the reintroduction of a spiritual principle into the vital centre of human life.

Western civilisation to-day is threatened with the loss of its freedom and its humanity. It is in danger of substituting dead mechanism for living culture. Hedonism cannot help, nor yet rationalism. It can be saved only by a renewal of life. And this is impossible without love, for love is the source of life, both physically and spiritually. But if physical desire is separated from its spiritual principle and made an end in itself, it ceases to be love and it no longer gives life. It degenerates into sterile lust. It is only when it is spiritualised by faith that it becomes vivifying love and participates in the mystery of creation. Love requires faith, as life requires love. The loss of faith ultimately means not merely moral disorder and suffering, but the loss of social vitality and the decay of physical life.

XIV

Religion and Life

It is often said that Christianity is out of touch with life and that it no longer satisfies the needs of the modern world. And these criticisms are symptomatic of a general change of attitude with regard to religious problems. Men to-day are less interested in the theological and metaphysical assumptions of religion than in its practical results. They are concerned not so much with the truth of Christian doctrine as with the value of the Christian way of life. It is Christian ethics even more than Christian dogma that has become the principal object of attack.

This is not altogether a misfortune, for it shows that people no longer treat religion as something that has no relation to man's daily life. The passive acceptance of religion as something that every respectable citizen takes for granted is no longer possible, and at the same time the self-satisfied bourgeois acceptance of the world as it is is equally discredited. To-day everybody admits that something is wrong with the world, and the critics of Christianity are the very people who feel this most. The most violent attacks on religion come from those who are most anxious to change the world, and they attack Christianity because they think that it is an obstructive force that stands in the way of a real reform of human life. There has seldom been a time in which men were more dissatisfied with life and more conscious of the need for deliverance, and if they turn away from Christianity it is because they feel that Christianity is a servant of the established order, and that it has no real power or will to change the world and to rescue man from his present difficulties. They have lost their faith in the old spiritual traditions that inspired civilisation in the past, and they tend to look for a solution to some external practical remedy such as communism, or the scientific organisation of life; something definite and objective that can be applied to society as a whole.

There is, however, little ground for supposing that the world can be saved by machinery or by any external reform. In fact, the great tragedy of modern civilisation is to be found in the failure of material progress to satisfy human needs. The modern world has more power than any previous age, but it has used its new power for destruction as much as for life; it has more wealth, and yet we are in the throes of a vast economic crisis; it has more knowledge, and yet all our knowledge seems powerless to help us. What our civilisation lacks is not power and wealth and knowledge, but spiritual vitality, and, unless it is possible to secure that, nothing can save us from the fate that overtook the civilisation of classical antiquity, and so many other civilisations that were brilliant and powerful in their day.

Now this question of spiritual vitality, whether in the case of the individual or society, is the very centre and essence of the religious problem. Religion is not philosophy, or science or ethics, it is nothing more or less than a communion with the Divine Life, whether it be regarded from within as the act of communion itself or externally as a system of beliefs and practices by which man brings his life into relation with the powers that rule the life of the universe.

Primitive religion is concerned, as we should expect, primarily with the powers of nature, and it finds its centre in the cult of the powers of fertility and generation on which the physical life of the earth and man alike was dependent. All the vital moments in the life of the tribe or the peasant community were invested with religious significance and sanctified by religious rites, and these rites were not merely magical in the utilitarian sense, but sacramental and mystical, since they were the channels by which man attained contact and communion with the divine powers that ruled the world. Thus, in primitive society there could be no question of any contradiction or conflict between religion and life, since the two were complementary aspects of the same thing. Religion was the vital centre of the social organism and governed the whole economic and political activity of society. Nor was there any contradiction between the material and the spiritual, for material things were regarded as the vehicles of spiritual forces; in fact, to the primitive the world is a vast complex of spiritual powers, good, bad, and indifferent, which affect his life at every turn, and religion is the trail that he has blazed out for himself through this spiritual jungle.

The coming of the higher religions changed all this. Religion no longer found its centre in the practical needs of human life. It became a matter of spiritual discipline and intellectual contemplation. Man realised the transcendent character of spiritual reality and freed himself from the terror of the dark and the power of the sinister forces that lurk in or behind nature. But this higher type of religion, with its clear realisation of the distinction between matter and spirit, also contained the seeds of a conflict between religion and life. There was no room for common humanity on the icy summits to which the path of contemplation led, and yet it was at the same time the only way to deliverance and spiritual life. This contrast is seen in its most striking and paradoxical form in Buddhism, for Buddhism is, above all, a direct and straightforward attempt to solve the problem of human life, and it does this by a radical denial of life itself. The Buddha professed to teach man the secret of happiness and the way of spiritual deliverance, but his noble, ethical teaching has its beginning in the realisation that existence is suffering, and its end in the peace of Nirvana.

This pessimism and turning away from life is characteristic to a greater or less extent of all the great religions of the ancient world; even the Greeks, for all their humanism and appreciation of physical life, did not escape from it. The first word in Greek speculation is the Orphic mysticism, with its yearning for deliverance from the sorrowful circle of birth and death, and its last word is contained in the Neoplatonic doctrine of the evil of matter, and the necessity for the soul to escape from the world of sense to the world of pure spirit.

It was to a World dominated by these conceptions, as well as by the decadent remains of the older tradition of nature worship, that Christianity came, and it also brought a message of deliverance and spiritual salvation. But it inherited a different tradition from that of either the Greek or the oriental world, and its dualism was not the dualism of the Indian yogi or that of the Hellenic philosopher. Jewish religion differed from all the rest in the dynamic realism of its conception of God. The God of Israel was no metaphysical abstraction, like the Platonic Idea of the Good, or the universal Brahman, or the Chinese Tao, "not the God of the philosophers and savants, but the Living God, God of Abraham, God of Isaac, God of Jacob, *Deus meus et Deus vester*."

This Living God manifested Himself externally by the vital action of His creative Spirit—as the breath of Divine Life that brooded over the primordial chaos and which inspires the prophets with the word of life. In the Hellenistic language of the Book of Wisdom it is the power "that reaches from end to end, ordering all things sweetly and strongly, which, being one, has power to do all things and remaining in itself renews all things, and from generation to generation passing into holy souls makes men friends of God and prophets."

Thus the Christian idea of salvation was not deliverance from the body and from the sensible world; it was the salvation of the whole man, body and soul, by the coming of a new life. In no other religion is the conception of *life* so central and so characteristic as in Christianity.

From the beginning, Christianity was regarded not as an intellectual gnosis or a new morality, but as a new life: as the communication of a new vital principle, which transformed human nature by raising it to an objectively higher plane of being. In the eyes of the primitive Church the Christian was a new creature, as different or even more different from the natural "psychic" man as the latter was from the animals. This conception is absolutely fundamental alike to the Pauline and the Johannine theology. To St. Paul Christ is the second Adam, the first born of the new creation, and it was from the organic and sacramental union between Christ and the Church that the new spiritual humanity was born. And so, too, in the Johannine writings Jesus is not merely a teacher or a moral exemplar; he is life and the source of life, and the essence of Christianity consists in the grafting of this divine life on the stock of humanity by a vital sacramental act.

This sacramentalism has led many modern critics to compare Christianity to the contemporary mystery religions, which also laid emphasis on the conception of a new birth. But, whereas the pagan mysteries were simply the rites of the old nature religions invested with a new metaphysical, or rather, theosophical significance, the sacraments of Christianity are organically connected with its essential nature. The humanity of Jesus is a sacrament, the visible church is a sacrament, and the vital moments of the Christian life necessarily manifest themselves in sacramental acts. The mystery religions and Gnosticism were alike powerless to bridge the gulf between human life and spiritual reality. They were ways of escape from life, not ways of regeneration. Christianity defeated its rivals because it was felt to be an historical and social reality, capable of transforming human life.

Primitive Christianity is instinct with a triumphant sense of spiritual vitality that has no parallel in the history of religion. "Awake thou that sleepest and arise from the dead and Christ will shine upon thee." The new principle of spiritual life that had entered humanity made it possible for men to face the harsh realities of existence with new courage. It did not free from suffering and death, but it subordinated them to vital ends. This is the greatest psychological victory of Christianity: the spiritual reconquest of that great part of life that had hitherto lain under the shadow of death. "Show us miracles," wrote Blake, "can you have greater miracles than these? Men who devote their life's whole comfort to entire scorn and injury and death." The Christian could accept what was unbearable to human nature, because the cross had become the token of life. As St. Paul says, he could rejoice in his sufferings because they were all extension and completion of what Christ had suffered for His body, which is the Church.

This heroic acceptance of suffering is, of course, rare. It is the mark of a saint. But it is only in the saints that the Christian life is completely realised. We cannot judge Christianity by statistics or by striking an average. One saint can do more than a thousand average men, however active and well organised they may be. In this respect Christianity is essentially aristocratic, since the quality of the individual is the only thing that matters. And yet, on the other hand, it is the most democratic of religions, for an uneducated beggar who is a saint counts for more than a thousand scholars or organisers. As St. Francis says, the brilliant preacher may congratulate himself on the effects of his sermons, when their success is really due to the prayers of some unknown saint, whose importance is realised neither by himself nor by others.

This is what St. Paul means in his famous panegyric of charity, for charity is nothing else but this mysterious power of spiritual life actuating the will. It is no human power or moral quality, but a supernatural energy that transforms human nature and builds up a new humanity. Nothing gives a more appalling idea of the difference between living and dead religion and of the apostacy of the modern world than the profound degradation that this word has undergone in modern times. It has lost all its vital significance and its mysterious "numinous" quality. It has become identified with the most external and spiritually barren type of social beneficence, and even this beneficence is tainted with the suggestion of social patronage and ethical self-satisfaction. And in the same way, that great saying of St. John, "He that loveth not knoweth not God, for God is love," has been degraded from the most profound of spiritual truths into a sentimental platitude.

These are but specimens of the way in which spiritual concepts can become emptied of their vital significance. We have only to compare modern ecclesiastical art with that of the past to feel that the life has gone out of it, and that what was once seen as living reality has become a dead formula. And this devitalisation of modern religion goes a long way to explain the anti-Christian attitude of writers like Nietzsche and D. H. Lawrence. For there is nothing so repulsive as dead religion; it is the deadest thing there is. As the Gospel says, it is not even good enough for the dunghill.

What is the reason for this state of things? There are plenty of people who will say that it is because Christianity has been tried and found wanting, that its promise of new life was a delusion, and that it never possessed any real power of changing the world or of transforming human nature. But is it possible to assert that in the face of history? Is it not obvious to any unprejudiced mind that Christianity has been one of the greatest spiritual forces in the history of the world, and that our civilisation would have been an entirely different thing without it? And even to-day it retains its power over the minds of those who come into vital contact with it. The trouble is that the channels of communication between Christianity and the modern world have been narrowed and diminished. The world has gone on its own way and left Christianity on one side, and it is only those who have a strong sense of personal religion that have the courage to surmount these obstacles and reestablish contact for themselves. And even these often find it hard to bring the whole of their life into relation with Christian standards. They are

Christian in heart and will, and yet a large part of their life—physical, economic and social—remains unchanged as part of the secular world.

The fact is that man is a social being, and his social environment conditions the greater part of his existence. He cannot free himself from social control by a mere act of will, and yet, on the other hand, the Christian cannot acquiesce in a division of life which makes religion a purely private affair that has no influence in social and practical matters. This has always been one of the central problems of Christian life. The early Christians were, indeed, forced to make a radical breach with the secular world because that world was pagan, and the mere fact of being a Christian cut a man off from civic life and public activity. The Christians were a race apart, with a social life of their own, which, like that of the Jews or the early Quakers, was the more intense for being repressed and limited. But with the conversion of the Empire the danger of secularisation at once became serious. It seemed as though the world was more dangerous as a friend than as an enemy, and as though the religion which had withstood all the attacks of the persecutors would lose its freedom and vitality now that it had become the state-church of the Empire. The new situation called for a new remedy, and this was found in the monastic movement which, beginning in Egypt, spread throughout the Christian world with extraordinary rapidity. The monastic life was nothing else but an uncompromising attempt to realise the teaching of the Gospels in practice, to abandon everything that stood in the way of the literal fulfilment of the evangelical ideal, and to base the whole of life on Christian principles.

Men fled from the cities to the desert in order to escape from the atmosphere of secularism that pervaded social life. They built up a new social life outside the state—a life of the simplest possible kind without private property, without personal independence, without marriage; a communism founded on poverty, chastity, and obedience, which is the only true communism that the world has known.

Such a life could, of course, only be realised by a small minority. It was the inner citadel of the Christian life, a kind of reservoir of spiritual power on which the rest of the Church could draw, according to its needs. There was, of course, a danger that the cult of the monastic ideal would lead men to neglect or undervalue the life of the ordinary

Christian, as we see in the history of the Eastern Church, which lost
its power to leaven the world and became as static and unchanging as
the other religions of the oriental world. In the West, however, monasticism always possessed a sense of its apostolic mission. It was the
monks who converted the barbarians and laid the foundations of Western culture. Owing to the example and the influence of the monks, the
Western Church did not acquiesce in that dualism of religion and life
which was the natural result of the external acceptance of Christianity
by a barbarous and semi-pagan society. Mediaeval Christianity was a
dynamic force which strove against enormous odds to realise itself in
social life. However unsuccessful that effort was, it was at least a vital
movement that embraced all that was living in contemporary culture.
From St. Benedict and St. Boniface to St. Bernard and St. Francis, from
Bede to Alcuin, to St. Bonaventure and St. Thomas, the history of the
mediaeval church is the story of an heroic and tragic struggle for the
vindication of spiritual ideals and the realisation of Christian principles
in social life. We cannot of course regard mediaeval civilisation as the
model of what a Christian civilisation should be—as an ideal to which
modern society should conform itself. It is admirable not so much for
what it achieved as for what it attempted—for its refusal to be content
with partial solutions, and for its attempt to bring every side of life into
vital relation with religion.

Thus it is no accident that the loss of Christian unity in the sixteenth
century was accompanied by the loss of the unity of Christian life. The
attempt of the Reformers to spiritualise religion ended in the secularisation of society and of civilisation. The Reformation is a classical
example of the blunder of emptying out the baby with the bath. The
Reformers revolted against the externalism of mediaeval religion, and
so they abolished the Mass. They protested against the lack of personal
holiness, and so they abolished the saints. They attacked the wealth and
self-indulgence of the monks, and so they abolished monasticism and
the life of voluntary poverty and asceticism. They had no intention of
abandoning the ideal of Christian perfection, but they sought to realise
it in Puritanism instead of in monasticism, and in pietism instead of in
mysticism. And the result was that the practice of perfection became
the mark of a sect instead of the vocation of a minority. The late Canon

Lacey used to maintain that the sects in Protestantism correspond to the religious orders in Catholicism, and there is an undeniable element of truth in this view, for each new attempt to realise Christianity in practice, from the Anabaptists to the Quakers, and from the Moravians and the Methodists to the Plymouth Brethren, gave birth to a new religious body. But whereas the religious order was part of a universal whole, and had its *raison d'être* in the life of the whole, each sect set itself up against its predecessor and existed as an end in itself. The Puritans attempted to popularise asceticism by making it binding on every Christian, and the result was that they rendered it repulsive. The ordinary man was ready enough to recognise the self-devotion of the mediaeval ascetic, but he resented the claims of the Puritan saints as hypocrisy or spiritual snobbery. Consequently, every fresh assertion of the Puritan claim was followed by a reaction that tended to the secularisation of culture. Where Puritanism was defeated, as in eighteenth-century England and Germany, the state-churches became more secularised than the mediaeval Church at its worst, and where it was victorious, as in Scotland and New England, it had a narrowing and cramping effect on life and culture.

Meanwhile, in Catholic Europe, the Church still maintained the principle of spiritual unity and its claim to the control of social and intellectual life. It showed its vitality by the intense missionary activity of the new religious orders, and by the spiritual life of its saints and mystics. But it retained its hold on society only at the cost of immense strain. It was like a besieged city under the martial law of the Inquisition and behind the ramparts of state protection. And, even so, it was not safe from the attacks of sectarianism and secularism.

The Catholic world also had its Puritans in the Jansenists and its Erastians in the Gallicans. No less than in Protestant Europe, the bitterness of religious strife discredited the cause of religion and alienated the mind of society. The victory lay neither with Jesuit nor Jansenist, nor Huguenot, but with Voltaire; while the enlightened despotism of the eighteenth-century state made the Church pay heavily for the reliance that it had placed in the support of the secular power.

The Church no longer protested against social injustice. It had become the ally of the ruling powers and the tool of vested interests; and, consequently, the European mind turned away from a Christianity that seemed to have lost its spiritual vitality, and looked for a new ideal in the service of humanity and in the cult of Liberty, Social Progress, and Rational Enlightenment.

The age of the French Revolution was a time of boundless hope and idealism. Men felt that the world was being born again, and that they were witnessing the liberation of humanity from its age-long enslavement to superstition and oppression and the dawn of a new age.

In spite of its apparent rationalism, the movement was essentially a religious one, which drew its inspiration from Christian sources and clothed traditional ideas in new imagery. But it was a religion that substituted intellectual abstractions for spiritual realities that put imagination in the place of Faith, and Idealism in the place of Charity. Where Christianity recognised the reality of the immense burden of inherited evil that weighed on the human race, and the need for a real deliverance, the new religion shut its eyes to everything but the natural virtues of the human heart, and salved the wounds of humanity with a few moral platitudes. Thus the new religion became a religion of death and not of life. Instead of freeing mankind, it liberated the anti-spiritual forces of economic individualism and selfish nationalism, and left society free to drift to destruction.

All this was realised more clearly by that strange, unorthodox prophet, William Blake, than by the official representatives of Christian tradition. "He can never be a friend to the human race," he wrote, "who is a preacher of Natural Morality or Natural Religion . . . you, O Deists! profess yourselves the enemies of Christianity and you are so; you are also the enemies of the Human Race and of Universal Nature. . . . Your religion, O Deists, is the worship of the God of this World by the means of what you call Natural Religion and Natural Philosophy and of Natural Morality or self Righteousness, the selfish virtues of the Natural Heart. This was the religion of the Pharisees, who murdered Jesus. Deism is the same and ends in the same." "Rousseau thought men good by nature; he found them evil and found no friend. Friendship cannot exist without Forgiveness of sins continually."[1]

---

1. *To the Deists* in *Jerusalem*, p. 52.

But at the same time he was no less hostile to the orthodox Christianity of his age, which had abandoned the cause of the poor, and which used religious arguments to palliate oppression and injustice.

In the past Christianity had been a gateway to life, but it was so no longer.

> Once meek and in a perilous path
> The just man kept his course along
> The vale of death.
> Roses are planted where thorns grow
> And on the barren heath
> Sing the honey bees.
> Till the villain left the paths of ease
> To walk in perilous paths, and drive
> The just man into barren climes.
> Now the sneaking serpent walks.
> In mild humility
> And the just man rages in the wilds
> Where lions roar.[2]

He saw orthodox Christianity as the golden Church into which no one could enter because of the serpent that had defiled the altar, and so the just man turned aside to a pig sty and laid him down among the swine.[3]

Yet, in spite of the inroads of secularism, traditional Christianity was a far stronger and more vital thing than the fantastic Gnostic mythology in which Blake found his personal solution. His idealism was merely a butterfly under the wheel of modern civilisation, while the old Christian tradition still showed its power over the lives of men.

All through the spiritual decline of the modern world there have been men and women who refused all compromise, and maintained the ideal of the Christian life in all its fullness. The beggar saint, Benedict Joseph Labre, was the contemporary of the philosophers who preached the gospel of enlightened selfishness and of the industrialists who sacrificed human life to the power of money. The Curé d'Ars worked his

2. *The Marriage of Heaven and Hell:* Argument.
3. "I saw a Chapel all of Gold."

miracles in the midst of the self-satisfied bourgeois materialism of the age of Louis Philippe and the Second Empire. Father Damien served the lepers of Molokai when the economic exploitation of the subject peoples by European commercialism was at its height, and at a time when it seemed impossible to disentangle human life from the complexities of a mechanical civilisation, Charles de Foucauld left Paris to lead the life of the Fathers of the Desert in the inner recesses of the Sahara.

And, although this is an extreme instance, the case of de Foucauld is, in a way, typical of the situation of the Christian ideal in the modern world. It was forced to separate itself from the main stream of modern life, and so, in spite of its abiding vitality, it could not dominate or modify the circumstances that governed the lives of the majority of men. The life of the saints was a witness against the modern world, rather than an example to it. The life of the ordinary man was governed not by the rule of faith, but by the law of money. Business, not religion, was the norm of existence.

It is true that Christianity can never cease altogether to be social so long as it remains Christianity. This fact finds its most complete expression in the objective sacramentalism of the Catholic Church, but is not entirely absent even in the most individualistic forms of Protestantism. It is of the very essence of the Christian life to be social, for it is a communion with man as well as with God—the life of a Church.

Nevertheless, there is a danger in the modern world that the social life of the Church should sink to a secondary plane as compared with that of secular society. To the early Christians the Church was literally everything: it was the new humanity and the beginning of a new world. Even in the Middle Ages the Church was still the fundamental society which embraced a larger and deeper part of human life than the state or any economic society. But in the modern world, and especially among Protestants, the Church has become a secondary society, a kind of religious auxiliary or dependency of the primary society which is the state; and the secular and economic sides of life are continually encroaching upon it, until the Church is in danger of being pushed out of life altogether.

How is this state of things to be remedied? How can Christianity once more become the vital centre of human life?

In the first place it is necessary to recover the ground that has been lost through the progressive secularisation of modern civilisation. We must transcend the individualism and sectarianism of the post-Reformation period, and recover our vital contact with Christianity as a social reality and an organic unity. And this is impossible unless we transcend the subjectivity and relativism of nineteenth-century thought and recover an objective and realist sense of spiritual truth.

But even this by itself is not enough. It is merely the foundation for the essential task that the modern Christian has got to face. What the world needs is not a new religion, but a new application of religion to life. And Christianity cannot manifest its full efficacy either as a living faith or as an organic social reality unless it heals the maladies of the individual soul and restores the broken unity of man's inner life. As we have seen, human life to-day is divided against itself. But this division is not simply due to an opposition between the religious faith that rules the mind of the individual Christian and the secular interests that control his external activity. It goes much deeper than that, since it also springs from a disharmony and contradiction between the life of a spirit and the life of the body. Spiritual life and physical life are both real and both are necessary to the ideal integrity of human existence. But if a man is left to himself, without a higher principle of order— without Grace, to use the Christian term—this integrity, is not realised. The spirit fights against the flesh and the flesh against the spirit, and human life is torn asunder by this inner conflict.

The oriental religions attempted to solve this conflict by the denial of the body, and the radical condemnation of matter as evil or non-existent. They won the peace of Nirvana by the sacrifice of humanity. The Western humanist, on the other hand, tried to find a solution within the frontiers of human nature by the elimination of absolute values and the careful adjustment of man's spiritual aspirations to his material circumstances. He pacified the revolt of the body by sacrificing the soul's demand for God.

Christianity cannot accept either of these solutions. It cannot deny either the reality of the spirit or the value of the body. It stands for the redemption of the body and the realisation of a higher unity in which flesh and spirit alike become the channels of divine life.

It cannot be denied that Christianity has often appeared in practice to agree with the attitude of the oriental ascetic or with an equally one-sided ethical puritanism which allows insufficient recognition to the value of the body and the rights of physical life. Nevertheless, Christian asceticism rests in principle, not on the Platonic and oriental dualism, but on the Old Testament principle of a divine law of life that regulated every side of human existence—physical, social, and spiritual. The law was not merely a matter of external ceremonialism. It was a spiritual norm to which man must conform his thoughts and his actions and which made his whole life a liturgical act. And we see in the Psalms how this ideal was incorporated into religious experience, and made the foundation of the spiritual life of the individual as well as of the social life of the national Church.

It was on this foundation that the Christian ethic was built, and the Pauline repudiation of the Mosaic law was in no sense a denial of this ideal. The Christian gospel involved the substitution of the power of the spirit—the law of liberty—for the external legalism of the older dispensation. But it was equally comprehensive and universal in purpose. It was, in St. Paul's words, "The law of the spirit of life in Christ Jesus."

Hence the Christian life is not an ideal for the mind and conscience alone; it is a new life that embraces both body and spirit in a vital synthesis. It is not merely an order of faith; it is the order of charity fulfilled in action.

How can such an order be realised in the circumstances of modern life? We cannot go back to the strict formal asceticism of the past, any more than we can go back to the social law of the Old Testament. But, on the other hand, we cannot do without asceticism altogether—that is the fallacy of the Quietist and the sentimentalist. We need a new asceticism suited to the new conditions of the modern world—a strenuous training of body and mind in the new life.

As Father Martindale has pointed out in a recent article,[4] the needs of the new age have already called forth new forms of the religious life. The ascetic ideal no longer expresses itself in the external regulation of

4. In *The Month* of August, 1932.

life, but has become so intimately fused with the religious vocation that it finds its own spontaneous expression in the life of the community. It is, however, easier for the religious to solve this problem, since his whole life is ordered to a religious end, and he is not distracted by a division of aims. The position of the layman is inevitably more difficult, since the external forms of life are determined by economic forces which take small account of religious considerations. And not only is religion confined to the inner life, but that life itself is exposed to multiple distractions. Now even the poorest has opportunities for diversion which surpass anything that even the privileged classes knew in former ages. It seems almost absurd to expect people to bring the spirit of Galilee and Assisi into the environment of Hollywood and Chicago. No Christian can deny that it is possible. But it involves something more than pious platitudes and ethical idealism. It calls for an heroic effort like that which converted the Roman Empire. I believe myself that the need produces the man, and that the coming age of the Church will see a new out-pouring of spiritual energy manifested in the Christian life. But that does not acquit us of responsibility. It is not enough for us to sit still and wait for an apocalyptic solution of our problems. The saint, like every other great man, is the organ of a social purpose, and the success of his mission depends on the reserves of faith and spiritual will that have been accumulated by the anonymous activity of ordinary imperfect men and women, each of whom has made an individual contribution, however minute it may be, to a new order of Christian life.

XV

The Nature and Destiny of Man

I

In her doctrine of man the Catholic Church has always held the middle path between two opposing theories, that which makes man an animal and that which holds him to be a spirit. Catholicism has always insisted that man's nature is twofold. He is neither flesh nor spirit, but a compound of both. It is his function to be a bridge between two worlds, the world of sense and the world of spirit, each real, each good, but each essentially different. His nature is open on either side to impressions and is capable of a twofold activity, and his whole destiny depends on the proper co-ordination of the two elements in his nature: and not his destiny alone; for since he is a bridge, the lower world is in some sense dependent on him for its spiritualisation and its integration in the universal order.

In the early ages of the Church the main opposition to this view of man's nature came from those who, like the Gnostics and Manicheans, held man's nature to be purely spiritual and his connection with the body to be in itself an evil and the source of all evil.

This view, as held by the Catharists and Albigensians, was also the dominant heresy of the Middle Ages, and even to-day it has its adherents among Christian Scientists and Theosophists.

During the last four hundred years, however, Spiritualism has been a steadily declining force, and the materialistic view of man has become the great rival of Catholicism. It is true that during the last generation a strong wave of Spiritualism passed once more over Western civilisation, and showed itself both in literature and art, in philosophy and religion, not to speak of such lower manifestations as magic and table turning. Nevertheless, this movement did not rest on any clear view of the relations between spirit and matter. It was in the main a reaction of sentiment against the dogmatic scientific rationalism of the nineteenth century. In literature it is represented by the mystical materialism of Maeterlinck, as well as by the orthodox traditional Catholicism of Claudel and the vague symbolism of W. B. Yeats. It is neither a philosophy nor a religion, it is rather agnosticism becoming mystical and acquiring once more a hunger for the infinite. The resultant attitude towards religion is well expressed by one of the younger French poets, P. J. Jouve:

> J'ai dit Dieu—je dirais l'étoile
> Ou le vent dans les arbres nus;
> L'Univers, l'antique Raison,
> Athena bleu ou Christ en Croix,
> Et ce serait toujours plus vrai.

It may be that this movement is a temporary phenomenon, without any deep roots in the mind of the age, and without importance for the future; but it is also possible that it marks the beginning of a religious age and the permanent weakening of the rationalist and materialist tradition which has increasingly dominated Western civilisation ever since the fifteenth century.

The change that came over Europe at that period was too complex to be ascribed to any one cause. It was the breaking up of the social and religious unity of the Middle Ages. In every direction men were conscious of new power and new knowledge, and they used their new opportunities to the full in a spirit of ruthless self-assertion which took no heed for the rights of others and had no respect for authority and tradition. In this sudden and violent expansion, the genius of that age foresaw and traced out all the essential achievements of the modern as against the mediaeval world. Indeed, the mind of some of the great artists and humanists, above all of Leonardo da Vinci, is more modern than that of the philosophers of the eighteenth-century enlightenment, or those of the pioneers of nineteenth-century industry and science.

It is easy to understand that such an age should evolve a new view of human nature. The men of the Renaissance had turned their eyes away from the world of the spirit to the world of colour and form, of flesh and blood; they set their hopes not on the unearthly perfection of the Christian saint, but on the glory of man—man set free to live his own life and to realise the perfection of power and beauty and knowledge that was his by right. They returned to the old Ionian conception of nature, "Physis," a single material order, which, whether it be rational or irrational, includes in itself all that is. "Nothing is more Divine or more human than anything else, but all things are alike and all Divine."

It is true that few thinkers were sufficiently consistent or sufficiently bold to expound this idea explicitly, like Giordano Bruno. Nevertheless, it is implicit in the life and work of many of the men of the Renaissance. Rabelais, for example, may have been sincere in his professions of belief in God, but the true tendency of his ideas is shown when he substitutes for the spirit and the flesh, for supernatural grace and corrupt nature, the opposition of "Physis " and "Antiphysis": the joyous "Physis" of the humanist and poet, of the peasant and the soldier, of all that is real and carnal and unashamed of itself, and the hateful dark "Antiphysis" of the schoolmen and the monks, hostile to life and destructive of joy.

But it was only in the exceptional minds of an exceptional age— men like Bruno and Rabelais—that the new ideas attained to clear expression; the ordinary man, even if he lived like a humanist, still half belonged in thought and feeling to the Middle Ages. Moreover, the Christian Renaissance of the sixteenth century largely undid the work of the Pagan Renaissance, so that by the beginning of the seventeenth century the tide seemed indeed to have turned.

Nevertheless, the rationalist and humanist traditions were carried on, whether by unsystematic sceptics like Montaigne or dogmatic atheists like Vanini, until in the course of the eighteenth century they came at last into their kingdom. From that time the negative work of destructive criticism and the positive construction of a rationalist and natural synthesis have been carried on vigorously, especially in the more favourable environment produced by the political and industrial revolutions, and the passing away of the *ancien régime.*

The naturalist conception of man has above all been influenced by the Darwinian doctrine of the Origin of Species, and by the evolutionary theories to which this gave rise. The doctrine of a continuous de-

velopment through the whole of animate nature, and the gradual evolution of the human species under the influence of natural selection,
seemed to show that no principle external to the material world need
be invoked to account for man: he was of a piece with the rest of nature. Further, the theory of evolution was linked with the earlier liberal
theories of political and social advance to form the modern doctrine of
unlimited and inevitable material progress, a doctrine fundamentally
unscientific and based on an irrational optimism, but which has nevertheless become a part of the mental furniture of the ordinary modern man. As yet, however, the naturalist movement has not received its
definite philosophy. There has been no lack of ambitious attempts to
elaborate naturalistic syntheses, but none has been final. Neither Condorcet nor Holbach nor Bentham nor Comte nor Spencer nor Haeckel can be said to be the philosopher of the movement. Nevertheless,
in their doctrine of man there is a large element common to all these
philosophers. Whether they be Deists, Materialists, or Agnostics, they
generally agree that man is a part of the material world; that in the
knowledge, the control, and the enjoyment of this world he finds his
true end, and that no spiritual principle can intervene in this closed order governed by uniform physical laws. Taking it as a whole, however,
modern naturalism is due not so much to any philosophic theory, as to
the material triumphs of modern civilisation and man's conquest of nature. The realm of mystery before which man feels himself humble and
weak has withdrawn its frontiers. Man can know his world without
falling back on revelation; he can live his life without feeling his utter
dependence on supernatural powers. He is no longer the servant of unknown forces, but a master in his own house, and he intends to make
the most of his new-found powers.

The resultant attitude to life is well shown in the following extract
from Professor Bateson's Presidential Address to the British Association in August, 1914.[1] "Man is just beginning to know himself for what
he is—a rather long-lived animal with great powers of enjoyment if he
does not deliberately forego them. Hitherto superstition and mythi-
cal ideas of sin have predominately controlled these powers. Mysticism

1. *Report of Brit. Assoc,* 1914, p. 29.

will not die out: for these strange fancies knowledge is no cure: but their forms may change, and mysticism, as a force for the suppression of joy, is happily losing its hold on the modern world. As in the decay of earlier religions, Ushabti dolls were substituted for human victims, so telepathy, necromancy, and other harmless toys take the place of eschatology and the inculcation of a ferocious moral code. Among the civilised races of Europe, we are witnessing an emancipation from traditional control in thought, in art, and in conduct, which is likely to have prolonged and wonderful influences. Returning to freer, or, if you will, simpler conceptions of life and death, the coming generations are determined to get more out of this world than their forefathers did."

This view of life is clearly rather practical than philosophical. It is only possible to one who looks at the surface of life; if we look at man from within, its simplicity is easily seen to be delusive.

If man limits himself to a satisfied animal existence, and asks from life only what such an existence can give, the higher values of life at once disappear. It is from that very element of the eternal and the unlimited, which the materialist seeks to deny, that the true progress of the human race has sprung. Throughout his history, man has been led, not as Buckle taught, by the rational pursuit of practical and material ends, but by belief in a transcendent reality,[2] and in the truth of moral and spiritual values. This is to a great extent true even of the values of that civilisation which the disciple of naturalism accepts as his end. Even Professor Bateson himself demands of his ideal eugenist community that it shall not eliminate the Shakespeares and the Beethovens. Yet what value remains in Shakespeare's work if the doubt of Hamlet is a simple physical neurasthenia, and the despair of Lear but the reaction of a wounded animal to hostile circumstances?

Man's true excellence consists not in following the law of animal nature, but in his resistance to it, and in his recognition of another law. The law of the animal world is the law of instinctive desire and brute force; there is no room in it for freedom or right or moral good. In man alone a new principle comes into play; for he recognises that beyond the natural good of pleasure and self-fulfilment, there is a higher

---

2. *i.e.,* transcending the world of sense-experience, not, of course, the order of nature.

good which is independent of himself, a good that is unlimited, ideal, spiritual. It is true that man does not necessarily follow this good; it is easy enough for him to disregard it and to lapse into animalism, but even as he does so, he has the sense of choice, of responsibility, of something he has gained, or lost.

This contrast between man's moral consciousness and the world of sense-experience is one of the fundamental problems of existence, and it presents an obvious difficulty to the materialist or naturalist for whom this world of sense-experience makes up the whole universe. Yet some of the most thorough-going and clear sighted of materialists from the days of Huxley onwards have accepted it resolutely with all its difficulties. In one of his essays Mr. Bertrand Russell even makes it the foundation of his ethical theory.[3] He admits that the world shown to us by science is a world of blind force, and that man with his knowledge of good and evil is a helpless atom in a world which has no such knowledge. His origin, his growth, his hopes and fears, his loves and beliefs are but the outcome of accidental collocations of atoms, and are destined to be swallowed up again by blind material forces. Nevertheless, he rejects the conclusion that our moral ideals are worthless and that naked Power alone is to be worshipped. "If Power is bad, as it seems to be, let us reject it, from our hearts. In this lies man's true freedom: in determination to worship only the God created by our own love of the good, to respect only the heaven which inspires the insight of our best moments. In action, in desire, we must submit perpetually to the tyranny of outside forces; but in thought, in aspiration, we are free, free from the petty planet on which our bodies impotently crawl, free even, while we live, from the tyranny of death."

Thus he arrives at the paradoxical conclusion that we must love a good God Who does not exist, and refuse to serve nature which does exist, but is not good. It is not likely that a religion of this kind will ever become popular, since men will always be inclined to adapt their morality to their general conception of the universe. Rather than acquiesce in a flagrant contradiction between the real and the ideal, they will lower their ideal to the level of their conception of reality. In order

---

3. "The Free Man's Worship," reprinted in *Mysticism and Logic,* 1918.

to avoid Mr. Russell's dilemma, it becomes necessary for the materialist to deny the transcendence of the moral ideal, unless the difficulty is slurred over, as it is by Haeckel and so many others in an irrational and sentimental idealisation of nature.

On the other hand, when once the absolute superiority of the human spirit to the rest of the material universe is admitted, it becomes intellectually, as well as practically, difficult to halt at the point at which Mr. Bertrand Russell halts. For if it be once affirmed that in the human consciousness a principle, or an order of being, higher than anything that is found in the material world has made its appearance, it is difficult to suppose that that principle can be of so transitory and limited a character as he maintains.

Even in the limited field of experience open to our minds, the power of spirit is out of all proportion to that of other forces of nature. The force of conscious reason is able to mould and direct in a thousand ways the world of unconscious matter and animal nature. Thanks to the power of reason, man is like the god of this planet. He is able to dominate his environment and to co-ordinate the forces of nature in his own service. Nor is this conscious dominion over nature the only kingdom of man's spirit. The realm of abstract thought is greater than that of action. The riches of the kingdom of the spirit are inexhaustible, and here the greatest minds are often those that feel their own limitations most keenly, as though in all their science and philosophy they are no more than children picking up shells on the shores of an illimitable sea.

There is a point at which the world of spirit comes into conscious contact with the world of matter. That point is man. It is in the highest degree unreasonable to limit the whole world of spirit to its manifestation in the human mind, and to conceive of the universe as a vast material cosmos in which a solitary fragment of spiritual being exists in the case of one reasonable and moral creature. It is surely more rational to suppose that the world of thought and of spiritual values, on the threshold of which man has the consciousness of standing, is a real world, an order no less great than the material order, and that it is in this alone that we shall find a solution to the otherwise hopeless conflict between man's spiritual aspirations and the limitations of his material existence.

At first sight this problem is only accentuated by the admission of the existence of a spiritual world. For if man is spiritual, why does he not live by the spirit? By reason he is able to control the external world but not his own nature, and though he can recognise the supreme value of the moral order, he seems incapable of making it dominate his own individual and social life. Many of his acts spring, not from reason, but from impulse, and that impulse is grounded deep in his animal nature. Indeed, the main driving force behind human life seems to be a subconscious life instinct, in itself not essentially dissimilar from the life instinct of the animal world. This life impulse manifests itself in all the natural desires centering round the struggle for existence in all that serves the life of the individual or the species on the animal plane. It finds its central and most characteristic expression in the sexual impulse, and it is on that account named "Libido" by Jung and his school of psychologists; but it extends far beyond the limits of the sexual functions, and makes itself felt even on the higher levels of human experience, which are apparently very far dissociated from the primary physical needs.[4]

II

This life of unconscious or semi-conscious instinct is, however, far from covering the whole field of human activity. Not even the lowest savage lives entirely by instinct, and in civilised man the domination of other conscious and rational forces is plain enough. Reason makes it possible for man to review and judge his instincts, to foresee the consequences of his impulsive actions, and to restrain them in cases in which their fulfilment is disadvantageous to himself; for instinct is blind and may lead the individual to his ruin, as a moth is led to the candle flame. Nevertheless, as a rule, rational action is not fundamentally different, as regards its end, from instinctive action. For the most part the conscious motives that inspire the activities of the individual and the society are but a continuation of the physical life impulse on the rational plane. A conscious self-interest, the deliberate aiming at pleasure, wealth, and power, whether in the case of the individual or of the group, takes the

4. Cf. the extended use of the term *concupiscentia* by St. Augustine.

place of the obscure, physical impulses which dominate the life of instinct. The one may indeed conflict with the other, for success in the social competition of civilised life requires a self-suppression and a kind of asceticism which runs directly counter to physical instinct. This conscious self-seeking is in essence entirely different to animal instinct, although, from a moral point of view, it is no higher. It is in fact evil in a sense in which animal instinct cannot be, for it is not, like the latter, the natural activity of a higher, spiritual force. The life of animal instinct is better than that of rational self-interest in that it is less limited; for it serves not merely the purposes of the individual, but those of the species, and more, of the whole of nature. The individual is the servant and instrument of a universal impulse.

With the rational life, however, the individual has conquered impulse in so far as it makes him the servant of obscure and unrealised purposes. He serves not a universal and ultimate purpose, but some special and secondary end, *i.e.,* he uses impulse and material things generally for his individual pleasure and profit, and these may have no ultimate justification and serve no purpose in the general scheme of things. Now if the materialist hypothesis were true, it would naturally follow that the life impulse, whether as unconscious instinct or as rational self-interest, would be not only the dominant power, but the only power in man. For it is inconsistent to deny the reality of spirit as being and to continue to maintain it as a motive force in action. There would be no room for freedom or moral responsibility, but man would be the slave of physical impulse and self-interest, and as the life-force drove, so must he go.

Actually, however, as we have seen, man has a spiritual side to his nature. He is conscious of another good besides the good of instinct and self-interest, a good which is absolute, and spiritual, and he has some vague conception of a spiritual power to which he is responsible.

On the foundation of this spiritual consciousness, and in order to satisfy his spiritual needs, he builds up his systems of natural religion, systems which may be powerless to dominate the life impulse effectually and habitually, but which are at least able to modify it and to give man the desire for a higher and freer life.

In primitive society, where man is absorbed in a struggle for bare existence with the mysterious forces of nature, religion, like the rest of life, is more or less on the plane of instinct, and is concerned with material rather than spiritual objects. But even here the spiritual consciousness exists, though it is confused by the sense of mystery which overshadows the material world, and causes primitive man to look on all material things and forces as moved by indwelling spirits. So, as man advances in civilisation and in control over his life, the religion of nature becomes less important, and that of society takes the first place. The ordinary life of the people becomes rationalised and secularised, but their deeper needs remain. Although the religion of society seems to be utilitarian, a spiritual element is implicit in it. For example, if the religion of many early civilisations is directed mainly to success in war, the ultimate end of that success is not to gain material advantages for the society, so much as to exalt its god by its victory.

But it is only when civilisation is mature, when society becomes self-conscious and the struggle for bare survival is slackened, that the spiritual needs of man's nature exert their full power. It is then that he begins to reason about life and the end of life, and to contrast his actual existence with the ideal life which his spirit desires. He revolts against his slavery to the law of animal instinct and selfish desire, no less than against the law of death, which seems to render vain all the achievements of the human mind. He feels himself the plaything of physical needs and physical sufferings which make his individual life a selfish struggle for survival ending, in inevitable extinction. If he lives for his society as the one thing in his life which is permanent, and through which he may in a sense survive, he does but enter upon a wider cycle of the same life process. Civic life can only satisfy when the society itself subserves a spiritual end. There is nothing in social life as such which is more spiritual than individual life. Animalism can dominate the former as easily as the latter, even more easily. The group purpose is as well served when the human pack tears to pieces its weak or maimed member as when it throws itself with self-regardless courage at the throat of the common enemy.

It is, in fact, when we look at the history of mankind in the mass that the evils of human existence are most apparent. We see empires, built on oppression and the blood of the poor, by degrees melting into ruin, and being replaced by some equally bloodthirsty but more barbarous power which goes at last to meet the same fate. Nor does civilisation bring freedom; for the spectacle of a civilised society dominated not by one unconscious natural instinct, but by a conscious lust for pleasure or power or wealth, is even more horrible than the other. What wonder if some men have always turned away from the cruelty and greed and lust which seem to dominate the struggle for existence, and have refused life itself, if it is only to be purchased on such terms?

This is the fundamental problem which has pressed on the human race for thousands of years and which is as living now as it was in the days of the Buddha. The last generation, indeed, believed that Science had solved this problem like so many others. It was their boast that:

> Science has pierced man's cloudy commonsense,
> Dowered his homely vision with more expansive an embrace,
> And the rotten foundation of old superstition exposed.
> That trouble of Pascal, those vain paradoxes of Austin,
> Those Semitic parables of Paul, those tomes of Aquinas,
> All are thrown to the limbo of antediluvian idols.[5]

But who now would claim that "that trouble of Pascal" has been rendered any less insistent by the discovery of the fossils of Neanderthal Man, or the Pithecanthropus of Java? We have returned to the old problems which arise not from lack of scientific knowledge, but from the very conditions of our nature.

It was in India that religion first reached this stage, owing mainly to local and climatic conditions which at once forced on and limited the development of a self-contained civilisation. It is, however, a mistake to make these material factors responsible for Indian thought itself. The same process takes place eventually in every matured civilisation. Some peoples, like the Chinese and the Romans, have possessed a genius for social life, for organisation, work and practical achievements, but even these have experienced at last the inevitable dissatisfaction with human life as it is, and the need for deliverance.

In India, these phenomena were exceptionally strongly marked and widespread, and the fundamental postulates of natural religion enter

5. *Poems of Robert Bridges,* p. 421 (Oxford Edition).

more deeply than elsewhere into the life and thought of the people. The sense of man's bondage to animal life and desire, and to the law of death; belief in the fruit of moral action, Karma, as inevitable retribution or recompense; and, above all, the need for deliverance from the animal life and the law of death (Nirvana) are at the root of all the great Indian systems whether Buddhist or Vedantist, Sankhya or Yoga, Sivaite or Vishnuite, though all this is woven on a background of animism, polytheism, and magic.

The Indians picture the whole life process as an endless wheel of lives and deaths gripped in the claws of the monster Kama or desire; to be freed from that wheel is the end of all their efforts:

> Through birth and re-birth's endless round,
> Seeking in vain, I hastened on,
> To find who framed this edifice;
> What misery! birth incessantly.

But how can man escape from the domination of this power which seems the very power of life itself? Only, it was said, by turning his back on life, by seeing in the whole sensible world nothing but illusion, and by leaving the finite and the known for the unknown infinite. The sting of death is desire: destroy desire and you will destroy death, but you will destroy life also in so far as life is human and limited.

The classical expression of this attitude to life is found in Buddhism, which excelled all other Indian religions in the simplicity of its reasoning and in the austerity of its morals. "Two things only do I teach, sorrow and the ending of sorrow," said the Buddha, rebuking those who would know whether Nirvana was existence or non-existence. Life is evil, the body is evil, sense is evil, consciousness is evil. Only in the destruction and cessation of all these can the true good be found. This is no less the message of the other great spiritualist religions of the East. Whether they teach a spiritualist monism, like the Vedanta; a spiritualist nihilism, like Buddhism; or a spiritualist dualism, like Manichæanism—they agree in this, that what is wrong with man is not the disorder or disease of his actual existence, but his very life itself. Evil is not in man's will, but is essentially bound up with the existence of the body and the material universe. Therefore this life must not be spiritualised;

it must be left behind, and man must return to the one, absolute, un-differentiated Being, or Not-being, of which his spirit is a part.

This is the oriental solution of life, and with it all progress ends. Society loses its higher vitality which is transferred to the pursuit of the absolute, and man's spiritual energy is dissipated in theosophy and asceticism.

However progressive a civilisation may be, eventually it realises its natural potentialities, and then the tendency is for it to fall into an oriental or Byzantine state of fixity in which the life impulse turns to religion.

There is no reason to believe that the modern scientific and industrialist civilisation will ultimately escape that end any more than the great civilisations of the past. European civilisation was tending this way under the early Roman Empire, in spite of the scientific genius of the Greeks and the essentially "Western" spirit of the Romans. The oriental spiritualist attitude to life was dominant alike in philosophy and religion, in Neo-Pythagoreanism and Neo-Platonism, in the oriental cults, above all in Gnosticism and Manichæanism; and it was the great danger to the Christian Faith throughout the early centuries of the Church's life.

Yet these religions, with all their impressiveness and their fascination for minds that are satiated with material progress, do not solve the problem of human life. Man left to himself[6] is powerless to reconcile the antinomy of his spiritual and material natures. Either he may let himself sink back into the life of the body, disregarding the claims of the spirit, or he tries to satisfy these by the total rejection of the body and the life that it conditions. Yet man cannot be quit of his nature on such easy terms. In spite of his denial of it, the material world goes on, and the body must in time exact retribution from those who despise it.

Thus even Buddhism, the most uncompromising of all the spiritualist religions, was not proof against paganism and magic; and the way of renunciation and the law of moral discipline were succeeded by the superstition and obscenity of Tantric Buddhism which spread throughout Northern India and Thibet during the early Middle Ages.

6. *i.e.*, man in his present condition of fallen nature.

In the case of monistic religions, the process of degeneration is even easier, for the vagueness and antinomianism of the pantheist attitude to life are apt to idealise man's lower nature, and to throw a cloak of symbolism over the indulgence of physical impulse.

III

Such reactions and degenerations can be avoided only by a spiritualisation of the whole of man's nature, which will unite the life of the body and the life of the spirit in the service of a common end. Some force must be found which will spiritualise human life without destroying it, which will keep the life impulse at work in the world without letting it dissipate itself in the aridities of materialism, or die down in the emptiness of world-negation.

This is the claim of the Catholic Faith, that a new power has in fact been brought into the world which is capable of regenerating humanity; not merely by reconciling human nature with itself—which is the unattained goal of human philosophy—but by uniting organically the whole of man, body and soul, sense and spirit, with a higher spiritual principle, thus making of him a new creature.

This restoration or recreation of humanity is the essential doctrine of Christianity. Jesus Christ is to the Catholic not a prophet and teacher like the founders of other great religions, nor even is He only the divine revealer of God to man: He is the restorer of, the human race, the New Man, in whom humanity has a fresh beginning and man acquires a new nature. His work was genetic and creative in an absolutely unique sense, for it brought into the world a new kind of life which has the power to transmute and absorb into itself the lower forms of physical and psychical life which exist in man.[7]

It is the "new birth from above"[8] of which Christ spoke to Nicodemus, a mysterious force, the power and reality of which are manifest, while its cause and working are as invisible as the wind.

---

7. *i.e.,* the Christian does not simply acquire extrinsic supernatural faculties, his whole life becomes supernatural, and finally even his body shares in the new life. Cf. St. Paul, *Rom.* viii, 19.

8. *St. John,* iii.

This higher life was of course not entirely absent from humanity before Christ, but it existed rather as a potentiality awaiting realisation than as a force dominating the whole nature of man. For it is only through Christ, the second Adam, and in organic connection with Him, that the new humanity is to be built up. By the vital activity of the Spirit of Christ working through the Church and the Sacraments, mankind is remoulded and renewed; the disorder and weakness of human nature is overcome, and the domination of charity in spiritual love is substituted for the blindness of physical impulse and the narrowness and evil of selfish desire. The consummation of this work of restoration by the unification of humanity under the vital control of the Spirit of God may seem infinitely distant; since it involves the absolute conquest of matter by spirit, and the spiritualisation and immortalisation of the human body—in fact, a new world and a new humanity; but no lesser term is proposed by the Catholic Faith as the destiny of the human race.

Thus, the Catholic view of life involves a fundamental opposition between the new force that has entered human life through Christ and the disordered material activity which it replaces. This opposition shows itself in Christian asceticism, in the monastic ideal of perfection, the cult of virginity, and the mortification of the body, all of which seem to betoken as drastic a world-renunciation as that of the Hindu ascetic.

Consequently, many moderns regard Christianity as the culmination of that wave of oriental spiritualism which overwhelmed the ancient world. But this is a fundamental misconception. Christianity comes neither from the East nor from the West. It is, even as it claims to be, the fulfilment of a unique religious tradition which denied oriental pantheism and nihilism as obstinately as it refused occidental humanism and materialism. It is founded, not on a metaphysical theory which denies the body and the material universe, but on a historical and social revelation—the Jewish faith in the Kingdom of God.

From the dawn of their history, the Jewish people were marked by an intense religious realism; they possessed a social genius no less strong in its way than that of the Greeks, but their political ideal was narrowly and literally theocratic: they were the one people of God—Israel.

Many other nations of the ancient world—Assyria, for example—

likewise were governed by theocratic conceptions, but sooner or later these political religions gave way before the current of religious universalism, even as the states themselves were swallowed up in the Persian and Hellenistic world-empires. With the Jews alone, universalism did not destroy the national faith, but, on the contrary, strengthened and spiritualised their faith in their own God and in their peculiar destiny.

From the ninth century before Christ down to the final destruction of Jerusalem in A.D. 70, Israel passed through a long succession of misfortunes, crisis following crisis, and disappointment crushing hope time after time: and yet in the midst of these troubles and disillusionments the Hope of Israel was gradually revealed.

It was the belief of the mass of the unspiritual Jews—the stiff-necked people and kings against whom the prophets wrote—that the covenant of Yahweh with Israel was such that the temporal welfare of the people was only limited by the strength of their god. If his service was neglected he would certainly send plagues in vengeance; but it was inconceivable that he should allow his people to be destroyed or enslaved by another, for that would be equivalent to acknowledging his inferiority to a "strange god."

It was against this conception of the relation of Yahweh to his people that the first prophets wrote. The earliest of them, Amos, declared that the kingdom of Israel was destined to destruction not because Yahweh was weak, but because the people had broken the covenant of justice and had ceased to be a holy people. Their avarice and the oppression of the poor had brought upon them the anger of God, which was not to be turned away by sacrifice or external service. Therefore the destruction of Israel was decreed by Yahweh, and the Assyrian world-power was but his instrument, "the rod of his anger" in the words of Isaias. Yahweh's power was not limited to his own people and his own land; the Gentiles also were subject to him, though they knew him not. Their cruelty and oppression would be punished in due time, as the sin of Israel had been; but first they had a work to do as unconscious instruments of the will of Yahweh.

And so the prophet Jeremias in the last days of the kingdom of Judah saw the divine purpose behind the victorious power of the King of Babylon, and set his face against the national and religious patriotism which would defend the Holy City to the last. He laid the curse of Yahweh alike on those who trusted in the arm of the flesh—the help of Egypt—and on those who prophesied falsely that Yahweh would never deliver his people into the hands of their enemies. For years he faced the intrigues and hatred of rulers and people, announcing in bitterness of heart the destruction of all that, the traditions of his people held most dear. Throughout the siege of Jerusalem and after the captivity, among the remnant that remained behind and went down into Egypt, he never ceased to warn the Jews that they must submit to the foreign yoke. Only after long suffering and humiliation might they hope for a time when Yahweh should restore his people under a king of the house of David, and give to them a new covenant, "written on the heart," whereby he would be forever known with an interior and personal knowledge, in place of the external legal relation that existed under the old covenant of Moses.

This promise is perhaps the highest and most important utterance amongst all the sayings of the prophets, for it seems to anticipate, more than anything else, the Gospel teaching of the spiritual character of the Kingdom of God. It is, however, in the second part of the book of Isaias that the special vocation of Israel as the people of Yahweh is revealed in its widest and most exalted form. Here the prophet proclaims that Yahweh is not merely the God of Israel: he is the divine Governor of the universe who wills that all nations shall come to know him and to obey the law of his Justice, as manifested in his people Israel. Therefore he has brought Cyrus, "His shepherd" from the north, to "humble the great ones of the earth, to break the gates of brass, to set free the captives," that all peoples from the rising of the sun to the islands of the West may know that the God of Israel is the one true God, the Creator and Ruler of the world.

And the prophet teaches that the sufferings of Israel had been inflicted not merely in anger, but for the fulfilment of this divine purpose. In the words of a later writer, "He scattered you among the nations that know Him not, that you may declare His wonderful works, and make them know that there is no other Almighty God besides Him."[9] In like

9. *Tobias*, xiii, 4.

manner, the restoration of Israel and the manifestation of God to the
Gentile were also to be accomplished by suffering and obedience. Yahweh's chosen servant, on whom His spirit rests, is called to carry out
the divine purpose in the spiritual order, as Cyrus is called to prepare
the way for it in temporal things. The latter, unconscious of his call, has
a mission of honour, the former, who shares in the Divine Spirit, has a
mission of suffering and shame.

"By his knowledge shall this my just servant justify many, and he
shall bear their iniquities." "Thus saith Yahweh, the Redeemer of Israel
and his Holy One, to the soul that is despised, to the nation that is
hated, to the servant of rulers: kings shall see and princes shall rise up,
and adore for the sake of Yahweh because he is faithful, and for the
Holy One of Israel who has chosen thee."[10]

The passages of Isaias that describe the mission of Yahweh's servant
have been more debated by the modern critics than any other part of
the Old Testament, and every kind of interpretation has been suggested
with regard to the character of the suffering servant. Most of their difficulties have, however, arisen from the inability of the critics to recognise the essentially mystical character of this prophecy. The Holy Servant
is chosen from the womb to redeem the sinful Jewish people and to
be a light to the Gentiles. Yet at the same time, in so far as the nation
is holy and fulfils its vocation, it also is "the servant of Yahweh," and
shares in the redemptive work; there is a mystical solidarity between
the chosen individual and the chosen community, and the latter only
attains to its destiny through the work of the former.[11]

It is not to be supposed that the Jewish people, even at its best, realised the depth of meaning contained in these utterances. They looked
on the return from exile as the end of their trials and the beginning of
a glorious reign for the restored and purified theocracy. These hopes
were destined, at least until the Maccabaean age, to complete disappointment. The external prospects of the Jewish state grew darker and
darker, and the Gentile world-power grew ever more irresistible. Yet
the more the rest of the Mediterranean world became united in a com-

---

10. *Isaias,* xlix, 7.
11. Cf. especially chaps. xlix and lv.

mon civilisation and a common syncretistic religious tradition, the more passionately did the Jews cling to their separation from the Nations, and to their special national, religious vocation. Since the disproportion between the material power of Israel and that of the Gentile empires caused any natural realisation of this destiny to be inconceivable, pious Jews were driven to rely more and more on the supernatural character of the salvation which God had promised to Israel. As the prophets had foretold, the Kingdom of God would be established, not by the arm of the flesh, but by divine power alone; therefore it would be, not a mere episode in Syrian history, like the first kingdom of David, but a change in the whole world-order, the beginning of a new heaven and a new earth. So, too, the Messias would be, not a great prince like David, who would exalt Israel by successful wars, but One "like unto the Son of Man" whom the prophet saw in vision coming in the clouds of heaven, and whose everlasting kingdom would be the consummation of the whole world-age.[12]

It was to those who lived in the expectation of this supernatural deliverance, pious and spiritual Jews who, like Simeon, "waited for the consolation of Israel," that the preaching of Jesus was addressed and the revelation of His Messianic office was made. The kingdom that He announced was the kingdom that they had been looking for, but it was also something more, even as He, the true Messias, was greater than the Messias that had been hoped for. The Kingdom of the Gospel was not simply the restoration of Israel; it was internal and spiritual, as well as external and cosmic. Its newness lay not in the promise of a new world—that was the dominant hope of later Judaism—but in the conception of the new world living in germ in the bosom of the present order. It was like a piece of leaven hidden in a lump of dough, a seedling plant destined to grow into the greatest of trees, a hidden treasure; and the process of growth that these images foreshadowed was to take place in the human soul.

The Jewish expectation had conceived the Kingdom of God as a change in the external world coming from without, according to the decree of God's power, but the Gospel, whilst announcing an equally

12. *Daniel*, vii, 13–14.

objective change, taught that the coming of the new world was consequent on an internal spiritual change in man. Judaism had hoped for a
new world; Christ brought a new humanity.

Thus the primitive Christian idea of the Kingdom of God was essentially twofold. On the one hand there is the period of hidden life
and growth, the kingdom in seed; on the other the state of perfection
and glory, the kingdom in fruit. On the one hand there is the "little
flock," persecuted, poor and without honour in face of the triumphant
kingdom of this world; on the other the people of God reigning with
Christ in a restored universe. In short, to use theological language, the
Kingdom of God includes first the Kingdom of Grace, then the Kingdom of Glory.

Modern critics have as a rule failed to recognise this dual character of the Kingdom of God in the Gospels. Either they have realised
the spirituality and universality of the teaching of Jesus and denied its
supernatural character, or they have recognised the supernatural or pre-
ternatural nature of the kingdom, and, conceiving this in an exclusively
cosmic or eschatological sense, have denied its moral and spiritual character.

The organic connection between these two stages is set forth in detail in the writings of St. Paul, where for the first time the Christian
doctrine of man was fully elaborated. The Kingdom of God is shown
to be nothing less than the restoration of the whole creation in and
through Christ. The Church is the embryo of a new world, and the
Spirit of Christ, which dwells in it, is the principle of its life and the
source of its growth. With the Death of Christ, the old order came to
an end, and His Resurrection,[13] together with the consequent gift of
the Spirit to His disciples, inaugurated a new order which will only attain completion at His second coming "with power."

The life of the faithful during the present world-age is consequent-

---

13. St. Paul lays great emphasis on the position of the Resurrection in the economy of
the Redemption. "The Resurrection is intimately connected with the fruit of the Redemptive Death, and with the gift of the Holy Spirit. It is at the moment of the Resurrection
that Jesus becomes 'life-giving spirit.' Previously, indeed, He had the Spirit in its fullness;
but the Spirit, which dwelt in Him, bound by the limitations inherent to the economy of
the Redemption, could not then exercise all its vital power." Cf. *John,* xiv, 18, and xvi, 7;
Père Prat, *Théologie de St. Paul,* II, 301; cf. also *ibid.,* II, 453 and note.

ly of a double or intermediate character. They share in the life of two worlds, one dying, the other still in the womb. Their bodies are still "subject to the bondage of corruption," the powers of this world-age are against them, the force of spiritual evil is still unsubdued, but by their membership of the Church they already belong to the new world which is being built up invisibly under the veil of the old, and their possession of the Spirit and His gifts is a "pledge of the world to come," an assurance of the reality of the new life.

Thus the divine life that they possess now by grace is essentially the same as that which will be manifested in the next world in glory. Indeed, the true line of division runs not between Heaven and Earth, but between the natural and the supernatural orders in this present world. The gulf between the "psychic" or animal man who lives by the law of his body or by the law of self-interest, and the Christian who lives by the Spirit, is greater than the gulf between the Christian on earth and the glorified souls of the saints in Heaven.[14]

On this essentially divine and supernatural character of the Christian life all St. Paul's moral teaching rests. He established a far-reaching opposition between man left to himself, following his own will, and limited by his own nature, and man renewed by grace, living by charity and spiritual love and admitted to a participation in the Divine Nature. This is not a Manichæan opposition between the essential evil of matter and the absolute good of spirit. St. Paul teaches that man is naturally good, and that the material creation, as represented by the human body, is an unwilling slave to evil. Humanity has been wrecked at the very beginning of its history by a disorder of the will which has sacrificed spirit to sense, and God to self, thus breaking the fundamental law of spiritual being and depriving man of the divine life which is his by grace.

This great refusal was Original Sin, the effects of which have been perpetuated through the whole course of man's development, and have influenced every side of his nature; and this refusal is renewed in each individual by actual sin, every instance of which is a fresh self-determination in disorder, and a new seed of death to humanity.

14. As Père Prat remarks (*Théologie de St. Paul*, II, 25), the Apostle usually includes Grace and Glory in a single concept which he names sometimes "The image of the heavenly Man."

In a famous passage of the Epistle to the Romans, St. Paul gives expression to man's sense of this disorder in his nature,[15] and of the impotence of his spiritual will to dominate his lower nature effectually. The human will is free, otherwise there would be no room for these agonised feelings of struggle and of responsibility, since the physical instincts would meet with no resistance. But, on the other hand, the disorder, which has been caused by sin, and by the consequent loss of the higher life of the spirit, affects both the mind and the will, so that man is powerless to restore the harmony of his nature, unless some new spiritual force comes into his life to liberate the powers of his soul from their morbid weakness, and to reunite his nature on a higher spiritual plane.

IV

The Christian life, therefore, consists in the gradual reformation of nature from within by the operation of the Divine Spirit, which is the actuating principle of the new life, just as the human soul is the actuating principle of the life of the body. This power manifests itself in the mind by faith, which is man's participation of God's Knowledge, and in the will by charity or spiritual love, which is man's participation in God's Will.[16] This is the great dynamic force of the spiritual life, and upon it rests all Christian or supernatural morality, as opposed to natural ethics. It is not so much a virtue as the animating principle and motive of all virtues. Thus St. Augustine argues that all the virtues are nothing but love; Temperance is love, reserving itself for God, fortitude love, bearing all things for God, justice love, serving God by well-ordering the things that are in man's power, and so forth. Hence his famous saying, "Love God and do what you will."

15. *Rom.* vii, 14–24: " I do not that Good which I will; but the evil that I hate, that I do. . . . For I am delighted with the law of God according to my inward man; but I see another law in my members, fighting against the law of my mind and holding me captive in the law of sin that is in my members. Unhappy man that I am, who shall deliver me from the body of this death?"

16. *Caritas non potest naturaliter nobis inesse, neque per vires naturales esse acquisita, sed per infusionem Spiritus Sancti, qui est Amor Patris et Filii, cujus participatio in nobis est Ipsa Caritas creata.*—St. Thomas, S.T., 2a 2ae, Q. 24, A. 2.

When man is introduced by Faith and the Sacraments into that new world, which is the Kingdom of God and the supernatural order, this new force begins to move his will. There is, as we have said, a natural love of God, for how can man not love the "Good of all good, the Good from which is all good, the Good which is alone good," but this natural love cannot dominate his life effectively.

The new power is different. It may be felt as strongly and as suddenly as the passion of personal love, or it may grow up slowly and imperceptibly, like the love of children for their parents, but in either case it is a genuine new psychical force which aspires to unmake and remake the personality. It checks physical impulse, and it denies self-interest. If it is strong—that is, if the whole mind is open to it—it may cause intense suffering, the birth-pain of the spiritual man. Yet though its power is so real and so evident, its source is not easy to discover. "The wind blows where it wills, and its voice thou hearest, but dost not know whence it comes nor where it goes; so is every one who has been born of the Spirit."

There is something mysterious about the whole supernatural life, whether of the mind or of the will. Man is moving in a strange world in which his own faculties no longer avail him. God's Mind, to which he attains by Faith, is so far above his own that he is unable to see, he can only believe. But already, if he gives himself up to the operation of grace, God's Will moves his own, and he is drawn strongly and painfully to the denial of his own will and the sacrifice of his natural activities.

It is a common error, especially among the non-Catholic Christian sects, to confuse charity, or supernatural desire, with devout feelings and religious sentiment. Charity, however, belongs essentially to the deepest and most spiritual part of the soul, a region beyond the reach of feeling or of self-analysis, and it is only indirectly and accidentally manifested in the consciousness or in the emotions. As St. Teresa says: "It is certain that the love of God does not consist in this sweetness and tenderness, which we for the most part desire, and with which we console ourselves; but rather in serving Him in justice, fortitude, and humility."

In the case of the ordinary Christian this force has not reached its full development. It has not absorbed into itself the rest of the psychic life, nor acquired immediate control over the emotions and the desires; but it exists alongside of the lower psychic activity which continues to operate although the higher will has turned itself deliberately towards the life of the spirit.

If this ultimate self-determination is adhered to, the final reformation of the personality on the supernatural plane is assured; but, unless there is a continuous effort to bring the whole nature under the control of charity, this process may be so gradual as to be almost imperceptible. Moreover, there is always a probability that a resurgence of disordered natural activity may swamp the whole personality and detach the higher will from its adherence to spiritual love. With the saint—that is, the Christian in whom charity has fully matured—this is no longer so. The whole personality is unified. Every phase of the psychic life is animated by spiritual desire, which is no longer painful and unnatural in its operation, but has become instinctive—as instinctive on the higher plane as physical instinct was on the lower. Such is the charity of the saints, of St. Francis, St. Catharine or St. Philip, in whom the body becomes an almost transparent veil incapable of concealing the flaming energy of the spirit. The potentiality which the human soul possesses of becoming the vehicle of this supernatural spiritual force is the central point of the Catholic doctrine of man. Thus, St. Paul speaks very little of man as he is in himself, but very much of the two forces by which human nature rises or falls. He is concerned less with its original constitution than with its dynamic possibilities, its aptitude for being transformed by 'the spirit of supernatural love, or degraded by the spirit of self-love or of concupiscence.

This likewise was the standpoint of St. Irenæus when he had to meet the most profound of all the heresies that have ever attacked the Christian doctrine of man and his salvation. He describes the Christian as a threefold being consisting of Flesh, Soul, and Spirit: that is to say, the Christian has three lives, the life of the body, the life of the rational soul, and the divine life which is given to him in baptism. "Of these, one, the spirit, saves and moulds; another, the flesh, is united and moulded; whilst that which lies between the two is the soul, which sometimes follows the spirit and is raised by it, but at other times sympathises with the flesh and is drawn by it into earthly passions. The flesh without the Spirit of God is dead, not having life, and cannot inherit the Kingdom of Heaven, but where the Spirit of the Father is, there is a Living Man, living because of his share of the Spirit, man because of the substance of the flesh."[17]

Finally, in St. Augustine we have not only a system of psychology, but also a philosophy of history based on the conception of the two forces which may govern human nature. "Two loves," he says," built two cities. The love of self builds up Babylon to the contempt of God, and the love of God builds up Jerusalem to the contempt of self." And so he sees everywhere these two loves at work, moving the depths of the psychic life, and manifesting themselves outwardly in two great hostile world-orders.

> "*Ex amore suo quisquis vivit, vel bene vel male.*"
> "*Non faciunt bonos vel malos mores, nisi boni vei amores.*"

Such phrases are constantly recurring in his writings, and they show how deeply his thought was affected by this dynamic theory of the two loves. Yet he insists that both these loves spring from a single root, from the inextinguishable desire of man's nature for happiness—*vita beata*. All the difference between the two cities—between humanity as a "damned lump" and humanity as the deified Temple of God—depends on whether man follows the blind desire for life of his physical instincts and the dark wisdom of self-love, or whether he turns towards the true *vita beata* which is supersensual and infinite, "the Beauty which is ever ancient and ever new," "nearer to man than his own soul, the life of his soul and the life of his life."

Nevertheless, this doctrine of the two men and the two loves, which is so ancient and fundamental a part of the Catholic tradition, is liable to misinterpretation. These pairs of opposites do of course correspond to the opposition between fallen nature and supernatural grace, but if they be applied *sans phrase* to the natural and supernatural *orders,* whether in their actual relations, or in their essential nature, the way is at once open to the Calvinist and Jansenist ideas of the radical corruption of human nature. According to Calvin, the good of nature has

17. *St. Irenæus,* V, 9, 1, 2.

been literally killed by Original Sin, and nothing can restore it. God may shut His eyes to its corruption in consideration of the merits of His Son, but in itself it will always remain evil. Jansenism did not go so far. It admitted the objective restoration of nature, but it conceived this as an irresistible exercise of divine power, which found and left man passive, and which was, moreover, limited to the small body of the predestinate.

Both Calvinism and Jansenism shared the same practical error—a fatalism which excluded human nature from any co-operation in the work of its renewal, and which made of nature and grace two closed orders mutually exclusive and hostile to one another. At bottom it is the old Marnichæan enemy in a new form. From the Catholic point of view, it is just as false to treat nature and grace as mutually exclusive things as it is to oppose body and soul, or matter and spirit, to one another; for the union of nature and grace makes up the Christian, just as the union of body and soul makes up the natural man. The supernatural is not the contradiction of nature, but its restoration and crown, and every faculty of man, whether high or low, is destined to have its share in his new supernatural life.

Who has not felt that the life which is most truly *natural*—that is to say, most in harmony with man's true being—is not the life of the man who lives by sense-instinct, but that of the saint—of St. Francis, for instance—in whom the original innocence and harmony of man with himself and with outward things seem restored?

It is remarkable that this conception of the "naturalness" of the supernatural life was explicity held by the very founders of Christian asceticism, those desert monks whose austerities have astonished and sometimes scandalised the mind of future generations. To St. Anthony and to his biographer, St. Athanasius, the ascetic life is the true "life according to nature." It is a process of simplification by which the monk may, as it were, recover the actual rectitude and harmony of nature in which man left the hands of his Creator.[18]

18. Cf. Newman, *The Mission of St. Benedict,* 3.

V

Nevertheless, this quality of simplicity and naturalness in the highest spiritual life has only been attained by intense effort: it is the result of a remorseless process of destruction and reconstruction. The disorder of nature is very real and very strong. It has rooted itself so deeply in humanity that it has become, as it were, an organised whole from which the individual and the society can only detach themselves with difficulty. Against the Christian ideal of social order as a co-operative effort based on justice and animated by charity, we see the reality of a naked reign of force, based on slavery, war, or economic exploitation, in which the strong prosper at the expense of the weak, and primitive peoples become the natural prey of more civilised powers. The reign of social and international justice is an ideal which can only be reached by a spiritualised humanity—a humanity set free from the domination of lust and avarice and cowardice, which drives men and nations blindly into disorder and cruelty. Hence the struggle between the spirit of Christ and that "spirit of the world" which is so real a force.

It is a common modern objection, and one which is widely accepted as a damaging criticism of Catholicism, that our religion neglects the real things by which the progress of the human race is advanced—science, industry, and political organisation—in the pursuit of imaginary goods of a visionary kind. In reality Christianity creates the motive power—spiritual will—on which all true progress must ultimately rest. Without this spiritual foundation, all progress in knowledge or wealth only extends the range of human suffering, and the possibilities of social disorder. All the great movements, which have built up modern secular civilisation, have been more or less vitiated by this defect. Whether we look at the Italy of the Renaissance, the England of the Industrial Revolution, or the Germany of the last forty years, we see in each case that the progress and wealth which are founded on individual or national selfishness lead to destruction and suffering. A civilisation which recognises its own limitations, and bows before the kingdom of the spirit, even though it be weak and immature like European civilisation during the Dark Ages, has more true life in it than the victorious material civilisation of our own age. There is no hope for humanity in science and economic organisation: these are but instruments, which may be used for death, instead of for life, if the will that uses them is disordered. Civilisation after civilisation in the past has stagnated and fallen into ruin, because it is tainted at the source, in the spiritual will which lies behind the outward show of things. The only final escape for humanity from this heartbreaking circle of false starts and frustrated hopes is through the conquest of the world by charity—the coming of the Kingdom of God.

The Catholic sees in the life of the Church the progressive development and application to humanity of this supreme remedy. It is not, of course, a process which is susceptible of scientific demonstration; the forces at work lie too deep for reason to measure them, neither can we follow the action and interaction of human and divine activities. From the beginning the Church has taught that it is impossible to judge the inward growth of the Kingdom by outward signs; it is the field of wheat growing with the cockle till the time of harvest: but no less has she recognised the complementary principle, that where there is inward life there must be outward manifestation.

Critics of Christianity are apt to judge of it as though it were an external system of law. This system is applied to a nation or a civilisation, and if these prosper, well and good; if not, Christianity is a failure. They do not realise the infinitely tenuous and delicate nature of the supernatural life, which works as continuously and infallibly as a natural force through the sacraments and operations of grace, but which can only realise itself in man and transform human nature by the consent and co-operation of the individual will. Where it is accepted in a merely natural way as a law, as part of a human system, it is powerless to act.

Only in the saints, with whom the process is exceptionally advanced, is the whole external life conformed to the new inward principle. In the ordinary Christian, the natural life goes on almost unchanged, based on its own principle and following its own laws. It is to this region that much of what we are accustomed to look on historically as Christian civilisation belongs. But behind all this the supernatural principle carries on its seminal activity and forms the embryonic life, which is destined eventually to absorb into itself and remake the whole nature, mental and physical, with all its vital activities.

Thus, although we cannot trace in society, as it is, even in Christian society, the clear evidence of the progressive development of the divine life in mankind, we can still see in every age new manifestations of the charismatic activity of the Spirit in the Catholic Church. Every age sees the Kingdom of God conquering fresh territory—the supernatural order more closely interpenetrating the natural world. Sometimes the conquests of one age seem to be lost by the next, but this loss is superficial. The achievement remains to be drawn in and represented at some future period.

The secularist naturally regards this kind of progress as unsubstantial and unsatisfactory. The end is never completely reached. Humanity keeps its old nature, whilst it loses the perfection that is really within its reach, in the pursuit of abstractions. But the goal of the Christian progress is far, because it is final. The Christian faith alone offers man a perfection which is not relative and transitory, but absolute and eternal. The Christian faith alone has measured how deep is the need of humanity and how great is the possibility of restoration. If it seems to neglect the material world, that is not because it treats the material world as unimportant, but because the restoration of the spirit must precede and condition the restoration of the body. The divine life that is in the Church is not limited in its effects to the human soul, it overflows onto the body, and hence onto the whole material universe:

Terra, pontus, astra, mundus
Hoc lavantur flumine.

In the present order of the world, the relation of spirit and matter, as well as the relation of the natural and the supernatural, has become dislocated. The unification or harmonising of the two former will follow eventually on that of the two latter. Then the body, and with it the whole material world, will be brought into a true relation with the soul, so that everywhere matter is the extension of spirit, and not its limit; the instrument of spirit, and not its enemy. St. Paul speaks of the material creation groaning and travailing in pain until the time in which it also will be delivered from the service of corruption and will have its share in the liberty of the perfected and glorified supernatural order.

This transfiguration of the material world is of course most vital in the case of the human body. That is why the Church has, from the beginning, attached such importance to the doctrine of the corporal resurrection, even though that doctrine was a source of difficulty and misunderstanding to the mentality of Hellenistic civilisation, as now it is to the mind of modern Europe. Nevertheless, without this final restoration of the body, the Christian doctrine of man would remain incomplete. Man was created to be the soul of the material world, the link between the two creations; that through him, as St. Gregory of Nyssa says, the divine might shine as through a glass into the earthly world, and the earthly, elevated with the divine, might be freed from corruptibility, and transfigured.[19]

The very essence of man's nature and his true *raison d'être* consists in this union of body with spirit. That is why death, the temporary dissolution of the compound, is a thing of such real horror for every man, even for the Christian. For though in one respect death brings the soul nearer to God, delivering it from the veil of sense and from the dominance of animal needs; yet on the other hand it is a kind of annihilation, a loss of an essential half, even though it be the lower half, of his nature.

If that separation were final, a central purpose of the Incarnation would remain unfulfilled. In place of the Christian theory of redemption, we should have the Gnostic or Manichaean idea of the salvation of man by the separation of his true nature from its material envelope or prison—the return of the Alone to the Alone, as we find it in the typical Indian philosophies. "But," says St. Irenæus, "since men are real, theirs must be a real restoration. They do not vanish into non-existence, but progress among existent things. Neither the matter nor substance of Creation is annihilated, the form alone passes away. When this form has passed away and man has been renewed, there shall be the new heaven and the new earth in which man shall remain, ever new among the new, and always in communion with God."

19. It may be objected that this view of man's function implies an anthropocentric view of the universe essentially bound up with the conception of the earth as the unmoving centre of the stellar heavens. But this function of man depends not on his being the ruling creature in the central sphere of the universe, but on the essential duality of his nature. The truth and importance of that duality is in no way affected by the progress of astronomy.

In nothing less than this does the destiny of humanity consist, according to the teaching of the Catholic faith. Without losing his own nature, man is brought into an inconceivably close relation with God, so that he lives by the Divine Life, sees God with God's Knowledge, loves God with God's Love, and knows and loves everything else in and through God. The life of the Divine Trinity externalises itself in the completed life of the Church, in humanity eternally and immutably deified. To that end, the Church on earth moves infallibly, irresistibly. In the Sacraments, in the life of faith, in every act of spiritual will and aspiration of spiritual desire, the work of divine restoration goes ceaselessly forward. In that work is the whole hope of humanity.

Ναί ἔτχομαι ταχύ. ἀμήν ἔρχου, Κύριε Ἰησοῦ.

Index of Names

Index of Subjects

Enquiries into Religion and Culture was designed and typeset in Galliard by Kachergis Book Design of Pittsboro, North Carolina. It was printed on 60-pound Natures Book Natural and bound by Thomson-Shore of Dexter, Michigan.